'A solid, eminently useful text that will awaken curiosity, orient future study, and provoke classroom discussion' – James Peck, Associate Professor, Department of Theatre and Dance, Muhlenberg College, USA

Is theatre direction a craft?

Why did theatre directors only start to appear at the beginning of the twentieth century?

These questions and more are answered in this survey of the art of theatre direction. Its scope ranges across the theatres of both America and Europe, looking at practices from Stanislavski up to the present day. Alongside descriptions of rehearsal-room practices, the text describes the history of directing, how it has been defined and the types of theatre it has made. It also reflects on the controversial nature of the role. Packed with quotations and examples, the book offers insights into the work of many different practitioners. It enables students to gain an in-depth understanding of directing, and sheds light on mysteries such as why theatre directors so often sit behind tables.

SIMON SHEPHERD is Professor of Theatre and Deputy Principal (Academic) at Central School of Speech & Drama, London. His recent work includes *The Cambridge Introduction to Modern British Theatre*, *Performance Research 14.2 'On Training'*, and *Theatre, Body and Pleasure*.

READINGS IN THEATRE PRACTICE

Series Editor: Simon Shepherd

At the heart of every performance lies a tension, a tension between the material object and the magical transformation of theatre. Taking elements of theatre such as sound, puppetry and directing, the series explores this relationship, offering both the vocabulary and the historical context for critical discussion and creative practice.

Published:

Ross Brown: Sound

Jon Davison: Clown

Penny Francis: Puppetry

Scott Palmer: Light

Simon Shepherd: Direction

Forthcoming:

Jane Boston: Voice

Alison Maclaurin and Aoife Monks: Costume

Joslin McKinney: Construction

Readings in Theatre Practice
Series Standing Order
ISBN 978–0–230–53717–0 hardcover
ISBN 978–0–230–53718–7 paperback
(*outside North America only*)

You can receive future titles in this series as they are published by placing a standing order. Please contact your bookseller or, in case of difficulty, write to us at the address below with your name and address, the title of the series and the ISBN quoted above.

Customer Services Department, Macmillan Distribution Ltd, Houndmills, Basingstoke, Hampshire, RG21 6XS, UK

Direction

Readings in Theatre Practice

Simon Shepherd

palgrave
macmillan

First published 2012 by
PALGRAVE MACMILLAN

Palgrave Macmillan in the UK is an imprint of Macmillan Publishers Limited,
registered in England, company number 785998, of Houndmills, Basingstoke,
Hampshire RG21 6XS.

Palgrave Macmillan in the US is a division of St Martin's Press LLC,
175 Fifth Avenue, New York, NY 10010.

Palgrave Macmillan is the global academic imprint of the above companies
and has companies and representatives throughout the world.

Palgrave® and Macmillan® are registered trademarks in the United States,
the United Kingdom, Europe and other countries.

ISBN 978–0–230–27621–5 hardback
ISBN 978–0–230–27622–2 paperback

This book is printed on paper suitable for recycling and made from fully
managed and sustained forest sources. Logging, pulping and manufacturing
processes are expected to conform to the environmental regulations of the
country of origin.

A catalogue record for this book is available from the British Library.

Library of Congress Cataloging-in-Publication Data
Shepherd, Simon.
    Direction / Simon Shepherd.
       p.   cm. — (Readings in theatre practice)
    Includes bibliographical references and index.
    ISBN 978–0–230–27622–2
    1. Theater—Production and direction.   I. Title.
    PN2053.S42 2013
    792.02′33–dc23   2012032278

10   9   8   7   6   5   4   3   2   1
21   20   19   18   17   16   15   14   13   12

Printed and bound in Great Britain by
CPI Antony Rowe, Chippenham and Eastbourne

Contents

Acknowledgements

For their comments, perceptions and information I'd like to thank: Experience Bryon and Geoff Colman, Central School of Speech & Drama; Janette Dillon and Brean Hammond, University of Nottingham; Maxine Doyle, Punchdrunk; Chris Goode, Chris Goode and Company; Mischa Twitchin, Shunt.

The editor and publishers wish to thank the following for permission to reproduce copyright material:

Farrar, Straus and Giroux and LLC for excerpts from *Brecht on Theatre* edited and translated by John Willett. Translation copyright © 1964, renewed 1992 by John Willett. Reprinted by permission of Hill and Wang, a division of Farrar, Straus and Giroux, LLC; Anne Bogart and Taylor & Francis for extracts from pp. 44, 46, 67, 85–6, 120, 131, 134, from *A Director Prepares: Seven Essays on Art and Theatre* by A. Bogart, copyright © 2003. Reproduced by permission of Taylor & Francis Books UK; Calouste Gulbenkian Foundation for extracts from pp. 19, 24, 93–4, 165–6, from K. Rae, *A Better Direction* (1989); Cambridge University Press for extracts from pp. 28–9, 32–3, 56–7, 68, 69, from D. L. Hirst, *Giorgio Strehler* (1993), © Cambridge University Press 1993, reproduced with permission; Cambridge University Press for extracts from D. Kennedy, 'The Director, the Spectator and the Eiffel Tower', *Theatre Research International*, 30.1, pp. 36–48, reproduced with permission; David Higham Associates for extracts from pp. 13–14, 15, 233, 259, 279, 280, 281, from N. Marshall, *The Producer and the Play*, Macdonald (1962); Faber & Faber Ltd., Gabriella Giannachi and Mary Luckhurst, and St Martin's Press (permission/acknowledgement to be confirmed) for extracts from pp. 27, 32, 70, 123, 137, from G. Giannachi and M. Luckhurst, *On Directing: Interviews with Directors* (1999); Manchester University Press for extracts from pp. 73, 90, 91, 98, 139, 142, 187, 188, 210, 225, 228, 247, 253, 264–5, 272, from M. M. Delgado and P. Heritage (eds), *In Contact with the Gods?: Directors Talk Theatre* (1996); Andrew McKinnon and Calouste Gulbenkian Foundation for extracts from pp. 13–20, from A. McKinnon, *The Training of Theatre Directors: 1995 and Beyond*, A report to the National Council for Drama Training and The Gulbenkian Foundation (unpublished); MIT Press for extracts from C. Weber, 'Brecht As Director' reprinted from *TDR*, 12.1, Bertolt Brecht (Autumn, 1967), courtesy of The MIT Press; Taylor & Francis for extracts from pp. xviii, 30, 53, 56, 58, 61, 74, 86, 152, 165, 184, from *On Directing and Dramaturgy: Burning the House* by Eugenio Barba, copyright © 2010 Routledge. Reproduced by permission of Taylor & Francis

Books UK; Taylor & Francis for extracts from pp. 115, 118, 176, 223–4, 225, 235, 249, 262, from *My Life in Art* by S. Konstantin, translated and edited by J. Benedetti, copyright © 2008 Routledge. Reproduced by permission of Taylor & Francis Books UK; Taylor & Francis for extracts from pp. 2, 9, 11, 12, 13, 15, 29, 30, 36, 39, 62, 85, 123, 126, 129, 131, from *The Director's Craft: A Handbook for the Theatre* by K. Mitchell, copyright © 2009 Routledge. Reproduced by permission of Taylor & Francis Books UK; University of Pittsburgh Press for extracts from pp. 39, 42, 47, 50–6, from 'Plot and Practice' from *David Garrick, Director*, by Kalman A. Burnim, © 1961. Reprinted by permission of the University of Pittsburgh Press; University of Toronto Press for extracts from pp. 4–8, 70–4, from W. R. Streitberger, *Court Revels, 1485–1559* (1994), © University of Toronto Press, 1994. Reprinted with permission of the publisher; Society for Theatre Research for extract from John C. Coldwin 'That Enterprising Property Player: Semi-professional Drama in Sixteenth-Century England', *Theatre Notebook*, 31, pp. 5–12, reproduced with permission.

Every effort has been made to trace rights holders, but if any have been inadvertently overlooked the publishers would be pleased to make the necessary arrangements at the first opportunity.

Series Preface

This series aims to gather together both key historical texts and contemporary ways of thinking about the material crafts and practices of theatre.

These crafts work with the physical materials of theatre – sound, objects, light, paint, fabric, and – yes – physical bodies. Out of these materials the theatre event is created.

In gathering the key texts of a craft it becomes very obvious that the craft is not simply a handling of materials, however skilful. It is also a way of thinking about both the materials and their processes of handling. Work with sound and objects, for example, involves – always, at some level – concepts of what sound is and does, what an object is and does . . . what a body is.

For many areas of theatre practice there are the sorts of 'how to do it' books that have been published for at least a century. These range widely in quality and interest but next to none of them is able to, or wants to, position the *doing* in relation to the *thinking about doing* or the thinking about the material being used.

This series of books aims to promote both thinking about doing and thinking about materials. Its authors are specialists in their field of practice and they are charged to reflect on their specialism and its history in order, often for the first time, to model concepts and provide the tools not just for the doing but for thinking about theatre practice.

The series title 'Readings in Theatre Practice' uses the word 'reading' in the sense both of a simple understanding or interpretation and of an authoritative explication, an exegesis as it were. Thus, the books first gather together people's opinions about, their understanding of, what they think they are making. These opinions are then framed within a broader narrative which offers an explanatory overview of the practice under investigation.

So, although the books comprise many different voices, there is a dominant authorial voice organising the material and articulating overarching arguments. By way of promoting a further level of critique and reflection, however, authors are asked to include a few lengthy sections, in the form of interviews or essays or both, in order to make space for other voices to develop their own overviews. These may sit in tension, or indeed in harmony, with the dominant narratives.

Authors are encouraged to be sceptical about normative assumptions and canonical orthodoxy. They are asked not to ignore practices and thinking that might question dominant views; they are invited to speculate as to how canons and norms come into being and what effects they have.

We hope the shape provides a dynamic tension in which the different activities of 'reading' both assist and resist each other. The details of the lived practices refuse to fit tidily into the straitjacket of a general argument, but the dominant overview also refuses to allow itself to fragment into local prejudice and anecdote. And it's that restless play between assistance and resistance that mirrors the character of the practices themselves.

At the heart of each craft is a tense relationship. On the one hand there is the basic raw material that is worked – the wood, the light, the paint, the musculature. These have their own given identity – their weight, mechanical logics, smell, particle formation, feel. In short, the texture of the stuff. And on the other hand there is theatre, wanting its effects and illusions, its distortions and impossibilities. The raw material resists the theatre as much as yields to it, the theatre both develops the material and learns from it. The stuff and the magic. This relationship is perhaps what defines the very activity of theatre itself.

It is this relationship, the thing which defines the practice of theatre, which lies at the heart of each book in this series.

Simon Shepherd

Part

I Introductions

Preface: This Book and the Others

Throughout the history of theatre there have been people in a company who have taken ultimate responsibility for overseeing how the show gets on stage. Arguably, therefore, all sorts of people have done what we would now call directing. But the existence of a role called 'director' really only emerged substantially at the turn into the twentieth century. And it is the practice done by a specific designated role with which we are concerned here. Hence this book is concerned with *direction* as the practice done by directors.

From here the general *aims* of the book follow. The intention is to:

- describe the range of the practice now associated with the formal role of director;
- account for the historical emergence of this role and its conditions of practice;
- reflect upon and critique the issues thrown up by the practice of direction;
- attend as much to organisation as to creation, and the relations between the two.

This book joins a fairly extensive literature on directors and directing that has accumulated over several decades. Those familiar with this literature may well already have expectations as to what a book on direction might contain. It seems to me important therefore not only to lay out what the book is trying to do but also to be very clear about what it is not trying to do.

The literature about directors and directing falls, crudely speaking, into the following categories: how-to-do-it books of method; personal accounts by directors and others of individual directorial practices; academic studies of the methods and productions of particular directors and companies. These can be broken down into sub-categories.

The how-to-do-it books might describe the whole process or specifically the handling of actors. They consist in the main of:

- books of exercises and/or analyses (such as that by Mike Alfreds 2007, possibly one of the more thoughtful – and readable – of these);
- pithy observations about or extended commentary on the production process (Hauser and Reich 2003 or Robert Cohen 2011, who is one of the most sensible and readable);
- dictionaries of terms and keywords of use to directors (John Caird 2010).

It is worth here singling out one of the earliest how-to-do-it books, not only because it is possibly the finest of them but also because it comes from an interesting place. Based on Alexander Dean's course for first-year students at Yale University, Dean and Carra's *Fundamentals of Play Directing* was published in 1941, after Dean's death. The 'five fundamentals of directing' are specified as 'composition, movement, picturization, rhythm, and pantomimic dramatization' (Dean and Carra 1974: 25). These fundamentals are then broken down into basic, and often very simple, elements: 'There are five designations in the relation of body position to audience'. Of these 'Full-front position is very strong', and others less so to varying degrees (Dean and Carra 1974: 102). It is, in historical terms, nicely tidy that the first of Dean and Carra's fundamentals, composition, is precisely the topic which, in 1909, heads up the published observations on staging of one of the supposed founders of directing, Duke Georg of Saxe-Meiningen.

While *Fundamentals* has a section on 'elementary stage techniques' for the actor, the book is mainly focused not on the business of getting performances out of actors but on the creation of the whole staged entity. Few of the how-to-do-it books since Dean and Carra have achieved the same sense of analytic simplicity and dispassionate objectivity. Too many of them are bound up in the projection of the personal identity of the author-director. This difference is possibly explained by the fact that, while Alexander Dean was a professional educator, a number of the how-to-do-it authors since then have been directors trying their hand as teachers.

The status of the personality of the director, and indeed the celebrity, has over time had its shaping effect on books about the craft. The personal accounts have always been popular from Stanislavski onwards, but they have ranged from methodical analysis to fluffy anecdote. They are often published within collections of interviews or talks. In this respect there is very little framework or apparatus which encourages critical reflection on the account being offered. Sometimes they are personal accounts written by rehearsal-room observers, usually academics of some sort. The amount of critical reflection remains variable however, perhaps because the observer has acquired, and loyally cherishes, the status of trusted friend.

The academic studies of particular directors may include accounts of production processes, representation of the director's philosophies in general and theories of theatre in particular, and descriptions, more or less analytical, of productions. The balance of these elements can alter. So too the study may tend towards celebration or critique, with the former being most frequent. Such single-director studies work alongside the personal-account texts in that between them they consolidate a canon of 'great' directors, the people thought to be worth interviewing and studying.

While this book finds great value in the accounts of methods and processes, it doesn't set out to privilege the work of any one individual or to keep in place dominant beliefs. Since the book tries to concentrate on showing and analysing the rich variety of a practice it seems important not to limit the potential of that variety. Such limitation might occur when we assume, or impose, certain sorts of evaluative hierarchies. It's worth challenging such assumptions. Thus, for example, we might question if the methods of a famous director are necessarily superior to, or more interesting than, those of anyone else. And in the face of generally accepted norms of rehearsal-room practice we might insist, rather pedantically, that these are, after all, merely that, generally accepted norms. They are not necessarily better or more productive than minority, albeit abnormal, practices – and if they are, we would want to demonstrate how and why. And finally here we should take issue with a tendency to embrace a habit of mind which imagines that the new and contemporary, the activities of the present, are automatically more interesting, enlightened, useful – and indeed newer – than practices long gone. The designer and director Achim Freyer explicitly criticises attempts to make work 'modern', noting how limited, and limiting, this can be as an approach (http://www.goethe.de/kue/flm/prj/kub/lit/en(3951)016.htm).

The commitment to recognising variety also informs the book's understanding of the director's role. There's a definition of that role that says a director does two basic things: organises the process and shapes the acting. It could also be said of course that the directing role designs the stage picture, teaches textual analysis and runs a company. But let's pause for a moment over that activity of shaping the acting. I consciously use the word 'shape' here in order to gather together some pretty divergent possibilities. There are, in general terms, three of these. Some directors expect the actors to arrive fully equipped to do everything they are asked to do: the responsibility for acting technique is that of the actor, who puts it at the service of the director. The director then shapes what the acting does within the mise en scène. Then there are the directors who seem not to have any use for acting technique and its potential, who in some ways work against it: the earlier Robert Wilson comes to mind here. Such directors may be said to shape the acting insofar as they disallow familiar techniques and solutions, or override them with other instructions. And lastly there is the most famous group, the directors who felt they needed to interfere with the technique of their actors in order to be able to make the sorts of shows they wanted to make (this is argued in more detail on p. 55 ff). The director as actor-trainer begins most famously with Stanislavski and his contemporaries, Meyerhold and Komisarjevsky, and, as we have noted from the how-to-do-it books, some directors still regard the development, if not training, of their actors as the most important part of the directorial role. Declan Donnellan's 2005 book is, for example, primarily about the development of actors. These directors shape the acting insofar as they shape the actor, literally modelling a set of techniques and attitudes.

Alongside the long and distinguished tradition of director as actor-trainer we can place another tradition that begins before Stanislavski's books appear. This is the tradition of director as textual analyst, and from at least Harley

Granville Barker onwards, through such as Brecht and Strehler, it has provided exemplary models for ways of understanding the operation not only of verbal text but of the whole language of mise en scène. As Louis Catron puts it, 'The play director seeking to achieve good theatre must begin with accurate play analysis.' For Catron, dealing with text takes precedence over dealing with actors: 'directorial vision, based on careful play analysis and interpretation, takes priority over working with performers' (Catron 1989: viii, 24). A more extreme, or perhaps more mechanical, version of this is found in Whitmore's *Directing Postmodern Theater* (1994). Somewhat assiduously obedient to semiotics, Whitmore describes the director's task as analysis of the script so as then 'to orchestrate signifiers in order to communicate to the spectators her interpretation' (Whitmore 1994: 20). The actor becomes one of an undifferentiated bunch of signifiers. Dean and Carra, in the early days of the how-to-do-it books for directors, had, by contrast, made a careful proviso: their emphasis on the five fundamentals 'is not meant to diminish the importance of acting requirements in the total expression of the play' (Dean and Carra 1974: 101).

That this analytic tradition is less celebrated than that of actor-trainer is, I suspect, less to do with its lack of functional efficacy than with the disciplinary structures within which we think about direction. Within the UK at least, but perhaps also further afield, directors tend to be studied by those associated with the disciplines of drama/theatre/performance studies. These disciplines also have an interest in the work of acting. They tend to define themselves against more book-based disciplines by placing the emphasis on 'practice' (usually thought of as anything but the practice of writing). Textual analysis per se tends to sit more firmly in the territory of a book-based discipline such as literary studies. And while literary studies often encompass the study of the dramatic script, the methodologies invoked for such study tend to be those of literary critics rather than directors (partly on the basis that directors, being engaged with practice, can't be expected to approach written text in a way appropriately refined). Whether this analysis is right or not, and I'll defer to others more expert, the point remains that we make assumptions about what directors do which are perhaps more ideologically driven than factually based.

All that said, much of this book remains interested in the relationship between directors and actors. But it is not necessarily interested in the particularities of one method over and against another. Detailed debates as to different actor-training regimes seem more properly to be the business of a text about acting, where the voice of those being trained can be heard alongside those who are imposing the regime of training. For this text about direction the task instead is to observe how particular interpretations of the role assume that it involves training actors, and how this assumption contains several others: assumptions about what actors and acting are for, what the relationship between acting and other theatre elements is, why it is necessary for directors to interfere, the right by which they do so, and the effects of that interference on people, structure and process. Some exploration of these assumptions properly belongs with our thinking about direction. An analysis of the process by which an actor experiences the character's emotions or comes to inhabit the physical regime of a mask, on the other hand, does not.

There is another area of exclusion yet more slippery. It is possible to argue, as I do, that direction should only be considered as such when the role of director structurally emerges in a major way towards the end of the nineteenth century. But it also seems apparent that this separated role which is responsible for the work of direction comes under pressure in the final decades of the twentieth century. In some collaborative companies (although by no means all) the work of directing is not fixed within a single role but is shared around. And in very different sorts of theatre, such as established opera companies, directing might be done by someone who is, at base, a designer. This historical process is reviewed in one section of the book, but insofar as the formal role of director turns into something else – such as a facilitator or executive – then I have excluded those figures from detailed consideration.

We shall come back to several of these points in different guises in the chapters that follow. But before we do so there is a last point to be made about aims and expectations, and that is to do with how this book works. It is part of a series called 'Readings in Theatre Practice'. As the series preface explains, the objective is to combine many different examples and quotations taken from a diverse range of sources and then to frame them within overview arguments. You will find that the majority of the directors named are British, but many of these are simply passing mentions. Where directing practices are more fully discussed there is, I hope, much more of a balanced spread across cultures and national institutions, though there is a conspicuous lack of engagement with Eastern practices. Insofar as there is a bias it is towards the area of my specialism, namely British theatre.

The short quotations through the text are intended to illustrate a range of practices and thinking. They are also used to prompt critique so that any one account of a practice might be used – or read – in different ways. That critical distance is then intended to inform the framing narratives. Alongside those there are two new essays by other scholars, Christophe Alix and James Reynolds, commissioned for this volume, and two new interviews with directors. The book is structured more or less into topics, but within the account of a topic the quotations might well be positioned so that they have itchy relations, rubbing up against each other. For the one thing that should be clear overall is that there is no orthodoxy about the director's role or art. To sustain this sense of there being no orthodoxy I have isolated the directors' interviews from the rest of the book. In these the two directors were asked a number of the same questions I asked myself when I was doing the research. Their responses don't necessarily lead them into the places where

I ended up, so their interviews sit in a potentially tense relationship with the rest of the material.

Overall, as the book trundles on, you'll find certain figures or practices keep popping up. There is no extended account of Stanislavski, for example, but Stanislavskianism appears in various places. So too you'll note we keep coming back to the topic of organisation, which seems rather under-represented elsewhere. If you're reading from beginning to end you'll find this starts with Goethe as a civil servant in Chapter 1 and culminates in the whole Part V. But there are clearly various ways of engaging with a book and mono-directional linear progress is but one of them. Reading this through its index, tracking highly specific topics, may be as good an approach as any. Please do take your own, so to speak, direction.

Chapter

1 Finding a Name for It

Stage manager, Regisseur, producer, metteur en scène, metteur en jeu, Intendant, director: they are all names, at some time or another, for the person that does a particular sort of activity. That activity is, in its basic form, the process of organising a performance: both getting it on the stage and shaping its contents. And it's not just the roles named above who have had this responsibility. Throughout the history of theatrical practice there have been different members of a company who have taken on the job of organising the performance. The people who did this most frequently, over the ages, were the leading actor and the author.

Directing as an activity, therefore, can be seen to have been done by many people besides those called 'directors'. In the cases of leading actors and authors directing was part of their job, and often a rather marginal part of it, as opposed to creating a text or show. It was not necessarily thought of as a separate activity, a discrete practice in its own right. The change comes about when theatre practice invents a role that, eventually, it calls the 'director'. With this role in place, it is then assumed that there is something particular which a director, and nobody else, does. One could say that the invention of a named role, director, calls into being something that can be thought of as a specific practice: giving 'direction'.

This book is concerned with that specific practice, namely with directing as something done by directors. It therefore limits its scope, in the main, to accounts of theatre practice in which there is a concept and role of director. To take the approach of tracking down every instance of anything that could be said to be the giving of direction would mean writing about actors, authors, impresarios and designers. It would also mean losing focus on the director as a specific structural and artistic role in its own right.

The emergence of that role is described later in this book. But by way of introduction to it here, let's look at some of the other names for it and see how they operated within their own theatrical context. On the way we shall see how their activity might differ from that of the people now called theatre directors, which in turn should help us reflect on our assumptions about the role of the director. We're less concerned here, then, with the 'art' of directing than with the job of directors, not trying to describe how they set about their work but trying to define what sorts of things they are meant to do.

SOME THEATRICAL NAMES

An early example of the name for someone who organises a performance, recorded around the sixteenth century, is the metteur en jeu: Cole and Chinoy give the example of the superintendents who were appointed at Valenciennes in 1547 to stage the Passion play (1963: 6ff). This person sets up the play, creates the game, leads the entertainment. The role was often taken by a performer who led from within the performance. This model is perhaps most familiar to us from eighteenth-century music, where the band was led from the keyboard or from the chief violin. In Shakespeare's theatre the show seems to have been put together by the leading actors, the shareholders of the company, of whom the dramatist, in Shakespeare's case, was one. His fictional creation Quince in *A Midsummer Night's Dream* is, as Geoff Colman has pointed out to me, more concerned with imposing order than art, but the relationship with actual practices at the Globe Theatre has to be moot. That practice of the dominance of leading actors continued into the eighteenth century where a division becomes clear between the leading actor heading up the company and working with the players while stage effects and materials were organised by the machinist. The figure of the actor-manager who emerged as a celebrity in the nineteenth century, what the Italians call the mattatore, presided over teams of stage staff. By the time we get to the actor-manager, but apparent also in Shakespeare's theatre, there's a crucial difference from that metteur en jeu at Valenciennes. That person was appointed to the task whereas the actor-manager was the person with the power. But in other respects there is continuity from the metteur en jeu, the person who organises the spectacle of which they themselves are a part. This is the most ancient, and indeed most persistent, theatrical model for getting a show onto the stage.

While the actor-manager dominated the scene in Britain and Italy (until very recent times in the latter), in Germany another role had emerged. This was the Regisseur. Patterson defines it as 'a post similar to that of stage-manager in the British theatre of the period [late eighteenth century], i.e. the person responsible for the organization and supervision of rehearsals, including entrances and exits and basic moves' (Patterson 1990: 72). In the eighteenth century, theatrical performances were staged by two main groups of performers. There were, first, the travelling companies. Their most secure source of income came from residencies at the court theatres among the collection of small dukedoms which comprised what would later become 'Germany'. Theatre was also put on by courtly amateurs at those ducal theatres, as a way of making their own entertainment. Such acts consisted of shadow plays, operettas and spectacles as much as plays. The person entrusted with overseeing the arrangements for the production of such plays and events was known as the 'Regisseur'. In the case of the travelling players the Regisseur might be the lead actor and head of the company.

The general arrangements of the court theatres in Germany were similar to those of the official Russian theatre. The Russian director Theodore Komisarjevsky (1882–1954) describes these:

> Until the end of the XIXth century there was no such person as a real producer in the Imperial Drama and Opera. The pieces were staged by the actors themselves under the supervision of a Stage Director (Chief Régisseur) whose real interest lay more in the administrative side of the Theatre than in the business of putting on the plays. A Stage Director was usally [sic] promoted to that post from that of Prompter or Stage Manager, as in the Army a colonel is promoted to the rank of general for long and zealous service. Eventually leading actors began to produce plays themselves which led to the engagement of special producers, an example which was set by the great Russian producer Stanislavsky in his Moscow Art Theatre.
>
> (Komisarjevsky 1929: 26)

Mention of Stanislavski takes us forward into familiar territory, but before we get there we need to look at two new terms.

While régisseur is a French word, it's not what the French call the directing role. The régisseur in France is a stage manager in our modern sense, the person who operationally organises the thing on the stage. Used in this sense, it seems to have a very long history, with the medieval mystery and passion plays being organised by régisseurs: a production of a religious 'mystery' play done in Belgium in 1501 is recorded in *Le livre de conduit du régisseur* (Komisarjevsky 1935: 28). By contrast to this, in overall aesthetic control of the elements of the show is the person who creates the fictional world, the metteur en scène. That name and the assumptions about what it does are very closely associated with the practices of cinema, and in particular the idea that the director of the film is like a sort of author. For scène is rather different from skena. Skena is the Greek word for the thing you perform in front of. Scene came to imply not simply the architectural space of the playing but what was played. So in theatre practice, a metteur en scène doesn't simply organise the stage elements, manage the stage, but creates from them a fictional scene.

The division of roles between régisseur and metteur en scène has its parallel in English. It was described in 1910 by P.P. Howe, who saw the emergence of new drama, 'plays more elusive in their spirit', as requiring a new role:

> the stage-manager has seen the rise of the producer.... The stage-manager retains control of all the mechanical work of the stage. The producer is the new supplementary authority who assumes responsibility for the artistic unity of the whole. It is a simple matter of allotment of function. The dramatist supplies both letter and spirit. The stage-manager is competent to deal with the letter, and the producer's business is to interpret the spirit.
>
> (Howe 1910: 185)

In antithesis to the stage manager, the 'producer' is responsible not so much for the organisation of the mechanics and materials of the event as for its 'spirit'.

Howe's distinction of tasks seems to make things clear, until, that is, one turns to a text published five years before, and perhaps a lot more famous. In his *Art of the Theatre: The First Dialogue*, published in 1905, the British designer and polemicist Edward Gordon Craig (1872–1966) calls for theatre to be reformed by attending once again to the importance of all elements working in harmony, where the visual aspects are as important as words. A key agent in enabling the recovery of the Art of theatre is a 'stage-director', technically trained 'for his task of interpreting the plays of the dramatist'. As Craig goes on to explain what he sees as being included in the work of interpretation, his name for this role silently shifts: the 'stage-manager' will design the scene, design the lighting and then arrange the bodies on the stage (Craig 1980: 147, 155).

What Craig calls the stage manager, Howe calls the producer. Certainly in Britain this was the word most consistently used throughout the twentieth century, although it was not a word that always satisfied those doing the job. In 1935 Komisarjevsky objected that the English word 'producer' meant 'a farmer, a husbandman, an agriculturalist, and *not* an artist who interprets plays on the stage and directs all concerned in the interpretation' (Komisarjevsky 1935: 15). This is quite an early use of 'directs' in a specifically English context, and it seems to appear as a deliberate attempt to insist on the artistry of theatre directing. But most people seemed unconcerned by the snobbish distinction between the production of things you could eat and things you couldn't, and the word 'producer' remained in general usage. Even in the mid-1990s Jonathan Miller (born 1934) was referring to himself as a 'producer' (Delgado and Heritage 1996: 162). But during the century Komisarjevsky's preferred word, 'director', began to filter into more general usage in Britain. Writing in 1938, the British playwright and novelist Somerset Maugham (1874–1965) described the new term as an Americanism. A generation earlier, the Americans had been blamed for invading the British theatre and commercialising it at the expense of its art. Maugham replays this when he sees directors as replacing authors' work with creations of their own. Directors, Maugham feels, should be merely concerned with the 'mechanics' of the staging, much like Howe's stage manager from 1910 (Maugham 1961: 148). Certainly it was true that in the United States the word 'director' was in more common usage – but here too it remained slightly slippery. In 1919 David Belasco described himself as a 'producer of plays and director of theatres' (Belasco 1969: 5). That distinction of words maintains a separation between art and management, putting the show on and running the theatre. Within the history of theatre it is often a false distinction, for the person that ran the theatre frequently put on the shows. But as the director role was emerging, it needed to define itself as having responsibility towards a particular sort of art. And the success of that is marked when we hear a yelp from a dramatist: 'the preposterous claim has been made that the author's script is to be looked upon merely as a vehicle for the director to express his own ideas' (Maugham 1961: 146). Maugham's protestations were in vain. The director's power and art were there to stay. In 1954 Hugh Hunt published *The Director in the Theatre*, though in 1957 Marshall published *The Producer and the Play*. The term hadn't settled down, but the role it was describing now seemed clearly established.

Here we can pause and look back across the various words that have clustered together. As I noted at the start, these words are associated with activities that look, initially, pretty similar. But the distinctions between these apparent similarities are crucial. A Regisseur in one place is a stage manager in another. A metteur en scène is rather different from a metteur en jeu. A producer of plays is not – and yet sometimes is – a director of a theatre. In each case the difference points towards a distinction between organisation of materials and aesthetic arrangement, between planning and vision, between 'letter' and 'spirit'. The sliding about of the terms is an indication as to how, in the early days, it was not all that clear that the organisation of materials wasn't also the organisation of aesthetics. When Howe articulates the distinction between the two so clearly and forcefully it was because he was writing as a polemical defender of a new system of theatre. The repertory model, which provides the name for his book, was an organisational device that, according to its supporters, would strengthen the quality of the art as well as democratise the theatre. Repertory theatre was making a break from the commercialism and banality of the actor-managers and semi-industrial impresarios. But, despite Howe's polemical clarity, the roles of planner and visionary, metteur en jeu and metteur en scène, manager and artist, keep sliding together.

THE STORY OF A BUREAUCRAT

The mingling is very apparent in the role which is sometimes seen as one of the earliest precursors of the modern director, the Intendant of the German court theatre. This role takes us back to the ducal theatres, travelling companies and aristocratic amateurs of the second half of the eighteenth century. We have already noted that in this theatrical culture the person who took responsibility for getting the show on was the Regisseur. But alongside the Regisseur responsibility of a slightly different sort was taken, not just for one show, but for a whole series of shows, by the Intendant. Now that organisational arrangement, it should be quickly noted, has similarities to a much earlier system for overseeing court entertainments, exemplified in the office of Master of the Revels in the Tudor court in England (see pp. 110–14). The German Intendant seems to fall into place as a specific point of origin, however, because we have clear evidence of engagement with the aesthetics of performance under the supervision of an acknowledged artist, the writer Johann Wolfgang von Goethe (1749–1832). This, unlike the activity of Master of the Revels, seems to be identifiable as something which works free of merely servicing the aristocratic employer, becoming an aesthetic project in its own right.

The role can be illustrated with the example of Goethe, who was active in Weimar from the 1790s onwards. Carlson (1978) gives the narrative: Goethe was already famous as a young writer when he was introduced to the even younger Prince of Weimar. He joined the household, where he was both fêted and sniffed at, in that although he was a literary genius of considerable charm, he was without proper social status, and yet was a close intimate of the ruler. That ruler insisted, against some opposition, that Goethe join his privy council. In 1779 Goethe took on responsibility for the War Commission and for the Commission of Highways and Canals. At the same time, like everybody else, he also participated in court theatricals by way of an amusing sideline. He contributed scripts, acted in shows and organised entertainments. But these were all secondary to the business of being a privy councillor.

In 1785 he went to Italy for a period and on his return was given responsibilities for Science and Art, and oversight of museums and botanical gardens in Jura. In this capacity he arranged for the appointment of a director for the new theatrical activity in Weimar – who then would once again engage a travelling company, after years of intermission, to play in the newly built court theatre. The administrative organisation Goethe put in place consisted of a supervisor, the Regisseur, to which role he appointed the actor Franz Joseph Fischer, with two sub-directors, one to put on music events and the other theatre (the latter was an actor from a travelling company). The Regisseur 'organized, scheduled, and supervised the rehearsals, made the final decisions on his readings in the early reading rehearsals, and later determined the placement of the actors on the stage. He also was responsible for general company discipline' (Carlson 1978: 59). Goethe did his preparatory work in such detail, however, that he himself ended up being the director of the new theatre society as well as 'intendant' of the court theatre.

As Intendant, he oversaw what was put on in the theatre. This job had several elements to it. He was responsible, first, for ensuring the artistic quality of the work. While as a writer he had definite views on the quality of written text he extended this aesthetic control into the practice of performing. This led to him formulating his 'Rules for Actors', written in 1803. The Rules contain instructions on how to speak, use the body and organise the stage – for example, 'Recitation and Declamation', 'Gesticulation', 'Grouping and Positions Onstage'. The 'Observations for Rehearsals' begin by specifying 'one should never rehearse in boots' (Carlson 1978: 316). So, in Goethe's version, the role of Intendant had more to do than monitor aesthetic quality.

It had also to do with developing a mechanism for reforming aesthetics, and thereby making a difference to how theatre was done.

All of this aesthetic work was, however, itself a function of a larger responsibility, namely the appropriate discharge of ministerial duty in order to assure high quality work in the court theatre. This was about more than entertainment. The court theatres of the princes of Germany were shop windows that displayed the taste, civilisation and wealth of their aristocratic owners. The young Prince of Weimar took as his model the Versailles of late eighteenth-century France, the paragon of absolutist royal rule, the power and control of which were exercised through appropriate taste, behaviour and display. The Intendant of the court theatre of Weimar, as everywhere else, was, above all, a bureaucrat in the service of an absolute ruler. He had to ensure that theatrical productions both established taste and disseminated decorum. Just as it was for Versailles, the theatre was an instrument that implemented rule by other means. Theatrical production was bound by, and communicated the force of, aristocratic values. To the extent that the Intendant can be said to be their precursor, theatre directors have a point of origin in the role of a bureaucrat employed by a late-feudal aristocratic society.

There were, of course, other points of origin. But the Intendant reminds us forcefully that theatre directors are allocated powers within specific structures. That allocation is specifically visible at the historical moment in Britain when the term 'director' was formally inaugurated. Norman Marshall, writing in 1957, tells the story:

> A year or two ago the Society of West End Managers firmly put the English producer in his place (or at least in the place which they think he ought to occupy in the English theatre) by taking his title away from him and assuming it themselves. Henceforth, according to the official announcement, the title of producer was to belong to 'the actual responsible management which provides the money and exercises complete control'. The duties of those who used to be called producers were defined as [']acting as liaison officers between the workers and the management' and being 'physically responsible for the correct and appropriate interpretation of the playwright's intentions. It can then,' graciously allowed the Society of West End Managers, 'be stated that "The production is directed by Mr. —" ['].
>
> (Marshall 1962: 279–80)

As much as it was for Goethe as Intendant, the role of the director is conceived as the agency for the transmission of that which is correct and appropriate. Thus the artistry and organisation of directors play a designated part in the communication of values and beliefs that underpin the conduct and arrangements of the culture within which they work.

Both terms in the phrase 'artistry and organisation' are important. While this book will, like many other accounts of directors, explore the artistry of the role, it will also give time to considering organisation. This forms a persistent thread through the chapters that follow, culminating in Chapter 10. As that thread is followed, artistry and organisation are shown to be interwoven, and indeed it becomes apparent that organisation may be the crucial and defining activity of direction.

Part

II Being a Director

Chapter

2   What is it Directors Do?

The short answer to this question is that it depends on whom you ask. Kenneth Rae's report for the Calouste Gulbenkian Foundation in 1989, *A Better Direction*, asked people from across the 'profession':

> The responses indicated that the role was seen primarily as interpretive rather than creative, although it was recognized that the job requires a creative temperament. At the same time there is a strong feeling that the director is there to draw out the best from the creative efforts of the rest of the team. The job therefore involves setting up the conditions in which people can do their best work.
>
> Some of the most common definitions were: 'an enabler,' 'a catalyst,' 'a co-ordinator,' 'the trustee of the writer,' 'an organizer,' 'a collaborator – the first among equals,' 'a chairman of the committee,' 'the one who stands outside,' 'a team leader,' 'a person who creates an atmosphere in which other people can create'.
>
> (Rae 1989: 19)

But some will also say that the role of director doesn't amount to very much. The contemporary French director Ariane Mnouchkine (born 1939) describes a polemically prosaic version of the job: 'My work involves seeing that the food is good, that there's no rain coming through the roof, and dealing with the money we have.' Insofar as there is an art to it, she describes it as a 'minor art...Because a play exists without a director. A painting doesn't exist without a painter, and a play doesn't exist without the writer. So, yes, it is a minor art.' This sense of things managing quite nicely without a director is also there in Declan Donnellan's advice: 'you need to bear in mind that there shouldn't have to be a director, but you're almost a necessary evil'. There is, says the Italian director Giorgio Strehler, 'no such thing as pure "directing", or at least there should be no such thing' (Delgado and Heritage 1996: 187, 188, 91, 265).

In the early days of directors, Huntly Carter suggested 'Perhaps the simplest definition of a director is a leader.' (Carter 1964: 23) He says this in the context of his 1914 book about the German director Max Reinhardt (1873–1943) – which makes it even more interesting that his suggested definition has next to nothing in it about making art. And in that respect it resonates with Mnouchkine's opinion from the other end of the century. Between the two there are the decades of texts which attempt to define what directors do. As we saw in the Preface (p. 4), Dean and Carra assert confidently that it's about art and that there are five fundamentals to it. But the focus shifts beyond art when, nearly 50 years later, Catron, in a sort of echo, defines the director's 'five functions'. This now has in it the idea that the director does a number of things besides providing art. How much is done of what activity remains, however, unsettled. So the general observation has to be this: there are many different ideas about what directors do and it is very difficult to arrive at one precise overall description. Take, for example, Samuel Leiter trying to describe 'the salient aspects of the director's art' in the introduction to his two volumes on directors. Reviewing the common features of his selected subjects his list includes:

- 'diversity of taste and accomplishments';
- many of them begin as actors;
- in rehearsal methods some are autocratic and some democratic;
- some use a Regiebuch while others do not;
- most have embraced the repertory model;
- great directors are distinguished by 'the multiplicity of their theatre talents';
- they have a fascination with 'shape and function of theatre space';
- many have written about their 'theatre ideas'. (Leiter 1991: xii–xv)

It's a list which has to be so baggy that by the end we are hardly any wiser about these 'salient aspects' of directors. So we may have to accept that a feature of the practice of direction is that it's very difficult to fix on a definition of it. And also that this practice is not always about making art.

It may be that the most secure starting point is one that acknowledges slipperiness of definition. This is what Eugenio Barba does: 'Directing is peculiar in so much as it is a practice that can be defined only *in relationship to a particular theatre milieu.*' He then goes on to list the varieties of approach:

- looking after the 'critical-aesthetical representation of a text';
- conceiving a performance from scratch;
- an artist with a vision developed through a series of different shows;
- a 'competent professional' who reconciles 'heterogeneous elements';
- 'an experienced coordinator';
- 'the performance's true author'. (Barba 2010: xviii; emphasis in original)

Barba's book on the subject is about directing and dramaturgy, where one always overlaps the other. But quite a lot of his account is also about dealing with people and process.

Later on in this part we shall look at the arts of direction when we look in some detail at the rehearsal room. But what a director does in the rehearsal room is predicated on what that director understands the role of giving direction to be. So before we look at what goes on in rehearsal, we perhaps need to think about how the director has come to be there in the first place. In approaching it that way it becomes clearer why there are so many varieties of definition as to what the role of director is.

BECOMING A DIRECTOR

Unlike actors or designers, the route into theatre for directors often bypasses any formal training. Directors came into being in a world which had invented conservatoires for actors, on the model of conservatoires for musicians. While there were some exceptions, which we'll look at later, in many societies for most of the twentieth century there was next to no formal training for directors.

The situation in Britain in the late 1980s was summarised in *A Better Direction*. Courses in educational institutions comprised drama departments, such as at Bristol, Kent or (based in English) Leeds, and drama schools, such as the Old Vic Theatre School, the Royal Scottish Academy and the Drama Studio. Alongside these were professional courses run by the British Theatre Association, the Directors' Guild, and Centre for Performance Research in Cardiff. There was also training by means of attachments run and funded by such organisations as the BP Young Directors Festival, the Regional Theatre Young Directors Scheme, the Scottish Arts Council, the Welsh Arts Council and the Arts Council of Northern Ireland. This report was updated by Andrew McKinnon in 1995: by then opportunities for training had increased, with up to 20 courses on which directing was taught. But McKinnon notes 'considerable, and to me alarming, variations in what different institutions consider to be acceptable' in terms both of quality and student proficiency. The same point had been made by Rae in 1989. McKinnon also reports 'widely differing views as to the necessary ingredients of a director's basic training and/or education', with 'no system for assessing against any agreed national professional criteria' (McKinnon 1995: 13, 15). This was of course a peculiarly British problem. Both at Yale University, with the work of Alexander Dean, and in the theatres of Moscow, directing had been taught in a formal way since the 1930s. But it's worth spending a bit of time on directors' training in Britain because the problems indicate something of the general oddities of the British.

The concerns reported by McKinnon had a larger problem behind them. Rae's Gulbenkian report had not been implemented and the proposed Directors Training Council had run into problems before it was even established. If there were variations in the courses, the profession itself had 'no agreement' as to what the training needs were. Indeed there was widespread scepticism about the value of formal training. McKinnon reported industry criticism of courses on the basis that directors don't get enough experience, with one saying there were 'too many "artists", not enough craftsmen/women' (McKinnon 1995: 14, 18). There was a sense that young directors lacked both knowledge and interest in the wider context to their show – its place in the season, its budget and technical planning, its relationship with marketing and educational tours. Directors, it was suggested, needed less art and more 'people management' skills. The Regional Theatres Young Directors Scheme was attacked for favouring 'intellectuals' (McKinnon 1995: 19, 20).

All of this evidences a mutual distrust between the academy and the profession, and that distrust seems to go back a long way. *A Better Direction* has a ten-page section which reports views on whether training is necessary. The Gulbenkian report from 1975, *Going on the Stage*, speaks of 'a general bewilderment... as to what, if any, training is appropriate for directors' (reprinted in McKinnon 1995). And certainly, for anybody who is aware of it, what the history of directing evidences, and not only in Britain, is that training is by no means the failsafe way of getting to become a director. In 1989 Rae noted that at that time many theatre directors in Britain had entered the profession before courses were available: 64 per cent had no formal training. Of those who did have training, 17 per cent got it at drama school. The majority (76 per cent) had come to directing after acting (though many had not been trained as actors either). Clearly the situation was different in other countries, such as Poland, the USA and the USSR, where there were well-established training programmes. It was the job of *A Better Direction* to bring Britain more in line with such countries.

Recommendations for the Teaching of Directing in Britain in 1989

Those considering a director training course should ensure that the following points are included:

i) Learning how to work with actors and understanding the actor's processes should be the primary focus of any course on directing.

ii) Experienced actors should be employed as teachers as well as performers in director training courses across all media.

iii) There should be an examination of how the trainers themselves acquire their skills.

iv) There should be adequate opportunities for professional updating by academic staff.

v) Any system of director training, whether in a university, polytechnic, college or a drama school, should build effective links with the profession taking particular account of local theatre companies and professional facilities.

vi) Similarly, professional theatres should show a willingness to make useful contact with director training courses in their area, and they should be prepared to play a part in that training.

vii) Director training courses should include adequate guidance on the special skills needed for working with children and young people, in performances and workshops.

(Rae 1989: 165)

To this, the report added:

13 (a) The managerial role of the director should be considered an integral part of director training.
13 (b) Appropriate ways should be found for teaching group dynamics and people management.
13 (c) Training opportunities outside the arts should be investigated, eg what the commercial sector can offer in management skills.

(Rae 1989: 166)

Those last recommendations about managerial skills were very much in the spirit of the late 1980s in the UK, a decade which had seen the government of Margaret Thatcher promote managerialism in various sectors but in such a way that 'management' seemed divorced from the actual knowledge of the core business, constructing a managerial caste (and indeed cost). As such the Gulbenkian report was not necessarily going to have much of an impact on a profession that had been hit by cuts to the arts and was politically opposed to Thatcher's Conservatism. That patchy impact was noted in McKinnon's follow-up in 1995.

Although by then more training courses had been set up there was a persisting culture of scepticism about what could be formally taught. Somewhat revealingly, the Gulbenkian report says that those who worked with directors favoured the idea of their being trained. Those who were much less in favour of formal training were some of the directors themselves. The report tries to explain this: 'What has to be taken into account here is that any admission of the need for a three or four-year professional training for directors implies that one's own background is entirely inadequate. So we were bound to encounter a lot of disguised defensiveness.' Now it could be argued that, where a director is successful, the 'inadequacy' of their background is not proven or at least not relevant. But the Gulbenkian report had a purpose, namely to recommend director training. And it claims that it is the absence of formalised training in the UK which has produced the informal way of doing things:

Those few who had been through a proper training, usually abroad, were convinced that was the answer. In the absence of this, most people favoured attachments and the assistant director experience, because that was the way they entered the profession. 'Probably the best training is not by "course" but by working as assistant, however humble, in a practising company,' said Lindsay Anderson, who had been rejected by both the Bristol Old Vic Theatre School and the BBC Television training course.

(Rae 1989: 93–4)

The implication is that if there were formal training then informal apprenticeships might not be necessary. Furthermore, there's a slightly more aggressive implication that people need to abandon their sentiment about their own life-stories to embrace the ideal of formal (management) training. But this all masks a deeper ideological division.

In the same year as the Gulbenkian report appeared, Howard Davies tells how: 'I did a post-graduate course at Bristol University which was supposed to teach you about directing, but it was absolutely useless because it was largely taught by academics who had never worked in the theatre' (in Cook 1989: 71). He in fact got his training via a much more familiar route, going into stage management and from there to directing. This was a fairly regular model. People learnt by observation and listening, they immersed themselves in parallel processes, they became a part of the same production machinery. The training within the 'profession' is seen to have a lot more relevance, and indeed reality, than the detached and artificial world of the formal course. Like a lot of binaries that pose reality against arti- fice, however, this one is ideological; and it performs a useful function. The apprenticeship in the 'reality' of the profession connects the director, that relatively new role, back into the ancient practices of the theatre. And indeed, deep in the history of directing, there are stories of organic emer- gence. As we know, many – from the Russian director Stanislavski (or indeed Meiningen's Chronegk) onwards – began as actors and then moved into directing.

But there is one other reason why the formal training for the director might be rejected as inappropriate. This also has to do with the uncertain position- ing, if not novelty, of the role, and it works to articulate one of the most powerful ideological assumptions about directors. Alongside the stories of organic emergence within the history, there are those of directors who got to their position by joining small companies, or indeed by forming small com- panies. As the very reverse of a training course, directors become directors by declaring themselves such.

When directors form a company of which they are the director, it is a mode of self-certification.

I had no idea whether I could be a director – I shouldn't think any of us have. How could we? And there's no way of training us to be one either, which is, I think, regrettable. Most of my generation became directors by having sufficient *chutzpah* to say in our early twenties, 'I'm a director'. If we kept saying it with sufficient *chutzpah* we were sometimes believed and then we directed plays. We became directors by directing.

(Peter Hall in Cook 1989: 15)

In this situation, then, what enables someone to think they can self-certify as a director? Characteristically it was because they had done a university degree. Hall read English at Cambridge, Peter Brook before him had read English at Oxford, Declan Donnellan read Law at Cambridge in a later generation. Typically a British university degree in the arts trains (or trained) students to work as individuals, to organise their own time, to shape their own investigations and draw their own conclusions. Thus a number of directors in effect prepared themselves for the art of directing by selecting their own material and doing their own research. William Gaskill read Stanislavski, knew of Brecht's work and was aware, through his colleague at The Royal Court Theatre, of the tradition that went from Jacques Copeau (1879–1949) in Paris through Michel Saint-Denis (1897–1971) to George Devine (1910–1966), there at the Court.

When Gaskill discovered Stanislavski and Brecht he was not being trained in their methods – as a Stanislavskian actor would be, for instance. He was instead selecting models for himself and thereby consciously establishing lines of influence. The structure of such lines of influence is one of the characteristic features of the world of directors. It is also a mechanism whereby practices are disseminated: Jonathan Pitches (2012) notes how ensemble practice was brought to Britain from Moscow by Komisarjevsky.

A few of the famous lines look like this:

- the Swiss scenographer and theorist Adophe Appia (1862–1928) influences Copeau, the Russian director Nikolai Okhlopkov (1900–1967) and the Berlin-based Leopold Jessner (1878–1945); Copeau then influences Saint-Denis and Giorgio Strehler (1921–1997); Jessner influences Terence Gray (1895–1982) at Cambridge ; Strehler also looks back to Brecht and the French actor and director Louis Jouvet (1887–1951); and in turn influences Patrice Chérau (born 1944).
- the Polish artist/director Tadeusz Kantor (1915–1990) learns about the Russian director Vsevelod Meyerhold (1974–1940), Oskar Schlemmer (1888–1943), the artist and choreographer associated with the Bauhaus school in Weimar, and Edward Gordon Craig.
- Copeau influences his contemporary, the actor and director Charles Dullin (1885–1949), who influences Jean-Louis Barrault (1910–1994), the director and mime artist (who also knows of Antonin Artaud and Etienne Decroux (1898–1991), the trainer and theorist of mime), who influences Lecoq (1921–1999), who through his performer school influences Mnouchkine, founder of Théâtre du Soleil and Simon McBurney (born 1957), founder of Complicite.
- Peter Hall (born 1930) read Stanislavski, studied the Berliner Ensemble, worked with Michel Saint-Denis, and knew the work of both Jean Vilar (1912–1971) at the Théâtre National Populaire and the Barrault/Renaud company.
- Reinhardt follows Appia (who looks back to Wagner) and Craig, and also develops techniques from the Meiningen company; Reinhardt's

work is seen by the British dramatist and director Harley Granville Barker (1877–1946), who also knows of Appia; Granville Barker in turn influences the actor and director Harcourt Williams (1880–1957) who influences John Gielgud (1904–2000), who also knows of Saint-Denis and Komisarjevsky.

Directors willingly talk about their models and thereby, each time, enact through repetition the consolidation of artistic genealogies. This suggests a culture in which individuals possess a certain basic level of cultural competence and independence of mind. They become self-taught in their specialism and in doing so they enter a network of other, similarly characterised, individuals. In 1989 'A large majority of British theatre directors are white, male graduates of public school background who have had no formal training as directors. Taking all ages, 71% are male, 29% female.' The majority under 30 were female; 92 per cent of those in their fifties were male. (Rae 1989: 24, 26) This network is informal rather than institutionalised, providing for transmissions of knowledge and, above all, opportunity in a way which seems entirely, but predictably, dependent on individual taste and feeling.

NICE PEOPLE

In his characterisation of the coming of the 'age of the director' at the end of the nineteenth century, Samuel Leiter suggests audiences became aware of 'a growing number of individuals who were virtually transforming the theatre experience by the application of their personal touch to stage production, even when they were neither in the play nor credited with its writing' (1991: 11). What is interesting about this formulation is that it proposes that a defining feature of direction, its precise historical distinctiveness, is a touch which is 'personal'. The personal in relation to becoming and being a director has a crucial status.

Here, for example, is Norman Marshall's definition, from 1957, of the role of the director:

A Definition of the Director's Role from 1957

It is now generally realised that producers are born, not made. The actual technique of production is really very simple. It is largely a matter of common sense and that indefinable quality called a sense of the theatre which nobody can acquire if he is not born with it. The ideal producer has an unostentatious, but immediately recognisable air of authority; he has a musician's ear for tone, tempo, and cadence; the painter's eye for the composition of grouping; the tact of a diplomat and the patience of a saint; and the comforting qualities of an old-fashioned nannie. He needs pertinacity and courage so that he does not show the slightest sign of despair to his cast however badly rehearsals may be going. He must be some-thing of a psychologist, not only to analyse the characters in a play but in order to know instinctively how best to handle each member of his cast. Some need to be coaxed and cajoled, some need to be flattered, some need to be deflated, others occasionally encouraged and a few are all the better for an occasional bullying. He must be able to use words to convey his ideas to his cast precisely and vividly. Yet a producer may have all these qualities and still achieve no more than a smooth and efficient performance if he lacks the ability to stimulate the imagination of his cast.

(Marshall 1962: 268)

The role seems to be defined here both as a set of skills and as 'indefinable' quality of temperament. To use the language of modern HR terminology, the personal 'competencies', as it were, become the job description. And this definition was by no means new in 1957. It had been in place in the discourse about direction since quite early on. Here is Kenneth MacGowan surveying the range of new directing and design practices in 1922:

The problem narrows down to the temperament of the artist *versus* the tempera-ment of the director. There is a difference; there is no use denying it. The director is ordinarily a man sensitive enough to understand human emotion deeply and to be able to recognize it, summon it, and guide it in actors. But he must also be callous enough to meet the contacts of direction – often very difficult contacts – and to organize not only the performance of the players, but also a great deal of bothersome detail involving men and women who must be managed and cajoled, commanded, and worn down, and generally treated as no artist cares to treat others, or to treat himself in the process of treating others.

(MacGowan and Jones 1964: 127–8)

The importance of 'temperament' in relation to the role of director can per-haps be illustrated from the man who, four years after MacGowan published his account, in 1926 co-founded the Festival Theatre, Cambridge. Terence Gray was an Egyptologist and his associate Harold Ridge was a metallurgist, an amateur actor, and had published a book on theatre lighting (1925). It was Gray who articulated the artistic mission of the theatre to attack Naturalism and it was Gray who presided over the making of the productions and indeed the remodelling of the theatre. Marshall calls him the 'director' of the theatre. Working for Gray were two 'producers', the first of whom was Herbert Prentice, an ex-railway clerk, and Marshall himself (who originally joined as 'stage director', doing stage management). In mounting a show such as the *Oresteia*, Gray was the one who had 'the whole conception of the production' but the 'actual production work', as Marshall describes it, was done by Prentice, while Ninette de Valois, Gray's cousin, produced the chorus (Marshall 1947: 59).

The problem was, apparently, that Gray's artistic project was undermined by his personal qualities. Marshall describes them in this way:

Although he was a bad judge of an actor, he had many other qualities to off-set this – immense originality, great courage, a wide knowledge of the European theatre, a tremendous capacity for hard work, a superb sense of showmanship, and a vivid and delightful personality. Added to this he was a man of considerable wealth. Nevertheless, his seven years of ceaseless experiment at the Festival had in the end little practical effect upon the English theatre. His great weakness was that he had an infinite capacity for attacking people, but little capacity for gathering and keeping followers of his own. He was too extreme in his views, too violent in the expression of his opinions, too obstinately uncompromising.

(Marshall 1947: 57)

The effect of his personal temperament was to destroy the brilliant group of collaborators which had produced the strikingly experimental productions: 'Gray's lack of any real capacity for leadership soon became obvious' (Marshall 1947: 59). At least that is how Marshall tells it: within a year Prentice and Ridge had left, and Marshall with them.

Into this story of Gray is tangled the definition of roles. Those interested in the history of theatrical terms can note the way in which the names of the roles slide across one another: Marshall joins as 'stage director', where the emphasis is on the word 'stage', much as it is in the term 'stage manager'. Prentice is clearly a 'producer', the one who works with the actors to embody Gray's conception, 'under the general supervision' of Gray. This is the role performed by Ludwig Chronegk (1837–1891) for Georg II, the Duke of Saxe-Meiningen, and it grows out of a form of managing the stage. In the gradually shifting distinctions between the names of the roles we can discern a larger tension between oversight and stage production, or, if you will, management and operation. And this tension carries with it a question as to the place of craft in directing, the 'director's art' as some have it. In Gray's work with his collaborators there would seem to be an unsettled relationship between the director's role and the craft over which it presides in that it is unclear whether the director's role itself has or needs craft as such. Gray had the 'conception' of the show and he had indeed designed screens and rostra, but his failure in leadership destroyed the artistic team. As director he gave direction to the show, as did Prentice and de Valois, but he alone as director oversaw and fixed the circumstances of the show, gave the process 'leadership'. At this stage in its life the incompletely resolved difficulty as to what the directing role actually does, and what its art is, can be felt in Marshall's interchangeable use of two words: 'It had not at first been Terence Gray's intention to direct any of the productions personally.' 'Gray was at his best as a producer of Greek tragedy' (Marshall 1947: 59, 62). When is a producer not a producer? When he is a director.

Thus for Bradby and Williams, setting out to describe 'directors' theatre', Gray is an excellent example of someone who can only be described as a director. In line with their observation about Duke Georg of Saxe-Meiningen, because Gray was not an actor 'he was able to retain an objective observer's eye' (Bradby and Williams 1988: 5). Indeed in Gray's case we should add that he was not only distant from the craft of performing but from all craft of theatre. A rich Egyptologist wanting to abolish theatrical Naturalism, he wasn't a person of the theatre either by training or experience. But it's that which, according to the director Komisarjevsky, might precisely have set him up for being a creative director:

> 'trained' actors are usually only capable of visualising the Theatre and its possibilities from their own narrow point of view, i.e., from the stage itself, and therefore often fail to grasp the significance of the Theatre as a whole. On the other hand, those who are not trained in any one particular branch of theatrical work, i.e., intelligent amateurs of the Theatre – as observers from the front – attain a much broader attitude towards the Theatre in all its aspects.
>
> (1929: 21–2)

The idea of director as 'observer from the front' was stated as a defining aspect of the role by Craig in 1905: 'the place of the actor is on the stage . . . and it is the place of the stage-manager to be in front of this, that he may view it as a whole' (Craig 1980: 174); and it resurfaces over 80 years later as Bradby and Williams' formula of the 'objective observer's eye' or indeed Barba's 'first spectator, with a double mind-set of estrangement and identification' (Barba 2010: 184). This coincides precisely with another director's formulation, also at the other end of the century from Craig: 'Making theatre without a director is finally impossible because the group needs an outside eye. This may be the dramatist or it may be the leading actor, sometimes it is the management. But the company demands to be lead [sic]' (Hall 1999: 47).

Although Craig did recommend that his stage-director be trained, that particular emphasis gets lost in the repeated assertion about the necessary separation of places which, for Craig as for the others, means that an actor cannot direct at the same time. So, if this notion of the 'outside eye' is a defining feature of the art of directing – which might be done just as well, but not simultaneously, by an author, actor or manager – we might say that the craft of the director seems to amount to an incidental structural effect. The director, working in an end-on theatre, happens to be the one who is physically in the position to look from out front, who can oversee what is going on. And that physical positioning duplicates the organisational positioning, in that the director, at the front of the team, oversees its work and carries forward the concept of the project, leads, as Hall says, the company. Remember that Huntly Carter's simple definition of the director is a 'leader', and that, as Marshall saw it, what brought Gray's project crashing down was that he could not lead.

And Gray could not lead, apparently, because of the sort of man he was, because of his temperament. Yet he was poised for a few years to revolutionise British theatre practice. So a question arises: he did not have the training, and he didn't have the temperament, and while the latter eventually let him down, for a while he was set for success. So what did he have?

The answer is culture. Historically directors have been able to have an 'objective observer's eye' not simply because they have been physically out front, but because they have been culturally out front. Let's return to Komisarjevsky's comments quoted above but this time give them with the lines which precede them:

> It is strange but true that for many years those who have done most for the Theatre as an art, and have encouraged new ideas on the stage have begun as amateurs. Among the latter we can name Antoine, the Duke George II of Meiningen, Stanislavsky, Diaghileff, Vera Komisarjevsky, Gordon Craig, Copeau, and the founders of The New York Theatre Guild. We need not, however, conclude from this that professionals have done nothing progressive for the Theatre, though it remains a fact that the big movements in the art of the Theatre of late years have been initiated by non-professional people. This seems to be mainly due to the fact that 'trained' actors are usually only capable of visualising the Theatre and its possibilities from their own narrow point of view, i.e., from the stage itself, and therefore often fail to grasp the significance of the Theatre as a whole. On the other hand, those who are not trained in any one particular branch of theatrical work, i.e., intelligent amateurs of the Theatre – as observers from the front – attain a much broader attitude towards the Theatre in all its aspects.
>
> (1929: 21–2)

In this analysis it seems that the decisive criteria are that the director has no training and no affiliation to any particular craft, that he or she is, bluntly, as David Mamet said of Stanislavski, 'a dilettante' (Mamet 1998: 15). What the director has instead is cultural competence, the unrestrained embrace of the amateur.

In most societies, cultural competence is acquired more or less by social osmosis, drawn from the discourse, knowledge and expectations of family and peer group. But cultural competence alone is not enough here: it has to be competence in the culture which is dominant, in the canonical, and, above all, it has to be competence which is assured that its rightful place is at the top. Such competence and its assumptions tend to reproduce the value system of a ruling group. And it may be for this reason that, historically, there have been all too few women directors. As Marshall notes of the early feminist Edith Craig (1869–1947) the theatre never gave her 'the opportunities she deserved, perhaps because in those days [1911–1920], when women producers were even rarer than they are now, there were too many prejudices to be overcome. Even to-day Irene Hentschel is the solitary woman among the established producers of straight plays in the London theatre' (1947: 81).

In Britain in the 1960s and 1970s, as in a number of other nations, the correct cultural competence was validated and concretised by attending a university. As we noted above, the power and range of the university degree are evidenced in its capacity to serve as the main formal route into direct-ing at that time. But it has now also to be noted that in those days a British university was very much more class specific, in social terms, than it is now and much of the informal learning amounted to transactions of, and con-solidation in, class values. The formation of the degree-trained culturally competent person is as much to do with social position as it is with tem-perament. We have then to listen to Peter Hall again: 'Most of my generation became directors by having sufficient chutzpah to say in our early twenties, "I'm a director." If we kept saying it with sufficient chutzpah we were some-times believed and then we directed plays' (Peter Hall in Cook 1989: 15). That 'chutzpah' is not simply personal manner. It is an assumption of the right to be out front, to lead.

TRAINING – FOR WHAT?

If the 'personal touch' in theatre was supposedly a mark of the new age of directors, we now have to see this idea of the 'personal' as an ideological construction. As an industry, theatre at a specific historical juncture sees the entry to it of a group of people who are simultaneously in powerful roles but without any training for the job beyond, perhaps, a university degree. Even by 1989, as we saw from the Gulbenkian report, there was divided opinion as to whether directors could be taught and, if so, how. So too there was division as to whether formal training was any better than learning on the job. One of those interviewed by the Gulbenkian author was the British director Peter Brook (born 1925), who said:

> One can't generalize. A director can only work out of his particular talent, person-ality, experience, attitude to life etc, so each director has to be considered a case apart. At the same time, he can be helped in his formation. In what way? There are two basic paths. The assistant (watching the work of someone more experienced) or the 'do-it-yourself' (learning by one's own mistakes in direct contact with the raw material). Again one path will suit one temperament, one will suit another. Per-sonally, I favour the second way. I think nothing develops more fully than trying and doing.

By way of example Brook instances his own practice: 'All our work with The Centre [International Centre of Theatre Research] playing improvisations in non-theatrical contexts convinces me that if a director gets together a few people, a would-be writer and borrows a room, and gets together a handful of people, he can start' (in Rae 1989: 94).

Note that Brook here is proposing something even less structured than learning on the job – simply a journey of individual discovery. And what legitimates that, according to Brook, is individual 'temperament'. In his specific case, however, this vision of starting by getting together 'a few peo-ple', by doing it oneself, is not the route he took. His early employment as a director was at those rather well-established houses, the Shakespeare Memorial Theatre at Stratford-upon-Avon and the Royal Opera House at Covent Garden. But that version of emergence is suppressed beneath the romance about the individual artist. For at the heart of that romance is an ideological assumption that the director, unlike an actor or instrumentalist, is one for whom temperament is all. Directors always already know best about their own training. They are, in essence, so to speak, equipped for the job simply on the basis of their personal characteristics. It is within this context that the rhetoric of the 'personal touch' acquires its attractiveness and value.

But the 'personal', as I've argued, is shaped by, and promotes, class values. The sort of cultural competence historically shown by directors has not been available to all. It is against that implicit assumption of the right to lead that training begins to become important. For to conceive of directing as a craft which can be acquired by developing learnable skills to a high standard is to imply that anyone can become a director, whatever their birth. This approach to directing also implies that even a leadership role requires training and that for management properly to play its part in production it has to be treated as a science. In this context it is significant that some of the earliest formal teaching of direction was established in the early Soviet Union.

When Norris Houghton visited Moscow in the mid-1930s, he found a general acceptance that directors needed to be formally trained. He would also, of course, have found the same opinion had he visited Yale, in the United States, in the mid-1930s. Everybody Houghton spoke to in Moscow about directing said 'a régisseur could direct capably only when he knew as much about the art of acting as could be learned from being an actor himself'. But it is significant that the directors were not being trained alongside actors. At the State Theatre Institute they were trained alongside scholars and managers of theatre. There were four departments (and 120 students): 'The first is devoted to the training of régisseurs, for drama and opera. The second is for scholars and scientific specialists in the history of the theatre. The third is confined to the preparation of managers of art sections. The fourth trains young people to become the managing directors of theatres.' Note the curriculum in the first department – and the presence of women:

> There are thirty young men and women preparing themselves to become theatre directors; they are among the older students of the Institute. They study the history of the theatre, of the fine arts, music, applied art, scenic design, stage direction, and something which is called the 'planning of theatrical economy' which was defined to me as 'the art of being able to organize a theatre'. One phase of it includes a knowledge of bookkeeping.

This emphasis on the seriousness of the craft of the director was apparently embodied in the arrangements of the Moscow theatres, which Houghton connects to contemporary theorisation about the role. He notes the 'long discussion in the theatre, brought to a head in recent times by the writings of Gordon Craig, about the relative importance of the actor and the producer' and then describes three sorts of theatre: 'those which exist for and are created by the actor [Moscow Art Theatre], those which exist for and through the producer, and those which exist for the actor but are created by the producer in closest association with the actor' (Houghton 1938: 62–3, 65).

But this sort of thing, as the journalist and critic Kenneth Tynan (1927–1980) saw it, could not come into existence in Britain, for the English, says Tynan, 'have never really warmed to theatrical directors'. The only English directors who had perceptible influence on English acting, he says, were Granville Barker and 'intermittently' Tyrone Guthrie (1900–1971). As such, the power in English theatre lay with the actor and that, goes his argument, accounted for the shabby state of English theatre at the time:

> If our theatres are filled with the kind of hollow semi-realism for which our authors write, much of the blame must rest with directors. Many of them are affable, intelligent men; but none of them measures up to the Continental definition – a dynamic compound of confessor, inquisitor and sage. The real art of the director, it has been sardonically observed, is his ability to get a script to direct: which involves charming a management and at least one star, who is quite likely, if the motivation of the performance is even remotely questioned, to round on the director with a chill request that he go easy on 'that Stanislavsky stuff'.
>
> (Tynan 2007: 42, 43)

Tynan's polemic wants to see a tougher form of directing which will then limit the power of that commercial commodity, the star actor. It is a replay of the polemic heard from avant-garde theatres across Europe in the early twentieth century. And in terms of the 'sardonic' definition of the art of the director it is not wholly accurate. George Devine at the Royal Court had worked with Michel Saint-Denis and knew the tradition back to Copeau. Copeau, who walked away from Parisian theatre to become a recluse in Burgundy, was himself untrained – just as were many European directors. Tynan's polemic is not, then, actually engaged with the 'art' of directing. What he wants is more directorial power and to make his case for it he perpetuates an idea that directing in Britain is simply an extension of the well-heeled amateurism of the English upper middle class, where charm is more important than wisdom. The irony is that when someone like Hall, from Cambridge University and self-declared as a director, later took over at the National Theatre there was deep resentment of his managerial power, which produced resignations, among which was Tynan.

Tynan's image of the English director as someone without much art or power has to do, I suspect, with an anger about the class system, both within the theatre and beyond it, rather more than with the precise artistry of directing. If you don't like that class system – and of course there's every reason not to – then one way of getting at it is to see it as being unskilled. This sense seems to inhabit the reflection on his own changing attitude of the British director Richard Eyre (born 1943):

> I think all directing is a skill which is acquired empirically. I've come more and more to think there is a real skill to it although I spent a long time believing the propaganda – that anyone can turn their hand to it, and oh, you've got leverage because you were at Cambridge, and you've had lucky breaks – a kind of con-spiracy of reasons as to why I might be a director rather than anyone else. Now, perhaps because I've more confidence in my own abilities, I do believe there is a real, measurable, *metier* which is directing, as there is with conducting, and one not to be derided but to be taken seriously . . . . So I do think it is a real craft which has to be learned, and how could it be anything else? But we're British and there's no proper training in this country, or at least not as there is in some of the East European countries where there are extraordinary theatre schools in which direct-ing is taken very, very seriously, and taught as a course over many years. Here, inevitably, you learn on the job.
>
> (in Cook 1989: 29)

What Eyre doesn't really say, but then he might not need to, within the terms of the opposition I have described, is what the craft actually is. Vague in definition, it is structurally precise, held in place simply by being the alternative to middle-class amateurism. Which then makes it equally viable for his younger contemporary Deborah Warner to say: 'I believe you can't really *train* to be a director' (in Cook 1989: 100).

In this division of opinion we come back to the question that has haunted this chapter: what do directors do? If you are going to train for something, you need to know what you are training for. If you simply have to provide cultural competence, an observing eye and leadership, then – arguably – certain sorts of people, from the right sorts of places, might well not need to train. It might come with the personal attributes. Yet, on the other hand, just because they are 'personal' – or, rather, just because they don't look specif-ically theatrical – there's no reason to suppose they don't require training. In an interview in 1995, Giorgio Strehler defined the personal qualities that he saw as 'specific' to the director function: 'the ability to communicate, to offer pertinent criticism, a deep and wide-ranging culture – by which I mean not merely a literary culture'. That ability to communicate and offer criticism was not to be conceived simplistically. Strehler had in mind a very particu-lar, and all too rare, talent: 'I think that without a certain dialectical frame of mind, the ability to see and argue through many diverse points of view, the ability to work collectively with actors, designers, musicians, and so forth, it would be wrong to take on a trade which is, in the last analysis, as imperfect and imprecisely defined as that of directing for the stage' (in Delgado and Heritage 1996: 264–5).

Now the implications of Strehler's position take us much further than the possession of an observing eye or the acquisition of transferable skills. We have seen that the discourse of the personal has had a positive effect in stressing the importance of the seemingly non-artistic aspects to the role – the need to include leadership and person management skills as a part of theatrical process. But the personal discourse also has a negative effect, a sort of solipsism. Strehler calls directing a 'trade' but one which is 'imprecisely defined'. That imprecision has allowed directors across the years to define the job as they want to do it. It is perhaps the only role in theatre which can be self-defined in this way, open to any sort of interpretation by those who take it on. Strehler's formula is one that requires not simply good communication skills but, and this is the crucial difference, 'a certain dialectical frame of mind'. It is the dialectical approach which allows for argument as a part of collective working, and ways of doing argument as an embrace, and working through, of opposites.

The Strehler formula is not necessarily, any more than any other, a recipe for how to be a director. But it is useful here because it enables us to arrive at a very simple, but not always stated, place. The leader is under obligation to possess certain skills and to be able to relate to others in a particular way. The relationship between leader and led has to be dialectical. View it this way round: an observer out front only exists as an observer because there is something to observe. The leader only exists insofar as there is something to be led. By agreeing to be observed and led, the directed allow the director to have existence. The facilitator is facilitated. The craft, if craft it be, is something to do with acknowledging this.

Chapter

3   Methods of Direction

There is no agreed method for directing a stage show. The reason for that is that people do shows for different reasons and think about theatre in different ways. Clarification of this is an important starting point. As the American actor trainer and director Lee Strasberg (1901–1982) put it on the Director's Unit which he taught between 1975 and 1982, 'We always question what we're working for and ask, "What are we trying to do?" ' (Cohen 2010: 80).

Although this is not always the place that the books of advice for would-be directors begin, it is a primary question. Peter Brook advises that a director 'needs only one conception ... which comes from asking himself what an act of theatre is doing in the world, why it is there' (Brook 1988: 6). When the American director Susan Stroman (born 1954) and her collaborators sought Stephen Sondheim's permission to develop an early work of his, *The Frogs*, he asked: 'Why? Why do you want to do it?' In recounting this Stroman rather sensibly comments: 'I thought that was interesting. He was less concerned about us rewriting a show of his that wasn't completely realized, and more concerned about the fundamental dramatic reason we wanted to do *The Frogs*' (in Viagas 2006: 95). It's a sensible comment, I think, because from this question, and its answer, all the other questions, and their answers, flow.

Of course the answer might appear to be very simple, namely that the director is doing it because she has been asked to and will get paid for it. But the question is slightly bigger than this and probes more deeply the director's relation with the show. To ask why one wants to do a show is to ask what one wants to do the show for: what does one want with the show? Indeed what, in brief, is this show for? Once that's sorted out one can ask: how, in order for it to do what I want it to do, do I want it to work? From here, what do the performing and design need to do? And, therefore, what sorts of performing and design are required? This then, as a number of directors note, cues the selection of the methods.

In this chapter there is a range of examples of methods of direction from key points in the process, but it's not aiming to cover every aspect of it. It has little to say, for example, about how people structure the rehearsal period or conduct the 'first reading'. Instead of giving advice as to how to do it, the main interest here is in the assumptions that lie behind the various ways it's done – and the consequences that they have. It therefore ranges across methods which contrast with one another, from regularly taught practice to the unusual and radical. The intention is that we think about what methods of direction assume and express.

FORMING THE COMPANY

The formation of the company is arguably the most important step in the process, since it establishes the agents through whom the performance will be made. That performance will in large part be shaped by their ideas, capabilities and commitments: 'by the first day of rehearsals I have taken a lot of decisions already: I've named the play, cast the actors and probably, with the designer, designed the set. These decisions are enormous and likely to represent the most significant choices a director makes' (Warner in Giannachi and Luckhurst 1999: 137).

The casting is crucial because, quite apart from the agents who will embody the finished work, it produces the relationships and attitudes of the workforce. These two are connected of course; as Richard Eyre observes:

> I would say the casting is sixty to seventy per cent, not just in type and the suitability of an actor's looks and ability for a particular role, but also that you feel you will have a relationship with the actors and that they will fit into some kind of social group. Part of the business of directing is to engage a group of people and engender a happy and homogeneous entity.
>
> (in Cook 1989: 29–30)

On the matter of relationship with actors, one directing manual advises against casting friends (McCaffrey 1998) but the American director Peter Sellars (born 1957) notes 'I cast people who I want to have dinner with, and who I want to know as friends for the rest of my life' (in Delgado and Heritage 1996: 225). Strehler founded the Piccolo Teatro with a group of friends.

But however the company is formed it does not necessarily require that the actors be cast straightaway. Indeed it is arguable that when an actor is cast immediately then they are from the very start locked into their role – their identity in the company is their role. Roger Planchon (1931–2009), the French playwright and director, did it differently, as described by one of his actors: 'The casting is never made definite at the start, except for one or two roles. We read the play out loud. We discuss it ... Roger sees each actor alone to see if the role which he had the day before suits him. Little by little, after fifteen days, the casting has crystallised' (Daoust 1981: 20). These tactics created a situation in which the actor had to be interested in the whole play rather than in her or his own role.

A perhaps more radical approach is one that recognises how the written text will always tend to structure the relationships between the members of the company, through the allocation of roles, and hence either eliminates the written text or keeps it at a distance until later into the process. Joan Littlewood (1914–2002) often did not let her actors see the script until after a sequence of physical exercises and improvisations. Famously, when the company worked on Behan's *The Quare Fellow* they spent hours tramping around the flat roof of the theatre: 'The day to day routines were improvised, cleaning out cells, the quick smoke, the furtive conversation.' When they came to the text they realised that they had already explored and developed the shapes and interactions of the play (Goorney 1981: 105). In other productions, even after they had been allocated parts, Littlewood got them to play parts other than their own.

While Littlewood pioneered methods for developing the skills of the company and opening up the pre-written text, the process still tended to be top-down in its organisation and delivery. When Peter Brook first formed his International Centre of Theatre Research in Paris in 1970 the initial focus was on getting the performers, from a range of different countries, to become aware of each other as individuals and to appreciate each other's skills. They began with yoga exercises and then Brook got them to transform the space, using any materials to hand. This was followed by whole-group work with bamboo sticks, a simple activity in which individual skill could be shown and shared while at the same time promoting physical and rhythmic interactions across the group. Vocal work also transcended the individual differences of a multi-lingual group by working with invented syllables (see the description in Smith 1972). The aim was to create *a group* without losing individual distinctiveness, and to ensure that the performers were always more primary than the show. The person doing the ensuring was, however, the director.

Brook's exercises seem to be at the opposite extreme from the early twentieth century practice of the American playwright and director, David Belasco (1853–1931). He started on a production by analysing and planning the scenes (ignoring written stage directions, whether the play was by himself or another). This led to sketches showing arrangements of furniture and best possible movement of characters within the scene. The scenic artist was then briefed and models were made. Then with the electrician he experimented with lighting. Then the scenes were built, always using real materials. Having got this far he then set about finding a cast: 'By the time I am ready to make my contracts, my conception of every character is complete.' The casting process is governed by a sense of overall design that seems to have next to nothing to do with characterisation: 'the quality of the voice is a strong persuading factor in my calculations. If I happen to have selected an actor with a deep voice for a certain part, I try to put him opposite an actress who has a high pitched voice, for when the talk floats across the footlights it must blend as in a song' (Belasco 1919: 63, 64).

Although Belasco's methods may look old-fashioned, the description of them takes us into slightly uncomfortable territory that Deborah Warner's brief account slides over. Belasco suggests that the actors, the human element of the stage, are, from one point of view, simply physical material for working with much like the scenery. We shall return to this later. But for now let's set Belasco's early twentieth-century approach to company formation alongside that of a 2011 book by Robert Cohen. He describes how 'As the concept begins to emerge, and is shared between director and producers, the artistic team is beginning to be put together.' This requires some care: 'in addition to their research on the play, directors should research their potential "playmates" – in particular the designers – so as to help guide the selection process and, afterward, the ensuing collaboration' (Cohen 2011: 85, 86). On this model not just the casting but the formation of the whole company – particularly the designers – are already framed within one person's concept.

THE DIRECTOR'S BOOK

In the earliest days of directors, Max Reinhardt planned his productions in detail in advance of any rehearsals. His ideas for stage activity and arrangements, for light and sound, were all written down in his Regiebuch, the direction book. The pages of the Regiebuch show diagrams and words, typed and handwritten, layered over one another (illustrated in Styan 1982). It is evidence of an extended process of thinking, researching and creating (see also Chapter 8).

Whether or not it exists as a physical object, the director's book exemplifies an approach to theatre production where part or all of that production is pre-planned by the director. A contemporary of Reinhardt, the English playwright and director Harley Granville Barker, is said to have marked out the stage movements of his play *The Madras House* (1910) on a system of squares laid over the floor. It was a very old technique. Goethe was meticulous about stage groupings: Patterson (1990: 81) says he asked his actors to think about the stage as a chessboard in order to make it easier for them to memorise movements, and Chinoy quotes a leading actor saying that the stage was 'marked out in squares' (in Cole and Chinoy 1963: 20). Chronegk apparently moved his Meiningen actors about at rehearsals 'on a floor marked out with chalk into squares and numbers, like so many chess men' (Komisarjevsky 1929: 59). And the technique persisted well beyond that. Actors describe how, in the mid-1930s, Michel Saint-Denis arranged the positioning of his performers to the centimetre, to a plan worked out in advance. In the post-war period in Britain directors associated with the radical new drama of the 1960s and 1970s, people such as George Devine, John Dexter (1925–1990) and Max Stafford-Clark, founder of Joint Stock theatre company, arrived at rehearsals with their stage pictures already worked out. In his 'director's book' Stafford-Clark had formulated the blocking (in Cook 1989: 241). And it doesn't need to be a literal book to work this way. Achim Freyer is a painter, designer and director. His productions might be a realisation of something painted. In this case the painting has the status of the book.

The appearance of the Regiebuch alongside some (but not all) of the earliest directors tells us something of its function not in getting the show on but in defining the remit, or more precisely the power, of this newly emerged figure. Stanislavski's wording is clear:

> I shut myself away in my study and wrote a detailed production plan...I gave directions to everyone at every moment of the action, and they were binding. [new paragraph] I wrote everything down in my plan, how, when, in what sense the role and the writer's directions were to be understood, what kind of voice to use, how to move, what to do...I made special little sketches for every entrance, exit, move, etc., sets, costumes, make-up, mannerisms, way of walking.
>
> (Stanislavski 2008: 176)

Note that specification that the directions 'were binding'. The Regiebuch was a mechanism for breaking the actors from their previous assumptions and habits by subduing them to the vision and plans – the text – of the director. Later on Stanislavski developed a way of working that was less dictatorial in mode, and more facilitative of the actors' personal development. By then, of course, he had made the break which he needed to make and had established his power as director.

But the director's book is not simply a device associated with the emergent power of the director. It is still with us. The preparation of a book as a mode of approach is recommended in a very recent publication by theatre director Katie Mitchell. In her director's book there is less emphasis on the arrangement of the stage, the design and blocking, and much more focus on the characters: 'Constructing a biography for each character before rehearsals begin will also help you when you are preparing to direct a new play.' But it is not only the characters who need to be written up, it is also the time scheme of the play. 'Write a chronology for the action between each scene or act. Then put each chronology on a separate sheet of A4 paper and slip in into your script before the relevant scene.' This chronology will help to suggest the passage of time since the actors will be able to have 'concrete pictures of the events that have taken place in between the scenes'. The scenes are then dropped, in advance, into the time-scheme: 'make decisions about when the scenes take place before you start rehearsing'. The construction of this chronology, and the concrete pictures, is much more than a work of analysis (of which more later). It is as much creation as the sketching of scenery and costumes: 'Put together a plan of time for the whole play by combining facts from the writer...with things you surmise or invent from the text' (Mitchell 2009: 30, 39, 36, 42, 41).

By contrast there are those who think that the book will simply get in the way of or collapse under pressure from the live interactions of the rehearsal process. The American director Alan Schneider (1917–1984) related how, while he tended to prepare a book beforehand, it didn't work when he was doing *Who's Afraid of Virginia Woolf*: 'I normally do [prepare a book] for the key scenes – I have some idea, but I try not to let anybody know I have the idea. But in this I couldn't do it – I tried, I gave up' (in Schechner 2002: 81). Anne Bogart suggests that this willingness to give up the book is itself a key lesson to be learnt: 'write everything down and then be ready to throw it all away. It is important to prepare and it is important to know when to stop preparing' (Bogart 2003: 134). More radical still in her attitude to the book is Liz LeCompte: 'I never bring blind reading or ideas about the mise en scène or ideas about blocking, or even come with ideas. I never work on them outside. If I do, I don't even bother to bring them in. Inevitably they don't work.' Although she notes she is usually 'making my own play', as opposed to the 'traditional' director (Schneider and Cody 2002: 334, 332), the book is not simply a repository for thoughts about a written text. It has been more often the mechanism for a particular approach to production, an organisational tool, where ideas are had in advance of the rehearsals and then the rehearsals are made to conform to those ideas.

DOING RESEARCH

The book is a place where creative ideas get recorded. But it is clear that for someone like Mitchell, her confidence in being able to 'surmise or invent' beyond the text is based on a very thorough understanding of that written dramatic text. Arrival at this understanding is the outcome of a period of intensive research. That research is necessary, Mitchell argues, because the director's primary task is to facilitate the actors in performing the play: 'No rehearsal process occurs without the actors asking questions about what has happened before the action of the play begins, and it is therefore enormously advantageous to have a firm grasp of this information.' The goal in preparing for rehearsals is therefore 'extracting information from the text that will help the actors to perform the characters and situations in the play' (Mitchell 2009: 12, 9).

Well . . . that is Mitchell's goal anyway. Bogart offers rather different advice:

> You need to find the right questions and discern when and how to ask them. If you already have the answers, then what is the point of being in rehearsal? But you certainly need to know what you are looking for.
>
> (Bogart 2003:131)

It is sound advice that directors should know what they are looking for. But directors look for different things, and each director will think that she or he is looking for the right thing. The thing the director looks for will tell us quite a lot about the director's assumptions about what theatre is and does.

For Mitchell research doesn't only answer the actors' questions, it also ensures that they perform what is in the play. This requires them to look for something particular. She notes that there is a problem with characters about whom there is little past information: 'If there are blank sections in their biographies, there is a danger that the director or the actor will invent information that will not help the actor act the play.' Research will ensure that only relevant information is brought to bear: it 'will root your understanding of the text in a strong sense of the historical period in which the play is set' (Mitchell 2009: 29, 15). The obtaining of that strong sense of historical period – or social setting or working environment – often requires field trips, historical explorations and biographical study of the author. When Max Stafford-Clark began preparatory work on Farquhar's *Recruiting Officer*, he and the company read both military and theatre history. At the Theatre Museum they looked at 'eighteenth-century acting styles': 'We began to study Garrick's advice on posture and Macklin's on Attitudes.' Then they looked at relations between the sexes. After this he notes: 'Started in on money. We had all undertaken to read a chapter of Roy Porter's *English Society in the Eighteenth Century*, and the task was to summarize relevant chapters for each other.' This led to an account of the wealth of the characters in the play, and sources of that wealth (Stafford-Clark 2004: 21–2, 41).

To give actors the task of summarising the chapters of a book is to treat the company as jointly engaged in research activity. It is a regular strategy. Adrian Noble, using a technique that goes back at least to Brecht, asked the actresses playing the witches in his *Macbeth* to bring in news images of outcast women. These in turn generated stage images. But research can often contribute as much to the company learning about itself as it can assist actors doing their roles. In his approach to plays set in a different historical period John Caird asks the actors to research a topic connected to their character:

> The actors then have to address their assembled colleagues on their chosen topic for ten minutes or so. In this way the whole company becomes expert about the period, and each individual actor becomes expert about the social, political and philosophical background from which their character was originally drawn. The purpose of this method is to inspire actors to base their choices in rehearsal on real knowledge of how their characters may have lived and thought. If actors are sufficiently steeped in the life and times of the period, then they will start instinctively reacting as people then would have done.
>
> (in Cook 1989: 44)

This stress on the importance of research, on really knowing about the play, has a long and revered history. One of the earliest and most influential examples is that of Stanislavski. In *My Life in Art* he tells how the company approached Gorky's *Lower Depths*. While his colleague Nemirovich-Danchenko did an analysis of the play, Stanislavski himself was in a muddle, 'as always at the beginning'. So they organised an 'expedition' to the Khitrov Market, 'Led by the writer Gilyarovski, who studied the life of down-and-outs'. Unfortunately that night there had been a theft and security was tight, but they nevertheless managed to get into and looked around the dormitories. The people they spoke to were the 'down-and-out intellectuals', the 'brain-centre' of the Market. They could read and write and 'copied out scripts for actors and theatres' (Stanislavski 2008: 223–4). In a similar process, preparing for Tolstoy's *Tsar Fyodor*, he visited the historical sites and bought authentic objects.

While a version of Stanislavski's fieldwork research is still done, let's recall Bogart's remark about directors needing to know what they are looking for, and the differences that might follow from how the object of the quest is defined. Research, on inspection, becomes slightly different things in different situations. Take the research questions that motivate the work done by Katie Mitchell and Max Stafford-Clark: for Mitchell's production of *The Seagull* questions include 'What season is it?' or 'Where is Sorin's estate in Russia?' From here one might ask: 'How large is the estate? What was the normal size of an estate at that time in Russia? What type of trees line the avenue? What size is the lake? What type of shrubbery is it?' (Mitchell 2009: 11, 13). For *The Recruiting Officer*, Stafford-Clark feels the need to explore a couple of relationships: 'How close are Kite and Plume? Is it anything like a relationship today between officer and sergeant? How intensely were Silvia and Plume involved when he was last in Shrewsbury? . . . How unusual is Silvia's determination to win Plume?' That last question wants to explore the conventionality of what is often a 'theatrical device' (Stafford-Clark 2004: 39–40).

These two sets of questions prompt some observations about the different approaches to research. First, we can note the parameters within which it is conceived and carried out. Mitchell's research, as with her whole approach, is located firmly within a commitment to Realism. Her book 'assumes you are interested in building an imaginary world for the actors to inhabit, using ingredients from real life and circumstances suggested by the text itself' (Mitchell 2009: 2). Her questions about *The Seagull* are all about 'facts', some of which the play might not be concerned to tell us. Her 'facts' don't, however, include speculation as to the status of 'theatrical devices'; they are not necessarily questions about the facts of dramatic form. Indeed David Mamet argues that such questions don't even understand the nature of the dramatic text. He imagines a situation where an actor is doing research: 'You have a character in the script say "I've been in Germany for some years." Exactly how many years would that be?' To this he responds that the playwright has no idea: 'The play is a fantasy, it is not a history . . . The character did not spend any time *at all* in Germany. He never was *in* Germany. There *is* no character, there are just black marks on a white page – it is a line of dialogue' (Mamet 1998: 60). Mamet provokes us to see that the method of research derives from, and reproduces, ideological assumptions, about text, about acting.

Second, we can note what people think they discover from the research. John Caird thought his actors would become very much more specific about a period, and therefore grounded in it. Thus, he thought, 'they will start instinctively reacting as people then would have done'. The assumption is that the actor can really feel like an eighteenth-century person. Similarly, of his expedition to Khitrov Market, Stanislavski says it 'aroused my imagination and creative process more than any discussion or analysis could have done. Here was nature that I could form and shape, living material for my work, people for characters.' In making his mises en scène, 'I was guided by living memories, not ideas I had thought up or suppositions.' And the reason he did not find it difficult to make his sketches was that 'I felt as though I was in the dosshouse myself' (Stanislavski 2008: 225). The research process can, apparently, take you subjectively into a different place.

This takes us to a third observation, which concerns the extent to which the research recognises and reflects on its own methods – or, to put it another way, the extent to which the research is shaped or coloured by the assumptions of the people who are doing it. Stanislavski remarks that the world of the down-and-outs was 'danger, robbery, adventure, theft and murder. That creates a romantic atmosphere around them and their own kind of wild beauty we were looking for at the time' (Stanislavski 2008: 223). So they come upon this evidence of the 'real' world of Gorky's beggars with a mindset seeking 'wild beauty'. This somewhat qualifies the terms on which Stanislavski felt himself to be like an inmate of the dosshouse. But it's a qualification of which he was himself quite astutely aware: he notes the dangers to his practice that come from 'the romanticism of the down-and-outs which encouraged my usual attraction towards being stagey' (Stanislavski 2008: 225). The excitement of the research might then be less to do with facts than with the combination of tourist trip and dressing-up, and has the effect of cancelling social and historical distance from what is being explored. Where it apparently gives subjective access to a different period or place the research might efface, or ignore, the realities of material difference. But there's something else it effaces.

Max Stafford-Clark points to it when he tells the author of *The Recruiting Officer* 'there does seem to be a real confusion here, in the twentieth century, about what kind of play you have written' (Stafford-Clark 2004: 37). Frequently research is seen as an activity which contextualises the written text of the play, looking to supply what it doesn't say, and sometimes adding new bits in. Research seems much less frequently to involve an engagement with the specific form of the text as written. We shall touch more on this below in the section on analysis (and it relates to issues raised in the chapter on Shakespeare: see Chapter 7), but what is relevant to note here is that the written text is as much part of the material circumstances within which the actors and director work as are 'real' objects and photographs brought into rehearsal.

It is 'material' insofar as it requires the development and use of techniques and has a physical impact on the performing body. This is recognised when writing hits people in the face, when directors feel they have to do work on dealing with 'verse'. But it is also there in prose. Restoration prose, for example, establishes particular patterns of breathing as does the nineteenth-century epigram (see Shepherd 2006). But this material impact of the written text is pushed to one side by a directorial method that encourages actors to ignore such things as punctuation, as in Strasberg's exercise where the actor 'doesn't keep literally to the sentence structure, but breaks through the words so the scene will reveal his thoughts' (Cohen 2010: 89). While Strasberg later says that no director should change a line's meaning, there seems to be an idea that syntax is not an integral part of the mechanism that makes meaning, and therefore can be ditched, in order to reveal not the scene's thoughts, but the actor's, and thereby perhaps, once again, efface difference.

But there is an additional issue here, which in turn has implications for embodiment. This is the need, all too infrequently mentioned in discussions of writing, to delineate precisely the range of different sorts of verse – and then to respond to them. In the Hamlet-Ophelia 'nunnery' scene, for example, there are several different forms of verse: the job is not simply to speak verse, but to recognise the different modes Shakespeare is quoting and then play them. And that general point can be applied to character. Dramatic texts will define and write characters in different ways. A single text might operate, or quote, different models of characterisation: Ibsen's *Doll's House* has Nora slide in and out of melodrama, and therefore the Nora actress needs to be prepared similarly to shift modes (see Wallis and Shepherd 2010). Research can ask the question, what kind of written object do we have here? What is being constructed and signalled by the writing? And such questions are clearly going to produce something very different from a question that asks what it was like being a middle-class woman living in that sort of house, of that sort of size, with that colour skirting board, in nineteenth-century Norway. And the answer isn't: 'It makes you feel a bit melodramatic.'

This point, like most good melodrama, can be taken one stage further. Directors and companies do a lot of research to find out about the world in which the play was written – and in which it is set – in order to try to discover more about the reality it imagines and refers to. What seems to receive less attention is the question of whether the play deliberately wants to misrepresent or distort that reality. There is an assumption that the play has an unproblematic relation to reality. Against that the counter-argument suggests that many plays deliberately, or indeed unintentionally, do their primary work as drama by wilfully interfering with ideas as to what reality is. It probably would not be helpful to do research for *A Midsummer Night's Dream* that explored what acreage of sixteenth-century England was given over to forest and the proportion of elms to oaks.

The capacity of research to (appear to) answer questions takes us to a fourth observation about it. Research can be seen not simply as a method for gaining knowledge about the play, but as a mechanism for organising the company, making them comfortable with the project and with each other. It is an instrument for achieving coherence. John Caird says: 'This kind of research is really just one of the starting points for a whole attitude towards rehearsing which will eventually help to build an arbitrary group of actors into something much more important – a company' (in Cook 1989: 45).

Research can also be, then, an organisational tool. It not only brings the company together, but it also offers to answer all the questions; it effectively brackets off the imponderables of historical or social distance; it allows free rein to subjectivity and instinct; and it ensures all gaps and silences are filled. Clearly, if you wanted to, you could do a production in which the gaps in the dramatist's text were staged: 'you will observe that Gertrude and Ophelia are never given a scene together'. But frequently the ideology behind research, and therefore production, is one that says coherence must be maintained and, if need be, invented.

Having made four general observations about research, we can close this section by recalling some of the different attitudes to what it is and does.

In his later years Stanislavski admitted 'we stuffed the head of the actor with all sorts of lectures about the epoch, the history, and the life of the characters in the play, as a result of which the actor used to go out on the stage with a head full to bursting and was not able to act anything' (in Magarshack 1950: 374). This seems to contrast with Katie Mitchell, who is closer to where Stanislavski started: 'the actor playing Agamemnon will research the number of ships in the Greek fleet; the actor playing Clytemnestra will find out about the walled city of Argos where the family lived . . . these research tasks are tailor-made to fit individual actors so that they only research what they actually need to know in order to play the scenes in the play' (Mitchell 2009: 85).

Research raises the question as to the relationship between actors and knowledge. What is or should be in the actor's head? 'In the early stages of rehearsal if an actor asks, "What am I playing here?" it occasionally helps to say, "You're trying to do this" or "You're trying to do that." But, really, in the end, I find this quite constipated. It can block the actors with theory because they start trying to find lots of different interesting verbs. It tends to become a rather cerebral exercise' (Declan Donnellan in Shevtsova and Innes 2009: 75–6). Research also raises the question about the relationship of director and process. What is or should be in the director's head? As Anne Bogart sees it: 'A director asks simple and meaningful questions propelled by curiosity. Curiosity cannot be faked . . . in pursuing an interest, we experience insecurity. Insecurity is not only OK, it is a necessary ingredient' (Bogart 2003: 131). Or, as Stanislavski more casually put it, 'when I arrive at rehearsal now, I am no more prepared than the actor and I go through all the phases of his work with him' (in Magarshack 1950: 374).

And, finally, research throws up a question about one other element. This is described by David Mamet:

'I want to know everything there is to know about the character and the times in which he lived,' the actor says. 'And if the author wrote, " . . . did smite the Sledded Polack on the Ice", I want to know the cause of the dispute between

Poland and Denmark which gave rise to that line, and I want to know the depth of the ice.'

Sounds like a good idea. But it ain't going to help. It will not help you in the boxing ring to know the history of boxing, and it will not help you onstage to know the history of Denmark. It's just lines on a page, people. All the knowledge in the world of the Elizabethan era will not help you play Mary Stuart.

(Mamet 1998: 62)

Research can produce a relationship to the dramatic text by making assumptions about what it is and how it functions.

ANALYSIS OF THE SCRIPTED PLAY

Commenting on his production of Trevor Griffiths' *Comedians* Richard Eyre notes:

... In respect of mining the characters, there wasn't anything terribly useful in keep watching stand-up comics in miners' welfare clubs, which is where we went. We talked a lot about stand-up comedy and watched a lot of it, but in the end the genesis of that production was a great deal of very, very detailed moment-for-moment work which involved a gradual accumulation of detail of movement and behaviour

(in Cook 1989: 31)

Many directors think the detailed movement will often emerge, not from research, but from detailed analysis of the written text. This depends on knowing the written text thoroughly. Mike Alfreds advises that a text should be approached so as to allow it 'to release its own life and imagined WORLD. Potentially it's a living organism.' Instead of seeking to impose a concept on it, the director should 'try to become one with the play, to immerse yourself in the material' (Alfreds 2007: 112, 113). But not everyone agrees with this version of the written text, let alone the director's relationship to it. Here are two other opinions: 'The best thing that can happen in the early stages of study is to find a "handle" for the play ("concept" is really too fancy a word at this stage)' (Black 1975: 5). A few years afterwards we get this: 'For contemporary directors the play is not a "given" – it is an invitation to undergo process.' This is the American critic and director Charles Marowitz (born 1934), writing about 20 years before Alfreds, and clearly with a very different notion as to how to be a contemporary director. For Marowitz the process has, necessarily, to be in critical relationship with the play and the director, by contrast with Alfreds' advice, is actually obliged to impose concepts: the modern director, he says, 'challenges the assumptions of a work of art and uses mise en scène actively to pit his or her beliefs against those of the play. Without that confrontation, that sense of challenge, the direction cannot take place, for unless the author's work is engaged on an intellectual level equal to its own, the play is merely transplanted from one medium to another' (Marowitz 1986: 4, 6).

As we embark on an exploration of different sorts of textual analysis done by directors, it is worth bearing in mind the division between Alfreds and Marowitz because it highlights assumptions about the relationship to the dramatic text, and, behind those, assumptions about the purpose of directing. But before looking more closely at written materials, we should observe that analysis also pertains to processes that do not begin with written text.

The construction of devised material, as Eugenio Barba sees it, is also capable of – and benefits from – extremely detailed analysis. His model identifies three 'dramaturgies' which organise the performance, each with its own protocol: 'The level of organic or dynamic dramaturgy' which 'concerns the way of composing and interweaving the dynamisms, the rhythms and the physical and vocal actions of the actors'; 'The level of narrative dramaturgy – the intertwining of events which orientate the spectators about the meaning'; 'The level of evocative dramaturgy – the faculty of the performance to produce an intimate resonance within the spectator' (Barba 2010: 10).

Barba's dramaturgies are of course, as the word implies, a mode of creation as well as analysis. This makes them slightly different from the work on scripted text for in this particular case analysis is done, in the main, to find out how it works, what suggestions it gives for its own staging. The process here is not about finding what one can 'do' with the script, and how one can add to it. It is about finding what is there already in the words. This is carried out very often on the basis of a model not drawn from the established procedures of literary analysis but instead from the techniques for working with actors developed by Stanislavski.

Let's take our summary of it from Norris Houghton who in the 1930s watched it in action in rehearsals at the Moscow Art Theatre. He observed that after the period of research was over the work entered a new phase:

> The régisseur has divided the act into a number of small pieces, or rather, he has taken up a short sequence of lines and grouped them together to create a small scene. Each fragment, kusok, has its place in the building of the act .... These kusoki are definitely marked and numbered in the script and, during this analytic period and even into the period of rehearsal which follows, it is the rehearsal unit.
>
> One might liken this dissection of the act to an analysis of a musical composition.

Houghton then acknowledges that in British or American productions there might seem to be a similar process of division, but with a crucial difference in how it is used:

> Usually the American or English producer makes the divisions on the basis of action: a scene may run from entrance to exit; often he picks up a new one at the entrance of a character, using the physical act of entrance as a motivation

for the announcement of a new scene ... . The Art Theatre's divisions are much smaller and more frequent because they are based not so much on movement as on unity of thought and emotion ... . A scene played across a table between two characters who sit there quite still for ten minutes would in all likelihood be rehearsed with us as a single scene just because there is no break in the action. In the Art Theatre these ten actionless minutes might contain six scenes, divisions being made every time a new chain of thought or a new emotional reaction is established between the two characters.

(Houghton 1938: 86–7)

A version of this became standard practice in British theatre, with its own name: when William Gaskill prepared for *The Sport of My Mad Mother*, 'I divided the play into units and objectives as laid down by Stanislavsky' (Gaskill 1988: 27). And the practice is still urged upon trainee directors in Britain. In one of the more persuasive of the how-to-do-it books (although his judgements aren't always beyond contest), Mike Alfreds demonstrates how to analyse a text for objectives, actions, beats: 'The more detailed the beats, the more vivid the performance' (Alfreds 2007: 82). But of course, as Marowitz might have argued, this will lead not just to vividness but to a certain type of performance, carrying certain assumptions and values.

So we need to re-state that, however widely disseminated, this is one particular sort of analysis. And two observations should be made about it. The first is that a search that looks only for thought and emotion is probably not going to want to attend to a text's tricks with form and convention, its changes of verbal register, its capacity to render itself as irony – that problematised relationship to reality that we noted above. Secondly, together with the kusoki, this analysis finds the play simply, and only, by finding the interior of the characters. Alfreds says that by doing analysis a director will understand how a play is made, which sounds commendable; but he explains that the purpose is 'to understand the structure; and to gather information about character' (Alfreds 2007: 120). Ah – that sort of information. But it doesn't all need to be a hunt for the supposed interiority of character. Mamet, among others, would say that, in fact, there is no such interior: it's just black marks on a white page.

A different sort of analysis was developed by Giorgio Strehler. It is based on 'three Chinese boxes'.

In the first box we approach the play on the level of reality: that is to say through the story of a family, its life at a particular moment; in the second we shift to a historical level and in the conflict and struggles of the individual characters we see reflected the social and political conflicts of the period; in the third we are operating in the context of universal – let us call them abstract – values ...

In *Per un teatro umano* Strehler explains this in much more detail: in the first instance we are dealing with ordinary human affairs: the buying and selling of a garden, people moving from Paris to Russia and back again; in the second we glimpse a wider panorama of Russia: of the classes which, like Firs, are disappearing or, like Lopakin, getting on; in the third we are aware of the eternal story of human existence, of suffering, resignation, the passage from birth to death. Strehler employs the image of Chinese boxes because each progressive interpretation is a broadening of the perspective, yet the three are interdependent, existing inside 'a fourth box which must contain all three'. The challenge ... is to realise all three levels of significance in equal depth.

(Hirst 2006: 28–9)

Now if those three levels are to function simultaneously within one production it implies a particular mode of performing, because the audience is engaged with more than the characters immediately in front of them. From here the larger implication is that, far from being a neutral mechanism, the kind of analysis that is done has its effect on creating the mode of performance. This is very clear in the work of Bertolt Brecht.

In his *Short Organum for the Theatre* Brecht recommends breaking the text down into units based on 'gestus'. He describes the 'realm of gest' in this way:

Physical attitude, tone of voice and facial expression are all determined by a social gest: the characters are cursing, flattering, instructing one another, and so on ... These expressions of a gest are usually highly complicated and contradictory, so that they cannot be rendered by any single word and the actor must take care that in giving his image the necessary emphasis he does not lose anything, but emphasises the entire complex.

By way of illustration he takes the opening sequence of his own play *Life of Galileo*: we see Galileo having a wash and then giving a lesson on the solar system to the boy Andrea Sarti. Of the milk Galileo drinks, Brecht asks: 'does he really drink it without care? Isn't the pleasure of drinking and washing one with the pleasure which he takes in the new ideas? Don't forget: he thinks out of self-indulgence ... Is that good or bad?'

After giving examples of how the embodied attitude of the gestus carries complex, and often contradictory, social attitude, Brecht notes the result of analysis: 'Splitting such material into one gest after another, the actor masters his character by first mastering the "story". It is only after walking all round the entire episode that he can, as it were by a single leap, seize and fix his character' (Brecht 1964: 198–200). It is not so much, then, that analysis helps develop the character; analysis may also define what sort of thing character is and does.

Brecht's mode of analysis attends very closely to what is in the written text (see also Chapter 7 for an example of his analysis of a Shakespeare play) but he is not inviting us to look for coherence, for 'unity' of thought and emotion. Instead: 'When reading his part the actor's attitude should be one of a man who is astounded and contradicts.' In order to consolidate this attitude on the part of actors Brecht recommends that they be held back from inhabiting the part:

To safeguard against an unduly 'impulsive', frictionless and uncritical creation of characters and incidents, more reading rehearsals can be held than usual. The actor should refrain from living himself into the part prematurely in any way, and should go on functioning as long as possible as a reader.

(Brecht 1964: 137)

The work of analysis thus produces an attitude to the material on the part of the actor. For Brecht this was important partly because he was trying to break with a previous method for doing things. But it is also important because of the logic of the process. Any mode of analysis takes place within a frame that lays down procedures, and very often also assumes what is being looked for. Thus the actor-analyst learns not only an approach to the text, but also develops a particular understanding of how the text works, as theatre. So, while it nominally takes apart the text, in order to understand it better, analysis may also be said to produce those who will perform it.

WORKING WITH THE FURNITURE

Implicit in Brecht's remarks about how Galileo drinks his milk there is an assumption that analysis doesn't simply focus on words spoken or not spoken. It also focuses on objects and furnishings. This is worth pausing over, for two reasons. The first has to do with enriching the understanding of how the written text functions; the second has to do with how the rehearsal space functions.

Fictional furniture

That great analyst of scripted drama, Harley Granville Barker, argued that in a naturalist text 'the actor's mere embodying of a character' needed to be supplemented, to become convincing, by the scene: 'Hedda Gabler's surroundings – she herself such a contrast to them – are very much part of the play ... And as for the studio and that queer garret in *The Wild Duck*, there is as much dramatic life in it, one could protest, as in any character in the play.' The need, therefore, is for the performer to understand the relationship to, and work with, objects and setting:

Rebecca sits crocheting 'a large white woollen shawl which is nearly finished'. Even in this (and even in the fact that it is a 'large' shawl and 'nearly finished') there is a touch of dramatic significance: for it is the occupation of a woman – of such a woman as we see before us, at least – who sits and waits and watches and thinks, and has been so sitting (since it is a 'large' shawl 'nearly finished') through long hours. She is waiting now and watching, her eyes turning every few seconds or so to the window. It is open, so that she may hear if not see the Pastor coming; she is listening intently too.

(Barker 1964: 27, 174)

The development of an appropriate way of crocheting has to be worked out between director and performer. Such working-out is not often recorded, but Weber tells us about Brecht:

> Sometimes it took an hour to work out whether an actor should pick up a tool one way or another. Particular attention was devoted to all details of physical labor. A man's work forms his habits, his attitudes, his physical behavior down to the smallest movement, a fact usually neglected by the stage. Brecht spent hours in rehearsal exploring how Galileo would handle a telescope and an apple, how the kitchenmaid Grusha would pick up a waterbottle or a baby, how the young soldier Eilif would drink at his general's table.
>
> (Weber 2002: 86)

These remarks about written texts raise two issues of interest for the director. The first has to do with the placing of bodies within scenic space; the second has to do with the expressive potential of that scenic space, and its furnishings, in their own right.

Meyerhold's staging exemplifies the first consideration, as described by Worrall:

> An extended arm or leg is never a gesture in isolation but is a gesture which repeats a pattern in the stage architecture. The rigidity of the structure imparts a rigidity to the gesture. A stance with the feet placed stably apart tends to be a repetition of an inverted 'V' pattern in the wooden frame. The individual figure fits into the literal framework like an organic part of it ... Thus the 'sufferer' in terms of the conventional action of the play – Bruno – can be made to seem caught in the structure as in a trap, as in a world in which he has not found his place.
>
> (Worrall 2002: 68)

Komisarjevsky had a more sceptical view of it however: 'Meyerhold tried to confine the actors in his productions to primitive picturesque movements and artificial intonations, making the acting subsidiary to the settings, and merely fitting the actors into the static picturesque décor' (Komisarjevsky 1929: 73).

Strehler exemplifies the second consideration:

> Where does the plastic/symbolic/realistic element reside for the characters in this room? In the chairs. These represent the crucial element that gives the action meaning. They speak volumes: they suggest the idea of property that has been squandered; an empty chair has a hidden, deeper meaning, it is a pointer to the present and the past. A chair on stage represents a most powerful alienation device – there's far more to it than just sitting down. A lot of empty chairs signifies tension, uncertainty, mystery. Who will sit there? Will anyone, ever? What are these chairs waiting for? and for whom? When they are empty they spell loneliness; when occupied, conversation, company, people. People capable of doing anything: making love or dying on them.
>
> (in Hirst 2006: 32)

Rehearsal room furniture

Many processes begin with the company – or at least the actors and director – sat around a table. So-called 'table-work' involves discussion of the play, sharing research, doing analysis. Nowadays it may form part of a sequence of varied activities rather than come in a block, but in the early days it tended to come first. Belasco had a large table in the 'reading-room' at the theatre around which everyone sat in the first few days while the play was read. There was a green felt-covered table for similar use at the Moscow Art Theatre. Louis Calvert recommends, in 1918, that a 'round table discussion' can solve the problems of different departments not knowing what the other is doing (he reports a clash between a costume designer and scenic artist) (Calvert 1918: 193).

This way of beginning can then have its effect on the process. Anne Bogart reports the method used by a Russian director to effect the difficult transition when the actors have to leave the safe 'comfort' of the table and move into open space:

> We were, at that moment, sitting together at a table. 'Imagine that we are at a table with a group of actors, studying a play,' he said and then picked up his chair where he and I had been seated together and moved it away from me to a certain distance. Then he placed the chair down and started to look at me intently. I felt exposed.
>
> (Bogart 2003: 134)

McBurney's solution is to make sure there isn't a table: 'I get people up on their feet immediately .... I'm not saying this is the answer, but the process is not always helped by sitting around reading' (McBurney in Giannachi and Luckhurst 1999: 70). Similarly Barba eschews the table, but instead does a performance of his own: 'I don't rehearse "around a table" in the sense of reading the text together with the actors and laying out my interpretation. Usually at the first rehearsal for a new performance, I expound its theme as I feel it. It is a sort of oral improvisation' (Barba 2010: 158). So there doesn't actually need to be a table for the space to be owned by the director.

Once the actors are free of the table, if they have been there, they don't return to it. The director, however, often ends up behind a table, looking at the actors. This piece of furniture comes to mark the difference between director and actors. In the case of Belasco, and before him Goethe, the table literally belonged to the director. Belasco's was part of the furnishings of his theatre. Goethe's was his table at home where he took the actors to conduct them in a read-through. Similarly Komisarjevsky's was in his London flat. Subsequently it may not have literally belonged to the director but the table was seen as part of the conventional attributes of the director. And as such it helps to define the director's role. Stanislavski notes that when he and Nemirovich-Danchenko began to go their separate ways, whereas previously they 'sat at the same table', now 'each of us had his own table, his own play, his own production' (Stanislavski 2008: 262).

Tables have to do with structuring relationships. Houghton reports a sequence of tables in Meyerhold's theatre. At the first rehearsal Meyerhold talked about his ideas: he 'sat in the centre at a large table'. In the phase of rehearsals when Meyerhold created the business: 'The stage was crowded. The centre part of it was set for the action. Meierhold sat at one table at the edge of it; his assistants sat at two other tables; the usual crowd of onlookers filled the wings and footlights.' In the next phase of rehearsals 'Meierhold leaves the stage and goes to the auditorium to begin his revisions and additions from there. For a time he makes constant interruptions and is continually dashing up the runway to the stage from his seat by a little table in the centre of the house' (Houghton 1938: 117, 128, 133). A director's table was clearly also a mark of authority recognised by outsiders: in the Moscow Art Theatre, at the formal dress rehearsals in front of invited guests, 'the director and his assistants, the designer and technical director of the theatre and usually one or two members of the Repertcom ["Board of Censorship"] sit at a long table covered with a green felt cloth, which is set half-way back in the house' (Houghton 1938: 97). For the censors' visit, a director's table needs to be staged.

In later years, as rehearsal-room equipment developed in complexity, the table begins to acquire new status, as the bearer of a new piece of kit. In the Builders Association show *Super Vision* (2005) a desk ran along the forestage. Here the operators sat along with performers who were not on stage, with performers sometimes acting to camera and the image projected onstage: 'The video operators necessarily have their laptops, which are functional. Positioning one at the actors' seats is a bit of set dressing – designed to enhance the sense that everyone in this production is online, connected' (Lavender 2010: 25). The 'desk' or table becomes part of the performance but when they move into this space the actors are treated as, put in the same scenic circumstances as, operators. The actors are given the equipment that comes with the desk. The table as it were absorbs the rehearsal activity into itself.

Thus although the table seems like a commonsensical way of providing for those whose work in the rehearsal room involves computers or books or pads of paper (and cups of coffee), its use sends signals. Katie Mitchell sensibly warns would-be directors, with or without table, to be careful how they sit in the rehearsal room: directors who sit slouched in a chair with crossed arms, for example, suggest to actors, albeit unconsciously, that they are judgemental or bored (Mitchell 2009: 131). The table doesn't come without ideological baggage. It was difficult, Stanislavski tells us, to get the dramatist Chekhov to sit at the director's table: 'We would make him sit down at the table, and he would begin to laugh. It was impossible to understand what made him laugh, whether it was the fact that he had become a stage director and sat at such an important table, or that he was inventing means of deceiving the stage directors and disappearing from their ken' (Stanislavski 2008: 417). The table is furniture that belongs with a role and it physically divides two groups of people in the rehearsal room. How any particular director uses the table and its meanings is always worth observing. And haunting that usage, echoing down the years, is Chekhov's imponderable laughter.

MANAGEMENT OF THE CIRCUMSTANCES

All the relationships in the rehearsal room – spatial, personal, material – are potentially shaped by the director:

> At that time they were rehearsing the *Urfaust*. [...] I walked into the rehearsal and it was obvious that they were taking a break. Brecht was sitting in a chair smoking a cigar, the director of the production, Egon Monk, and two or three assistants were sitting with him, some of the actors were on stage and some were standing around Brecht, joking, making funny movements and laughing about them. Then one actor went up on the stage and tried about thirty ways of falling from a table.... Another actor tried the table, the results were compared, with a lot of laughing and a lot more horseplay. This went on and on, and someone ate a sandwich, and I thought, my God this is a long break. So I sat naively and waited, and just before Monk said, 'Well, now we are finished, let's go home,' I realized that this was rehearsal.
>
> (Weber 2002: 85)

Weber's account of Brecht and Monk at work suggests a number of ways in which the director has an impact on the making process. These include expectations about what actors do – they try out, they analyse, they bring a particular attitude to the work – and expectations about directors – how they relate to actors, what hierarchy they sustain, how they physically occupy the space.

Now a number of directors are famous for developing programmes for training the sort of actors that their projects need. Most famously perhaps, Stanislavski had rather more to say about the practice of acting than he did about directing. This is because not just directing but the whole practice of theatre seemed to him to depend on the actor: 'I became convinced that there is a gulf between a director's ideas and putting them into practice and that theatre exists above all for the actor' (Stanislavski 2008: 249). For Stanislavski, as for other early directors such as Copeau, one way of making the break from a commercial theatre in which celebrity actors were dominant was to develop a company in which all the actors were alike subject to a disciplinary regime which had its origin in the vision, and indeed the person, of the director. But there is something that directors do – and all of them do it – which is bigger than training programmes for actors; namely the establishment of the conditions and atmosphere in which the company work.

In this section we shall look at three general topics: first the development of a sense of company and atmosphere of the working space, including what rehearsals are for; second the relationship of director and actors as the work is developed; and third the production of the acting. I shall have little to say about the training of actors, since properly this belongs in a book about the art of acting. The issue it does raise, however, is the director's attitude towards actors.

Company and atmosphere

As we noted early in this chapter, when Peter Brook established his international company in Paris in 1970 he began with group exercises and games. His contemporary Joan Littlewood and her company had already established a reputation for training actors during the rehearsal period. Part of this training was warm-up games, designed in principle to release the creativity of the company. This prompted a member of the company, Clive Barker, to develop a more purposeful and structured approach to games, which led eventually to his influential 1977 book *Theatre Games*. Over the subsequent decades steadily more companies have used periods of play. These model the interpersonal relationships by encouraging risk-taking and hilarity, breaking down various sorts of personal barrier. They also teach the members of the company to enjoy each other's skills and make it allowable for everyone to have creative ideas. Although it is often the director who runs the games, the sharing around of the creativity implies a different form of relationship between director and actors in relation to the material: 'Directors are really just manipulators of people, and their manipulation can be more or less subtle or aggressive. I prefer to be subtle.... Perhaps the difference in my work is that although there are roles, such as director, actor or writer, everybody can have a say in the process' (Spink in Giannachi and Luckhurst 1999:123). In companies that devise their own material, almost all of the creation is handled by the company, although the director, in the case of someone like Tim Etchells, retains a form of editorial control (see p. 156).

That control is both exercised and problematised in Eugenio Barba's version of the role of director of devised material. In his model both the actors and the director improvise: 'Once the actors had improvised and flawlessly assimilated their improvisations, then my own improvisation as director began.' The actors, often working as individuals, develop material. To this Barba then responds:

> My personal meeting with the actors took place through their fixed improvisations...I experienced them as stimuli...They appeared to me as a wealth of signals, obvious or abstruse symptoms, allusive information which had to be protected in order subsequently to be introduced in that work level where I elaborated interactions, connections, clusters of meaning.

In this work, he says, 'It was the non-conceptual part of my brain which decided. I had the feeling I was choosing these dynamic dialogues as a projection of my animal identity.' But, while he retains the right to trust his instinctive feelings about what he sees, he nevertheless invites the actors to question what he says: 'Anything I say, the contrary is equally true.' While this offering of himself to question might seem refreshing, or even unusual, in the role of director, it nevertheless, in the view of one of his long-term actors, doesn't put him beyond the practice of both editing and manipulating others: 'You cut and manipulate the actors' materials according to a taste and choices whose criteria are incomprehensible to the observer' (Barba 2010: 53, 56, 74, 61). Even though he shares in the work of creativity, allowing himself to be non-conceptual, it's the director's feeling which, unrationalised, presides over the work of others.

Not all Barba's actors see it that way and he himself, despite the odd romanticism about animal identity, has a commitment to hard work and continual questioning which underpins his approach to devising. This expresses itself in a healthy scepticism about the sentimental mystique which gathers, like lichen, around the notion of 'process'. 'A working process is not true, authentic or sincere, but only functional or usable in relation to a given person' (Barba 2010: 86). In a similar way games can be treated sceptically. The glowing jollity of the company comes to substitute for the work of engaging with text:

> I had a deep resistance to the kind of loose improvisational techniques used by many people working on the fringe in the different disciplines, whether drama or dance. They might be useful exercises for a warm-up but they had begun to be seen as a way of rehearsing instead of as an adjunct to it, and I didn't like that. In rehearsal I tended to work out exercises or exploratory projects which would fit the specific work I was engaged on.
>
> (Davies in Cook 1989: 74–5)

What is being produced in these circumstances, we might say, is the company's pleasure in itself rather than its capacity as a workforce to engage with alien material such as an historical scripted text. The method of approach thus has to be more exactly appropriate than generalised playing:

> Sometimes I spend two weeks on a text before beginning to move it, sometimes we will begin moving the play immediately, sometimes physically. Sometimes you begin with a whole series of related exercises or with a great deal of research. It's fluid and, again, I think you are relying on your instinct for what is right in terms of the combination of the play you are trying to crack, the company you are working with, the environment in which you are doing it and where you feel you are yourself – not forgetting the audience you think you will be addressing.
>
> (Alexander in Cook 1989: 63)

Most of this concern with detailed company interaction seems, however, to have no place within David Mamet's model: 'What should happen in the rehearsal process? Two things./1. The play should be blocked./2. The actors should become acquainted with the actions they are going to perform' (Mamet 1998: 72).

Whatever method is adopted, at whatever extreme of functionality, everything takes place within a particular rehearsal atmosphere (some of the wider implications of which are discussed in Chapter 10). Anne Bogart advises a sensitivity to atmosphere, and therefore a consciousness that directors might do the wrong thing out of fear: 'Many young directors make the big mistake of assuming that directing is about being in control, telling others what to do, having ideas and getting what you ask for.' But this, she says, is not good directing: 'It is about having a feel for time and space, about breathing, and responding fully to the situation at hand, being able to plunge and encourage a plunge into the unknown at the right moment' (Bogart 2003: 85). A similar, if more functionalist, point is made by Robert Cohen: 'The director's role is not to command an artistic collective to their duty, but to unite and aim them toward a shared challenge.' The shaping of material 'requires skills that reach into the emotional hearts and unconscious minds of those being directed' (Cohen 2011: 57, 56).

But control itself is also a necessary tool. Eugenio Barba says people become directors because of 'personal need' which makes them choose a 'role of power'. This power then enables him to make demands of actors in order to make them more excellent at what they do. It is, he says, a form of manipulation, but 'An actor accepts to be manipulated for personal reasons, if he has a feeling of breaking the limits of his ignorance, if he knows that there are no privileged colleagues in the group and if he is convinced that the director doesn't decide on the basis of selfish interests' (Barba 2010: 152, 165). Using a somewhat different language Declan Donnellan proposes a balance between law and love. Where an ideal world might be anarchy with love, laws become necessary to prevent people killing each other. In the microcosm of the world which is theatre, directing becomes a balance between love and law: 'when you direct a play you have to impose certain laws on what happens. In a scene between two people, or ten people, different amounts of laws are necessarily imposed by the director' (in Delgado and Heritage 1996: 90). That imposition is perhaps a different proposition from reaching into actors' emotional hearts.

Donnellan's formula is a conscious way of modelling the atmosphere. A key element of this modelling is the sense given out by the director of what they are like as a person. 'I know I have great power. Everything I do leaves traces: how I speak, with whom I speak, if I keep silent, if I smile or am serious' (Barba 2010: 152). Anne Bogart reminds us that whether they intend it or not, directors always communicate something to actors:

In rehearsal, a director cannot hide from an actor. Again, intentions are visible and palpable. An actor can sense the quality of interest and attentiveness the director brings into the room. It is real and it is tangible. If intentions are cheap, the actor knows this.

(Bogart 2003: 120)

Astute directors are conscious of their rehearsal persona and treat it as itself a work of production:

The encounter on the first day is always strange. The beginning is a very secret moment, I think. There is no formula for it. If I sense that people are embarrassed then I might do something really ridiculous to relax them; if they're over-relaxed then I might do something to give them a jolt; if they're tense I try to relieve their anxiety.

(McBurney in Giannachi and Luckhurst 1999: 70)

This control of persona is vital for handling the moment when the creative phase of rehearsal moves into the phase when stage business is fixed in place, when love becomes law. Houghton describes this at the Moscow Art Theatre:

with the final stage in the rehearsal period, the producer leaves the stage, drops his whisper, goes out into the house, and becomes at the same time audience and full-voiced master. He must now give the performance unity and form. The danger which the 'group of actors' theatre runs is that it may not recognize that eventually it will reach a point where it must yield its democracy to autocracy.

At this point, 'The producer's word is now law and the actor's comfort is little thought of' (Houghton 1938: 94, 95).

Working with the actor's body

When the director leaves the stage she or he puts a distance between themselves and the actors, in order to formalise the relationship. But it's not necessary to assume that just because directors are close to actors the relationship will be one of affection and enablement. Indeed historically the person in the directing role assumed rights over the body of the actor. Here is the Victorian satirist and librettist W.S. Gilbert (1836–1911) rehearsing the chorus: 'He issued his words of command as if he was on parade, and when they were not obeyed he stormed and shouted. Sometimes he would even seize the leader of the chorus and shake him into a Gilbertian view of his duties' (in Marshall 1962: 259).

This sort of directing is a useful mechanism for coping with, and concealing, bad acting, as Stanislavski noted of his own early practice. But the task was to develop beyond it. Houghton describes him at work: 'When rehearsals are held on the stage the producer is constantly there with the actors; he does not sit out front. Throughout this period he seems only to be trying to help the actors. He walks about with them on the stage; whispers suggestions to stir their imaginations.' This contrasts with Meyerhold: 'Meierhold is not searching for a reading that will satisfy the actor, as was Stanislavski, but for one that is as close as possible to the way he would read the line. He knows in advance the exact speed and intonation of each word.' Similarly, at the Vakhtangov Theatre, 'Every gesture, every move, is as carefully demonstrated to the actor by the régisseur, and the prompt-book plays almost the same important part' (Houghton 1938: 92, 127, 174).

Actors who are asked to copy may well have a different sense of themselves and their function from those who are treated as being more creatively potent. The latter approach became much more standard, with its vocabulary of sensitivity. Anne Bogart says: 'I direct from impulses in my body responding to the stage, the actors' bodies, their inclinations' (Bogart 2003: 85). A similar sort of sensitivity was attributed by Arthur Miller (1915–2005) to Elia Kazan: 'Instinctively, when he has something important to tell an actor, he would huddle with him privately rather than instruct before the others, sensing that anything that really penetrates is always to some degree an embarrassment' (in Kazan 2009: 40).

But this sort of instinctive sensitivity might also be problematic. Bogart asks herself whether, when she attends to the performers, she is in fact attending to herself: 'Am I attending with desire for success, or am I attending with interest in the present moment? Am I hopeful for the best in an actor or do I want to prove my superiority? A good actor can instantly discern the quality of my attention, my interest' (Bogart 2003: 74). Maria Fornes puts it more bluntly when she calls certain rehearsal techniques, 'manipulative' – and she points out how the rehearsal room atmosphere connects to the art that is produced:

> there is a lot of secrecy in rehearsal. The director speaks directly to each actor about the motivation and psychological manoeuvrings. Whispering. This makes the actor feel special, favoured, and the others feel left out.... Too often I see the director going and talking in the ear of an actor. Does this mean that the director is not saying anything that would be of benefit to the rest? ... The secrecy is divisive. Not just divisive between one actor and another, but also in relation to the character. What kind of character is going to come out of secrecy like that?
>
> (in Delgado and Heritage 1996: 98)

Presumably the kind of character that Kazan constructed.

Producing the acting

Indeed it is no surprise that a particular kind of character, a kind of acting, will inevitably emerge out of particular kinds of rehearsal atmosphere.

If games and exercises are seen as one way of encouraging creativity in performers, this encouragement can also happen in the work on scripted text – in the approaches to learning lines and staging, or blocking, the scenes, for example. All of this activity presents directors with choices, of which they may or may not be conscious. But even before it choices have to be made about regimes of training and preparation. For these not only produce particular sorts of acting, but also contain assumptions as to what acting consists of and what it is for. Barba's concept of 'subscore' is useful here: 'The subscore is an inner support, a hidden scaffold which actors sketch for themselves without intending to act it out.' The different ways in which a subscore can function 'depend on the actor's dramaturgy, which is different according to each specific technical tradition.' Thus Stanislavski's subtext is a form of subscore 'built up from the actor's personal interpretation of the character's intentions'. For Brecht 'the subscore is a continuous dialogue the actor uses to question the historical truth of the character'. In 'codified genres' the subscore has to do with the system of rules in a tradition (Barba 2010: 30). In other words subscore is not fixed or eternal but is entirely based in the ideology of the acting practice.

Now while it is not relevant to our purposes here to explore acting practices and what they do to actors, the questions about what acting does and what it is for can lead us into thinking about the variety of ways in which directors treat actors. These can be roughly bundled up into three: there are those who see it as their task to train or shape their actors' skills and attitudes; those who work with what they get, regarding the actor's skills as the responsibility of the actor; and those who affect to show no interest in the craft of acting.

We have already touched on directors who train. As we have seen, because Stanislavski felt there was a 'gulf' between directors' ideas and actors, actors needed to be trained. For him the theatre was primarily about acting. Ninety or so years later Mike Alfreds says the same thing. We should note, however, that when directors take on actor training this often serves the purposes of the director as much as it does the greater good of the actors. It is by training that Stanislavski and Copeau freed themselves from a commercial theatre industry dominated by celebrity actors. This of course can be of benefit to actors too, in that the formation of a company in which people develop longstanding relationships and share deeply held beliefs is very different from a form of employment which is based around temporary contracts for specific shows.

But it is nevertheless the case that when actors move outside a particular training regime or company they may encounter problems. Jonathan Miller notes that 'as a director I have never been able to reconcile the natural pride of the American actors in their own skills with the requirements of a play that demands...certain forms of artificiality and highly technical skills' (Miller 1986: 80). And among those American actors one of Hal Prince's performers notes that 'The so-called Method actors would have problems with Hal's fast-paced rhythm' (Hirsch 1989: 56). The point was put more polemically in relation to a training method that seemed to excite polemic: Stella Adler said those who went through Strasberg's Method ended up 'Crippled' (Adam 1980: 22). And, whether 'crippled' or not, these actors might not always be particularly useful to the play they are in: as the realist dramatist Arthur Miller saw it, 'The problem is that the actor is now working out his private fate through his role, and the idea of communicating the meaning of the play is the last thing that occurs to him' (Roudané 1987: 95–6). We may thus have to acknowledge that some directors' training regimes may only work for the particular purposes of those directors.

So for Alan Schneider what is important is the result rather than the process: 'any way of achieving the semblance of reality is, to me, legitimate'. The 'reality of the actor' was to him much less important than 'reality for the audience', regardless of whether actors found that artificial. What then becomes a point of difficulty is the assumption carried by actors who have been through a particular sort of training: 'The only real problem that I have with realistically trained actors is that, over the years, I've come to believe that there is no such thing as an abstract, rigid "reality" ' (in Schechner 2002: 75).

This takes us to the rather more knotty question of the status of the actors and their practice in the rehearsal room, and in dealing with this we're looking at the second group of directors, who work with what they get. When Schneider says that the reality of the audience is more important than the reality of the actor he is directly contradicting Strasberg's view that 'Only a reality that's the actor's reality – not mine, or yours, or the playwright's – can be relied on' (Cohen 2010: 87). As soon as the actor is moved away from having a privileged grasp on what the 'real' is, new relations are opened up. Directors may invoke a 'real' which the actors are simply required to provide, whether they feel it is 'real' or not. That requirement might involve helping the actor to deliver what is wanted or it might simply be a demand.

Although there is a thread that runs deep in the history of direction, from Stanislavski up to the 'how-to-do-it books' of such as Alfreds (2007) and Swain (2011), that it's part of the director's job to understand actors and their 'reality', the examples of successful practice that have ignored this indicate that it is not a given. Take, for example, the case of Hal Prince (born 1928), famously known as a director of musicals. Referring to rehearsal work on inner motivations, one of his actors, Lonny Price, says that 'Prince expects the actor to do all of that as part of his homework' (in Ilson 1989: 38). The different expectation comes from being outside a particular ideology of acting: Prince, we're told, doesn't 'personalize' as Method directors do. The actor is simply thought about in a different way. This doesn't entail obstruction or contempt, for, as another performer puts it, Prince 'allows actors to bring in their own choices, which he then edits'. But the different idea of the actor produces a different directing practice. This is described by Barbara Baxley:

Unlike Elia Kazan, who could be a teacher, a therapist – whatever the actor needed – Hal expects you to be a grown-up. He doesn't want to hear about the actor's personal problems in working out a character: he just wants you to get up and do it, and he'll tell you when you haven't found the right way.

(in Hirsch 1989: 56)

Now as we know Stanislavski said there was a gulf between the director's request that you get up and do it, and the actor actually doing it. Strasberg more or less repeated this: 'It's one thing to explain how to do something and another thing for the actor to be able to do it' (Cohen 2010: 87). Strasberg and a range of others would solve that as Stanislavski did, by helping the actor to get there. Another director, perhaps equally successful, such as the early Robert Wilson, might respond that it's of no interest to him what's going on inside the actor and that the actor's job is to do what is required. As one of his performers, Sheryl Sutton, observes, 'Bob never tells you what it's about. So you make it about something, working within the context of his coordinates. And you never have to explain what that is to him.' Not only are directors not necessarily obliged to facilitate actors, but they are also not obliged to have any respect for the craft of acting: Sutton as a trained performer says 'I had so much respect for my technique as an actor and I really felt confronted by not being able to use it.... What people have to find is a way to be people somehow in a very aesthetically defined space while performing minimalistic kind of actions' (in Shyer 1989: 12, 10). That might entail sitting still and counting until the precise time came to move.

Here we are a long way from Strasberg and respect for the interiority of actors. While Strasberg advises that 'Directly telling actors the results you expect or want leads to mechanical-like expression', Wilson throws the responsibility onto the actor: ' "You've got to find something," he once said, "that doesn't make it look like the director told you to do it – so it doesn't look stupid" ' (in Shyer 1989: 18). At the heart of this contrast of approaches is not simply the difference between the parameters, or 'coordinates', set by directors for actors, but the status of what Strasberg calls the actor's 'reality'. In his book Shyer likens Wilson's attitude to actors to Richard Foreman's view: 'I'm not interested in seeing actors' acts, but in seeing real people, awkward people' (in Shyer 1989: 10). For Foreman (born 1937), and most of those, like Wilson, influenced by the art movement that produced Happenings, the actor's reality is, by definition, illusory. Now, when we are in the territory where people make different definitions as to what reality is, we know we are dealing with ideology. In the contrasts between the different directorial approaches to actors we are looking at the management of value and at the definition of what is real, good and proper, at the definition of what 'works'. Notions like 'common sense' or 'real-world practice' evaporate. It is all ideology, nor, as the man said, are we out of it.

From directors' views of what they think acting is, let's look briefly at one of the key moments when they get actors to do it: when the actors start to move, the so-called 'blocking'. Insofar as it relates to 'composition' of the stage image, this takes pride of place as the first of Dean and Carra's 'five fundamentals' of directing (see Dean and Carra 1974). But of course this is far from being the only key moment. There is, for example, interesting division of opinion on the question of when actors should learn lines. Belasco 'insisted that my actors avoid trying to memorize their rôles until their conception of them is fully formed' (Belasco 1919: 72), and Strasberg followed him in that. Noël Coward insisted his actors knew their lines in advance of rehearsal. Peter Hall has moved from one position to the other. At the heart of it is a tension between fixing something early or having it debilitatingly unfixed, and that's all predicated on what is assumed about how brains work. But these sorts of questions, and their assumptions, cluster in an exemplary way around the matter of 'blocking'.

To some directors this is as crucial as lines, and in need of as much discipline:

> To Brecht, blocking was the backbone of the production: ideally, he thought, the blocking should be able to tell the main story of the play – and its contradictions – by itself, so that a person watching through a glass wall unable to hear what was being said would be able to understand the main elements and conflicts of the story. To work out blocking this clear takes an enormous amount of time; he would try out every thinkable possibility
>
> (Weber 2002: 86)

Doing the blocking is usually, however, one of the principal sites of negotiation between director and actors. Houghton watched this happening with Stanislavski:

> If the actor wishes to make movements of which the producer does not approve, he is allowed to try his way; perhaps he will eventually be led back to the producer's way if it is best; but he is never forced at this point to do anything which is not comfortable for him.
>
> (Houghton 1938: 92)

This led to a school of thought which believes that every movement should be motivated, on the basis that an actor can only move if the character has reason to do so. But the character, as David Mamet firmly says, is 'just lines on a page' (Mamet 1998: 62). And thus the movement might need to be made because the director or production logic has reason that it should do so: 'take a few steps over, darling, so we don't play center – I take everything off center'. This is Hal Prince who, in his persistent demonstrating of both gestures and intonations to actors, flies in the face of all Strasberg's advice not to tell actors the results he expects. Apparently he got away with it because he was 'delightful' (Hirsch 1989: 45). Less intent on being delightful

Joan Littlewood's response to an actor saying 'I don't feel right' was 'You don't have to feel right, you just have to do it. – Do it!' (in Goorney 1981: 167). Robert Wilson, going one step further, did not so much demonstrate as instruct: David Warrilow recalls being taught precise gestures, just as a dancer learns choreography, in a process that most actors would find insulting (Shyer 1989: 18). Blocking, then, is an activity where the actor's sense of the real or the workable, the actor's 'comfort' indeed, may be up for grabs.

This process may be seen, however, and Bogart invites us to, as not so much confrontational as contradictory and hence productive: 'I like to think of staging, or blocking, as a vehicle in which the actors can move and grow. Paradoxically, it is the restrictions, the precision, the exactitude, that allows for the possibility of freedom' (Bogart 2003: 46). That paradox about restriction producing freedom is something attested by actors who worked with the playwright Samuel Beckett (1906–1989) when he directed. Billie Whitelaw observes: 'It might seem as if his precision and insistence on the minutest detail should totally restrict the actor; but it doesn't. It gives you a marvelous freedom, because within this meticulous framework and I suppose surrounded by the feeling of compassion and safety, there is freedom to experiment' (in Knowlson 2006: 174). Similarly, in his reflection on being taught very precise gestures by Wilson, David Warrilow says: 'The more exact the parameters, the freer I became. Because once my body knows how to do these things, all the rest gets to be free' (in Shyer 1989: 18).

Obviously this is a very different approach from that of letting actors find their own way or creating conditions in which they can be freed of pressure or deferring to their reality. And it prompts a question. Where the books and courses advise directors to facilitate actors we need to ask: of what does facilitation consist? Declan Donnellan says that there only needs to be a good relationship between the performers, and then 'wonderful things will happen out of the scene because none of us have overburdened it with laws' (in Delgado and Heritage 1996: 90). By contrast the Beckett and Wilson actors quoted above suggest that it comes, not from freeing up the body or even understanding the text, but from the imposition of clear parameters, laws indeed. Both clearly work. That this is so presumably has to do with the understanding of the precise job of work in hand.

For Brecht, the blocking was important because it not only carried the story but communicated the attitude of the production. The way an actor stands is part of that actor's address to the audience. Whether there is any training or not, the analysis, the conduct of the rehearsals, the line-learning and blocking all culminate in a particular sort of acting. Very obviously the mode of acting is not in any sense necessarily or organically linked to the text being acted. Thus when he did *The Cherry Orchard* in 1974, Giorgio Strehler's approach consisted of: 'a critical application of the Stanislavski method; an alternation between moments when the actors allow their emotions to take over and moments of extreme self-control – with the actors simultaneously sustaining the two extremes. A game of internal versus external reactions, of participation and distancing, of absence and presence' (in Hirst 2006: 32–3).

Strehler's was a 'critical' application: it had a relationship of critique to the place where it started. This takes us to a final observation. One of the elements which shapes both rehearsals and the final production is the director's sense not just of what acting is but of what acting is for – why anybody is doing it in the first place. By way of illustrating the sort of issues here let's turn to one of the most articulate theorists of theatre techniques, Brecht. When Brecht wanted to demonstrate how epic theatre operated he used the example of a scene in the street when a witness to an accident demonstrates to bystanders what happened:

> the demonstrator should derive his characters entirely from their actions. He imitates their actions and so allows conclusions to be drawn about them. A theatre that follows him in this will be largely breaking with the orthodox theatre's habit of basing the actions on the characters and having the former exempted from criticism by presenting them as unavoidable consequence.

Acting, and hence blocking, in epic theatre are defined by a clear purpose, to encourage an audience to make judgements (Brecht 1964: 121, 124, 136). In this instance rehearsal process is definitely guided by a sense of what the production is for.

TECHNICAL REHEARSALS

When they speak about their work, directors often have more to say about the early stages of the process, the approach to the work and its rehearsal, than they do about the closing stages, the technical period and dress rehearsals. This is possibly because it seems to involve stepping away from what might be regarded as the more creative, emotionally involving activity into territory which is more straightforwardly organisational, the autocratic as opposed to democratic phase. Max Stafford-Clark says of the technical period: 'A director needs to focus on quite different priorities and develop a different range of skills during these three days. Above all, the director has to be pragmatic and objective' (Stafford-Clark 2004: 170).

Yet for some directors, at different phases of technological development, this change of focus allowed the space for a whole different sort of creativity: 'I utilize this time making the final adjustment to my lights . . . the timing of lights is quite as important as the timing of the movements of the players.' This is David Belasco, from the early years of the twentieth century. He was famous for his commitment to light as one of the primary expressive media of the stage. But in his discussion of light here he also directs our attention to the makers of light and thereby reminds us that this phase of the process is not simply about giving instructions to people who are brought in at the last moment but about seeing to fruition the work of those who are also part of the vision of the show:

> The perfect lighting of a stage can be accomplished only when the electricians become as familiar with the play as the actors themselves. I may say that I fully appreciate how great is the assistance my productions have gained from these small-paid men. They do not work mechanically, but with their hearts and souls, for, once having comprehended the spirit of the play, they are as dexterous with the appliances for regulating the lights as musicians with their instruments.
>
> (Belasco 1919: 80)

After he was satisfied with the lighting, Belasco attended to the make-up of the performers and then held a 'dress parade'. In his attention to each of these elements Belasco both marks his difference from previous modes of putting on shows and justifies his status as a director who was also theatre owner. He notes that he supplies the performers with every detail of their costume, rather than relying on them to supply it themselves as with earlier practices. And he tells us that in his theatres the dressing rooms 'are equipped with rows of electric bulbs of every hue' (Belasco 1919: 81) so that the actors can check properly the effect of their make-up.

Following the dress parade Belasco held a curtain rehearsal and, if there was music, he sorted it out with the musicians. The curtain rehearsal is another instance of the recognition that the whole company needs to engage with the spirit of the play. It also makes very clear that the newly emerged role of director views every material aspect of the production, and not simply the actors, as having expressive potential and thus brings these diverse aspects within an overall scheme of planning which ensures their productive interaction:

> I have sometimes experimented with a curtain fifty times, raising or lowering it rapidly, slowly, or at medium speed. The curtain men must be taught to feel the climaxes as keenly as the actors and to work in unison with them.
>
> (Belasco 1919: 83)

We might recall here that one of the memorable and distinctive effects of Harley Granville Barker's innovative Shakespeare productions at the Savoy in 1912 was the speed and sound of the fall of scenic drapes as dramaturgic punctuation.

Now ready for the first dress rehearsal Belasco ordered the space to be cleared and positioned himself, with his scenic artists, out front in an empty auditorium. Later he would invite guests to the final dress rehearsal in order to learn from their reactions.

AFTERWARDS

Directors have different behaviours after the show has opened. Deborah Warner likes 'to stay with a production in its early weeks of performance, I think a director should' (in Cook 1989: 105). Sometimes that staying with a production expresses itself as a form of vigilance. Clive Barker says of Joan Littlewood: 'There must have been some performances she missed seeing, but my memory of the production is that she came round every evening to distribute notes. The other actors got detailed notes. All she ever said to me was, "You weren't there" or "You still weren't there" ' (Barker 1978: 3). At the other extreme, with some finality, is Lluis Pasqual: 'I've never seen one of my own productions. It wouldn't agree with me' (in Delgado and Heritage 1996: 210).

An Interview with Ralf Richardt Strøbech

Ralf Richardt Strøbech trained at the Royal Academy of Fine Arts School of Architecture and also studied music and film at Copenhagen University. In 1995 he sang in the choir of Hotel Pro Forma's production *Operation: Orfeo* and after graduation started working with the company in 2004. As both architect and Artistic Director of Hotel Pro Forma he has produced work in a range of formats including exhibitions, architectural projects, graphic realisations and performance concepts. As a director Strøbech regards the space as something which performs, leading to work in airports, hotels, stations and transit halls. In 2010 he formed his own company, Loop Group.

Shepherd: Let's begin somewhere familiar: is there any value in regarding the director as an author?

Strøbech: It's related to personal branding. You have to have a particular aesthetic or something recognisable, otherwise you won't be able to do a production. What's the point of asking a person to do something if you don't know what you'll get? – It's related to the flow of money.

Shepherd: Because that product in the marketplace is not reproducible anyhow else.

Strøbech: And it's also related to copyright issues … It's very clear in painting: you know Jackson Pollock drips stuff and you know that [Georg] Bazelitz turns stuff upside down. It's to do with how you can reproduce that in the theatre so that you have something very recognisable – in order to be recognised as another auteur. It's a two-way thing. You need it in order to be recognised as somebody specific in that position, but it's also traditionally the way to recognise an auteur: it's a self-fulfilling prophecy.

Shepherd: Because there's no point in being an anonymous director because an anonymous director is inconceivable?

Strøbech: Actually I think it's a bit sad because it potentially takes away differences in the artwork. If, let's say, I was a highly branded director and I made a Shakespeare piece and a Goethe piece and a Virginia Woolf piece: they would look exactly the same because they are seven-tenths me and only three-tenths anything else. So it's really important to think about this role and where you want to position yourself between being at the service of or completely dominating the text. For me the notion of being an architect, as I am, is useful because the architect traditionally is the master builder rather than a design genius. What is unique about a production is the people participating in the project. The casting not only of the actors but of the entire team is the crucial moment because your recruitment will eventually define your product much more than what text or visual style you choose. But the interpretation of the role is very individual. You need to position yourself. I decided long ago that I really didn't want to brand myself at the cost of being able to make different stuff. The more prominent the branding the less liberty you have in the interpretation from one production to another.

Shepherd: So you get caught within your own persona.

Strøbech: Absolutely. You can see that in all the fashion houses. The more highly branded you are, the more difficult the escape.

Shepherd: Presumably one way of putting pressure on your own personal brand is deliberately to seek situations working with different companies or forming a company with different people than you worked with before rather than always keeping the same team.

Strøbech: I don't think you can say once and for all which is the better approach. The dynamic of it is that you need to be something specific in order to be able to produce something; but also you need not to be that in order to produce different stuff. It's paradoxical.

Shepherd: But it means then that there is always deep tension in there as well. When this role of director starts out historically it suggests there is somebody in charge of the process to keep it orderly, to make it work to schedule. That implies the role is in a clear-sighted and centred position of authority. What you're saying is that the role has deeply built into it a tension, an opposition – so it's actually perhaps the most structurally unstable role in theatre.

Strøbech: Isn't it linked to something that everybody feels all the time? If as an actress you produce the hysterical mother figure all the time, then you're only cast as this. The more we distance ourselves from the pre-modern conception of having a trade, being a blacksmith for example, or any role where you expect the output to be the same, the moment there's an emphasis on innovation, then you have this paradoxical situation: you need to innovate but you need to innovate in a predictable way.

Shepherd: So the market will recognise the object.

Strøbech: It's built into the society we have today, but it's very obvious in the role of the director.

Shepherd: Do you think it's a good thing that there's often no formal training for the job?

Strøbech: I think if there is an institutionalised role, then society should be able to provide an education for this role. The question of course is how to do it and what should they learn. When I said I come to the theatre as an architect, I meant that almost in a metaphorical sense – because I think that architecture is about making very large stuff that fits somehow inside a space. So you can have an architecture of thought or an architecture of computer programming. It is about organising a lot of different stuff in time and space.

Shepherd: As an architect you're interested in organising stuff in time and space – presumably if you were trained as a scholar of literature you'd be interested in your relationship with written text?

Strøbech: It depends how you look at it. You might also say that you have certain interests as a human being which drive you to be a literary scholar or drive you to be an architect. People act consistently with their basic substance as a human, no matter whether it's about what you order at a restaurant or how you would dress Carmen in the opera. But whether a particular person gets to do a particular piece is serendipity in the sense that people have to hire this or that person, or have to produce this or that piece, or put into production this or that play. This kind of Darwinian selection process is not necessarily healthy.

Shepherd: Would you say therefore that in terms of selection process directors emerge out of the social class that assumes its capacity to organise other people, that directors are habitually bourgeois?

Strøbech: To make a very broad generalisation, it's the bourgeois who have had financial liberty to incline themselves towards the arts. You will find the over-representation of the bourgeois class in the world of directing because it has power and in turn liberty, and it has decadence and yet has structure.

Shepherd: That's quite depressing?

Strøbech: I think it's very funny – in that every time you think you exercise your free will, it is of course circumstances that brought you to make that choice. It's actually very touching that the more you feel that you exercise your freedom, the less it means you do so. It's very beautiful and has a nicely resonant irony to it. Humankind is a very peculiar species in that it contains illusion within it, but this is the stuff that makes it in the first place. It relates to performing: I experience the liveness of it, but still I know it's highly planned. I really like that. It reflects how human beings function in the first place.

Shepherd: Tell me what you think the most important function of the director is during the process. Is that entirely individual as well? Does it depend upon who the director is and who the company is? Will the function change?

Strøbech: Whether it be expressed in terms of power or inspiration, the director needs to be a focal point in the way we produce theatre now. If you have an actors' collective, then somebody will assume that role anyway. In the production of the play somebody needs to be a focal point, but that's not necessarily the same as the centre. That's an important distinction. I would never think of myself as the centre of the production, but I would always think of myself as the focal point.

Shepherd: If the director is the focal point, is the whole thing organised into a direc-tor's vision or is it that there are other people's visions coming in to it as well? Is there a negotiation?

Strøbech: The word 'vision' is very problematic, though terribly over-used and very annoying. Mixed up within the concept of vision is a kind of exclusiveness. The way the word is used now implies something within sight but out of reach. So it kind of institutionalises the lack of need for process, because if you have a vision then you already know where you want to go. I would rather have a sense of direction in a physical sense: I know I'm going in this direction but I don't know where it will bring me. The version of 'vision' promoted by society is more to have a sense of goal than to have a sense of where you stand. It's invested in the future and linked to effectiveness, to efficiency.

Shepherd: Corporate missions and visions ...

Strøbech: I really really don't think it is healthy. What is the point of doing anything if you know where it will take you?

Shepherd: This might relate to the corporatisation of the director's role?

Strøbech: Recently there's been a pronounced tendency to professionalise theatre and theatre processes so that companies mimic corporate ways of doing stuff. That's very dangerous because art is not a commodity. It's not a product in the same way as cups and cupboards. It needs to be different, otherwise it becomes only entertainment. I have absolutely nothing against entertainment, not at all, but it is a different process and a different role for human kind. You need to focus on the process and not the goal – but that too can be misunderstood as a kind of seventies 'collective' cliché: 'let's have a nice process and nothing else matters'. But actually that isn't the right formulation – that you should focus on the process... because the process is not important either. You have to liberate yourself from the need to go somewhere specific, to be able to get lost. It's a little like Red Riding Hood diverging from the path. We need to diverge a bit more, because if we go down the beaten track then we know where it will take us. This is related to the paradox of innovation that we talked about earlier.

Shepherd: So the person who is the focal point has as part of their job to move laterally, to become no longer the focal point, as it were to mistake direction?

Strøbech: Yes, I really like to work in a way where I take the risk of following the enticing way – I don't know why and where it will belong but it will find its place eventually. It shouldn't be mathematical, it should be exploratory, inventive and joyous; it should be playful.

Shepherd: It's almost as if one should get rid of the English word 'director' and simply talk about direction. The thing will find its direction.

Strøbech: Yes, every production has a direction itself. Michelangelo would say that the sculpture is already in the stone and it's my job to liberate it. It's the same thing with the process in theatre. The finished piece is already there, it just has to be expressed.

Shepherd: So the art made by a director is the art of process or of company formation, an art which is capable of deviating. The art of a director is not necessarily simply making an end product but making all of the other things?

Strøbech: In Danish it's not called the director; it's called the instruktør so it has a completely different semantics.

Shepherd: And of course in English, as opposed to American, it always used to be 'producer'. You can almost say that the confusion, or perhaps the multi-facetedness, of the role is symptomised by the number of names it has.

Strøbech: In Swedish it's Regisseur, so it's similar to the German.

Shepherd: And then the metteur en scène.

Strøbech: I really like that French term. But I don't like the Danish one so much. Instruktør literally means telling somebody what to do. The crucial issue here, I think, is company values and how to promote them. But at the same time the really sad thing is that while ambition, mission and values are very important, once they are rationalised as insistently as they are now they lose significance. Of course you should have a mission or ambition or vision, but it shouldn't be a point – it should be a space. And remember that the nature of visions in the old-fashioned sense is that they dissolve, are enigmatic, like phantasmagoria. So I think a good way to understand vision is as being incorporated into a different world that emerges around you. Vision in that sense doesn't have a direction. It is a shared space and a collective experience of something particular or even peculiar.

Shepherd: Can I be extremely literal about vision for a moment: when you are working on a production, from where, physically, do you see it?

Strøbech: Very often at an optical distance. But nothing is innocent, so of course it makes a difference whether you make a production from the vantage point of the eighth row in the middle behind a table or whether you do it from the balcony. This is related to the fact that as a director you also have an obligation to the theatre, you know which seats are the most expensive. You are catering to certain needs, but you might not even be aware of this.

Shepherd: In terms of being aware of things – but on a different tack – what do you understand by the notion of research for a production?

Strøbech: I am in love with knowledge. But research is not having knowledge: it is to be inducted into a specific way of thinking. I would never research to know stuff but to be saturated in a specific way. To let yourself be taken over by the subject matter.

Shepherd: That would relate to what you said about being ready to take the wrong path in the wood.

Strøbech: You have to be in the middle of everything. It's a very nice place but very scary. In my opinion, that is something you can actually teach people. We are trained in this Cartesian mode of distancing ourselves. This continues with the whole positivist movement and the need to professionalise artistic processes and the aspiration to be worth as much as a scientist. The radical positioning of yourself and your cognition is what we need to teach directors – really to know when I am within a thing and when I am outside of a thing, and what the implications are of those positions. The two processes are complementary – one is inductive and the other is conductive, like breathing . . .

Shepherd: One can understand all of the pressures that resist that sort of ambiguity or restlessness.

Strøbech: It's very sad somehow.

Shepherd: Yes . . . And it prompts me to think about the relationship between subjectivity and structure, aesthetics and organisation. Does a production always show something of the process by which it was made?

Strøbech: If you work with a choreographer that works apart from the director then it will show in the final imagery. If you spend all the time with the lead and none of the supporting parts, then it will show. If I make a drawing with a piece of charcoal, then it will look like that, and it will be different if I use ink. It's such a fundamental truth.

Shepherd: But how does one show the evidence?

Strøbech: The more you work with something yourself you can see how other people have done the same thing. If you are a baker you can decipher this bread much better that I can, and if you are a director you really see the craftsmanship of other directors. If you listen to Mozart's symphonies now you might not be aware of sonata form, but his contemporaries would know this form intimately. Many audiences can't read the details and differences.

Shepherd: I'm interested in the exposure to those audiences of the artwork, and in particular the director's relationship to it once it has opened. It still hasn't really got to the end of its process, which may only come when the final show has been done. Some directors will have nothing more to do with it and others are very present, some even backstage.

Strøbech: The actors don't want me backstage. They're so sweet. It's actually because they don't want me to know their secrets. They have rites of their own, stuff they do – behave rudely or in a vulgar manner or whatever, and they don't want me to see that.

Shepherd: Like animals marking out their own space . . .

Strøbech: They should, it's theirs, they own it. Yes. There is another paradoxical thing about the role of the director which is the passing on of knowledge. It's a process of handing over what is in your head, a process of externalisation, translating the vision into the physical somehow. At the beginning of the process you know a lot about the show and you need to find a way to make everybody have that same feeling. And at the end, you have no role. On opening night, it's prerequisite that you don't have a role because if you're needed for something then the show is not ready to open. So you annihilate yourself in the process, you actively erase yourself from the piece.

Shepherd: It's a role which must experience a certain redundancy?

Strøbech: It's so awful, and especially on the most important night, the opening night, that you have absolutely no role. But this is how it needs to be.

Shepherd: Except that some directors get to a certain level of fame whereby on the opening night what they become is director as celebrity, always somehow connected to the show but now also detached as a star in their own right.

Strøbech: It's quite common in the movies.

Shepherd: Speaking of celebrity and power, would you ever seek to own your own building as director?

Strøbech: No, I wouldn't want that at all. That would be the same space all the time: it's not interesting.

Shepherd: Some people argue that it's the only way a director can get freedom. But presumably that takes you into the territory we were talking about earlier – is it actually a freedom or is it a form of entrapment?

Strøbech: Money can give you some kind of freedom and not having any expenses gives you another kind of freedom. So I think it's up to the individual to decide what kind of freedom it is.

Part

Histories of Direction

Chapter 4

The Beginning of Direction, and its Possible End: A Brief History

This chapter presents various accounts of the emergence of theatre directors: why and how they happened. It then speculates on the director's demise, or at least its apparent transmutation into something else.

THE STORIES OF ORIGINS

If you listen to the directors you would view the role as one that emerged out of nothing, a self-generating phenomenon of modernity. ' "Directing", stated Antoine in 1903, "is an art that has just been born. Nothing – absolutely nothing – prior to the last century prefigured its emergence" ' (Whitton 1987: 49). For such men as Antoine it was important polemically to insist that there was no pre-history, that they were a natural and inevitable part of the new. The historians, however, tell it differently. In one of the earliest anthologies of texts on directing, originally published in 1953, Toby Cole and Helen Crich Chinoy track the emergence of directing as a sort of natural evolution from a range of practices. These practices include some of those which are mentioned in the first chapter of this book, beginning with the medieval metteur en jeu, and their development, on Cole and Chinoy's model, happens across four 'ideas of theatre'. These are the 'pictorial' stage (from the Renaissance), the 'facsimile' stage (from the eighteenth and nineteenth centuries), the 'expressionist' stage and the 'theatrical' stage (twentieth-century 'subjectivism and relativism'). Thus, 'The emergence of the director followed these formulas for unity. His genesis lay in the pictorial stage; his first successes in the facsimile stage; and his triumphs in the expressionistic and theatrical stages' (Cole and Chinoy 1963: 14). The movement from one cultural moment to another is seen as a fairly straightforward progression, with a central conflict at its heart, that between production and written text: 'As production more and more usurped the power once held by the play itself, they [the "leading theatre artists" of 1750–1850] perfected the implements with which the director could work – the rehearsal, the co-ordinated acting group, and the scenic paraphernalia of accurate backdrops and authentic costumes and props' (Cole and Chinoy 1963: 17).

Cole and Chinoy's story of gradual emergence is generally corroborated by the research Norman Marshall did for his 1957 book, *The Producer and the Play*, although the detail of Marshall's work produces a slightly different emphasis. His exploration begins with an investigation of the actual uses of the word 'producer' and 'produce'. The earliest example he found was from Drury Lane playbills from 1828, which announced that the pantomime was 'Invented and Produced by Mr. Barrymore'. He observed, however, that the use of the word 'produce' tended to be confined to musical shows and pantomimes. By contrast the 1863 Drury Lane playbills for *Manfred* announced 'The general action of the Tragedy arranged by Mr. Phelps' (Marshall 1962: 13). The naming of Phelps makes it clear that what was happening was that, although someone may be credited with the arrangement or production, that person was always primarily in some other role, such as stage manager, author, theatre manager or actor. The first example Marshall found of a producer who simply did production was in 1890, at the St James's Theatre, when Lily Langtry (1853–1929), the actress and manager, did *As You Like It*, 'Produced under the direction of the Hon. Lewis Wingfield' (the cast, however, resented this outsider, who was something of an obsessive dilettante, and refused to play). It was another ten years, says Marshall, before the appearance of the first real producer whose job was specifically 'to work regularly as a director of plays with which he was not concerned in any other capacity'. This was Dion Boucicault (1859–1929), son of the famous playwright, who worked at the Duke of York's for the American entrepreneur/producer Charles Frohman (1856–1915) from 1902 until 1915 (Marshall 1962: 13–14).

In this narrative we see the word 'produce' coming uncertainly into existence to describe a function that is a regular part of the process of getting a certain sort of show on stage. The ambiguities hovering around that function can be observed in Brander Matthews' advice to actors in 1914. He notes that 'Many an actor strong in execution is weak in conception.' Consequently they need guidance:

> Here is the duty and the opportunity of the dramatist himself, or of the producer of the play, who need not be much of an actor, but who must know how the play ought to be acted in every part, and who can suggest to the several performers the various effects they are to accomplish.

And it is not simply the author that has this capacity: 'Sometimes the manager of the theater, or the stage-manager who brings out plays, has this power of suggesting and controlling and guiding' (Matthews 1914: 38, 39). Within this collection of roles the 'producer' remains slightly unfixed. Its vagueness of definition was further compounded by the ambitions of the actor-managers. As Marshall notes, the actor-managers, never slow in self-advertisement, acquired the new word and applied it to themselves: 'Produced under the direction of Mr. Tree' (Marshall 1962: 15). Of course actor-managers had always done this sort of production work, but at the opening of the twentieth century it became important to use this new part of the theatre vocabulary.

Before Marshall finishes his narrative he reminds us that, irrespective of the history of the word itself, 'modern methods of production date back to the eighteen-thirties' (Marshall 1962: 15). He is thinking in particular of the work of Madame Vestris (1797–1856), manager of the Olympic Theatre, London. She insisted on detailed rehearsals which, as manager, she led herself and, alongside this, she made innovations in the scenic arrangements of the stage, in the interests of greater realism. We shall come back to the importance of realism in the stories of directors in a moment, but for now let's enjoy this twist in Marshall's narrative, which has the effect of suggesting that, in the emergence of modern directing, the originary point was a woman.

When Marshall takes us back to Vestris as the originating point of modern methods, he is articulating what came to be one of the most persistent elements in the stories of the emergence of directing. Let's call it, for brevity, the 'Naturalism narrative'. As Cole and Chinoy tell it, the modern director came into being with Duke Georg II of Saxe-Meiningen, who was practising a particular sort of theatre aesthetic: the company used all the by-now familiar features, such as rehearsals, 'integrated acting' and accurate sets, to create 'realistic stage pictures'. This was followed, historically, by the independent theatre movement of the end of the nineteenth century: 'In the "free theatres" devoted to naturalism the director had his first sustained successes. Here he interpreted new plays in a new style for an organised public.' The proposition here is that as realism, or more specifically Naturalism, developed in the theatre, it was a form of such complexity that it required a specific director figure: 'A special art of production was ... developed to organize all the theatrical elements into a relatively harmonious illusory world, and with the art of production came the embryonic director.' Thus, at the heart of Cole and Chinoy's version of the Naturalism narrative is the idea that a theatre form has brought into being a new theatrical role: 'In this new "theatre of situations" the metteur en scène, the director, was essential' (Cole and Chinoy 1963: 22, 26, 16, 27).

The idea that a 'special art of production' was developed in order to organise a more complex form is one repeated by a number of scholars. Braun defines 'the coordination of expressive means' as 'the fundamental requirement of theatre production as we have come to understand it' and his book *The Director and the Stage* explains that this coordination becomes necessary within the framework of the new literary movements, Naturalism and, to a lesser extent, Symbolism; Whitton's account of French directors sees the emergence as a 'by-product of the trend towards Realism, of which Naturalism was the ultimate manifestation' (Braun 2000: 7; Whitton 1987: 13). The force of this hypothesis about the organisation of complex form is underlined when it is used to explain the emergence of a specific sort of directing. In the 1950s Broadway musical, according to Bering, the act of 'staging' gave way to 'directing'. Just as with Naturalism, he says, the emergence of the 'book musical' – such as *Oklahoma!* (1943) – 'required one person to be responsible for the artistic content' (Bering 2003: 42).

Being focussed on Naturalism this idea is itself a version of another narrative, that of theatre reform. This narrative was promulgated by the new generation of playwrights of the early twentieth century. It had at its heart the assumption that theatre had to be dragged back from its decadent and highly commercial flirtation with melodrama and pantomime and musical theatre and farce and made to become a more grown-up art form in the modern world by doing Naturalism. The agents of this change defined themselves as those who were tainted neither by decadence nor commerce, like the actors and managers, but who were instead a new breed of serious-minded theatre professional whose sobriety was marked not only by their literariness but by their readiness to face unpopularity as a consequence of their grimly modern shows. You can see how the story of the invention of directors slides into position alongside this narrative of theatre reform. But the logic of the position doesn't quite work. For it might be argued, to the contrary, that each new set of developments in the theatre has created a need to organise what in their own day may have appeared a complex array of elements. This was surely the case with the emergence of the court masque or early opera or the first gothic melodrama. Yet the director only came clearly into view as a specified role at the end of the nineteenth century. So it is perhaps the chronology here, rather than the theatrical form, which is the significant factor.

The period which saw the emergence of the theatre director, Modernism, has attracted quite a lot of generalisation about the change in outlook and feeling associated with a sense of the new modern age. Some of this was articulated at the time, by those who embraced the effects of, for example, mechanisation and speed. But modern scholars have also endeavoured to describe a change at this moment. This comes to bear on directors in the narrative of emergence told by Rebecca Schneider and Gabrielle Cody. They describe an increase in emphasis on the visual in 'modernity' which in turn sets the conditions for the new role of director:

> the mark of the individual eye, the signature of an individual visual guide, is often cited as *the* element distinguishing the modern director from what Chinoy calls 'stage manager only' ... the notion of a director ... is most often discussed in relation to the organization of disparate elements into something resembling a unified whole, and most often—in terms of the modern—a decidedly *visual* whole.

They argue that 'the primacy of vision' is a familiar concept in the theorisation of Modernism and that, while it may be contested, 'it is nevertheless relative to the general Western habituation to the perspectival (or pictorial) stage that the earliest modern directors plied their newly named trade'. It is 'relative to the inherited visual thrall to perspectivalism that we see the distinct appellation of "director" congeal' (Schneider and Cody 2002: 4).

Alongside the idea of a new emphasis on the visual within Modernism runs another cultural assumption. This proposes that the modern period (and by 'modern' here we're meaning the years from around 1890 onwards) experienced an increase in social alienation, a sense of fragmentation and loss of coherence. At this point the story of Schneider and Cody and that of Cole and Chinoy converge. Thus by way of development of their argument around visuality Schneider and Cody suggest: 'The increasing polarization between viewer and viewed, a byproduct of technologies of vision and "alienation" in industrialized urban society, contributed to a drive toward a director who could produce a "communal" experience (Cole and Chinoy 1963 3) — either through visual unity or through ritual effects' (2002: 5). This theme, already foreshadowed in what they say about the production of realism's illusory world, forms the conclusion to Cole and Chinoy's narrative:

> The absence of shared values and a casual rather than a consecrated audience meant that integrated theater could not spontaneously emerge. Missing from our depersonalized society were the collective experiences basic to the theater that we take as our ideal. The director as a single creative force tried to organize the conditions necessary for 'theatre in its truest form'.
>
> (Cole and Chinoy 1963: 77)

The only problem with this general narrative, however, is that almost every period describes its experiences of the present as being alienated and fragmented. The world is always getting bewilderingly faster and messier. And if that is the case, there would have been nothing stopping directors emerging in the conditions of extreme alienation and fragmentation that led towards the English Civil War and revolution of the 1640s.

The version of the emergence of directors that we have so far encountered is summarised by Dennis Kennedy:

> It is normally explained by detailing the growing demands of realistic and naturalistic production in Europe and North America after 1850, the spectacular demands of both romantic and urban melodrama, and, crucially, the rise of a theatrical avant-garde in the 1890s that emulated the avant-garde in literature and the visual arts and wished to transform the nature of the performative experience.

It is a narrative in which 'the significant assumption was that modernist approaches – most clearly formulated by Craig – were fundamentally conceptual and scenographic, based on the need for a controlling eye to forge the messy aspects of theatrical production into the unified vision associated with a painter or sculptor.' The flaw in this 'standard treatment', according to Kennedy, is that it has a 'tendency to underplay larger social issues'. For the emergence of the director occurred in conditions which 'paralleled the development of European capitalism and were requisite to it. To put this succinctly, we might see the director not as a creation of modernism but rather as a logical result of modernity' (2005: 37).

Kennedy characterises modernity as a period in history that consciously breaks with its past. At this break-point, bristling with its manifestoes for future practices, there appears the director as a self-defining artist – just like we saw, as a specific instance, in Antoine. But, says Kennedy, while the effects of Modernist aesthetics may articulate a break, what lies beneath is a form of continuity in which directors 'can be seen as inheritors of nineteenth-century industry, both the theatre industry and the manufacturing industry' (2005: 38).

Many of the histories of directing draw on the manifestoes written by Modernist directors and thus share their ideological standpoint. This in turn gets disseminated, notes Kennedy, to generations of students, and goes through that form of discursive sedimentation which then comes to be taken for truth. In fact, as Kennedy lists them, Meiningen behaved as 'a theatre owner in the German tradition of Franz von Dingelstedt, while removing himself from daily operations that were not appropriate for a prince' and Lugné-Poë, Granville Barker, Stanislavski and Antoine all acted in their own productions (with Lugné-Poë's being far from the unity of elements suppos-edly created by the modern director) (2005: 39). A consequence related to the fetishising of the new director by modernist histories is that they 'underplay how useful the director was to commercial theatre. On the deeply indus-trialized stages of the United States, it can be argued that the director had appeared in the last quarter of the nineteenth century, well before modernist reforms reached those shores' (2005: 40).

Kennedy's argument is a very useful corrective to the 'standard treatment' of the emergence of directors told by 'modernist histories'. Far from being a break with the past, the earliest directors, he suggests, were in continuity with it, even though that continuity was augmented by the conscious performance of a role that saw itself not simply as an aspect of Modernism but as producer of modernity itself. Recall here Antoine: 'Nothing – absolutely nothing – prior to the last century prefigured its emergence' (in Whitton 1987: 49).

There is, though, yet another narrative. This argues, again, that the role of the director did indeed evolve in relation to need, but this time it is not the needs of an art form but those of the structure and cultural arrangements of civil society. This narrative crops up at various points through the twentieth century, appearing relatively early with MacGowan in 1922 and in the new century with Innes in 2008. It usually begins as an attempt to explain the association of the role of directing with Germany in particular. Let's look at the version of it as told by the German director Peter Stein (born 1937).

He starts from the specific formation of German society. As I noted on p. 10, Germany before its unification consisted of a set of principalities and dukedoms. Each court had its theatre and in turn each major town in the principality developed its theatre, all usually as a point of civic pride. The gradual transition from aristocratic rule to that of bourgeois cultural power saw an insistence, 'a kind of religious need', not only that each city had a theatre, but that such theatre was also subsidised. This led to a practice of stable ensembles performing regularly in a fixed place. This, Stein argues, gives to German theatre the basis of ensemble, from the eighteenth century onwards, and thus provides for the emergence of directors. From here Stein the director invokes the idea of ensemble to argue for reform of a theatre practice in which actors had the same status as civil servants, protected, as he saw it, by a powerful rightist trade union which cut rehearsal time. The solution was a 'renewed idea of the ensemble' with actors themselves running the whole theatre (in Delgado and Heritage 1996: 247). This renewal can be seen as a sort of return to bourgeois ideology, in both its promise of liberation and its class power. In the narratives of the emergence of directors, then, continuity with the past has as much value as rupture.

SCIENTIFIC MANAGEMENT

In Britain, when William Archer and Harley Granville Barker published their proposal for a National Theatre in 1904, they suggested such a theatre should have its own training school. While the national theatre was to take decades to appear, a theatre training school, the Academy of Dramatic Art, was founded in 1904. Two years later it was followed by The Central School of Speech Training and Dramatic Art. These institutions could be seen to be modelled on colleges for the training of musicians, which preceded them by a number of years, but they were novel in Britain in that they suggested theatre was an art that could and should be trained for. In Germany there had long before been an initiative in this direction, albeit very short-lived: in 1753 Konrad Ekhof had established an academy with the Schönemann company 'to discuss repertoire, the art of acting, and the social status of the actor' (Meech 2008: 75).

The historical context, then, is one in which training comes into the cultural foreground as a notion, formalised by institutions, and it gets there because of a sense not only that theatre needed rescuing from the effects of commerce but also that there was a proper way of doing theatre, a proper basis of doing the art. The effect of this context can be mapped in the particular example of Jacques Copeau. His background was in literary studies, and as a young man he co-founded the *Nouvelle Revue Française* in 1909 but, although his colleagues were mainly interested in the novel, he was committed to theatre as a form. This commitment led to his establishing a theatre, the Vieux-Colombier, in 1913. He had next to no experience of work in the theatre, but he believed that theatre should be reformed, and to coincide with the opening of the Vieux-Colombier he published in the *Nouvelle Revue* 'Un essai de rénovation dramatique'. This attacked the degradation of theatre that resulted from its take-over by speculators producing only commercial entertainment, but it was also carefully modest in tone, being committed only to the restoration of 'good' theatre: 'We do not stand for any school, nor do we pretend to offer any formula in the certainty that from this embryo the theatre of the future will emerge' (in Whitton 1987: 57–8). Copeau's programme for action in a new theatre would include the formation of a conservatoire and the mechanisms for training for theatre. At his Ecole de Vieux-Colombier there would be no stars and actors would be trained in a country retreat away from the city. It was conceived as 'a troupe of young, unselfish, enthusiastic actors whose aim is to *serve* the art to which they are dedicated' (in Whitton 1987: 60).

Now in one respect Copeau's manifesto was functioning like Antoine and the others to self-declare, along the lines suggested by Kennedy, his own modernity. But the Copeau example also invites us to attend to the fact that a number of these new directors were driven by a shared impetus to renew theatre through both training and planning. That training, in Copeau's eyes, would produce those who would be servants of their art. As we see elsewhere, what impressed Stanislavski about Meiningen's Chronegk was that he was a disciplinarian. The new director intervenes into the celebrity competitiveness of the commercial theatre in order to produce orderly service. When Granville Barker, with Archer, wrote a detailed planning prospectus for an English national theatre he dealt not only with training but with budgets and schedules. This drive to train and plan is, I think, a symptom of something rather larger than anything we have noted hitherto.

In the United States, as in Germany, towards the end of the nineteenth century a new 'service' class, neither aristocrat nor plebeian, came into being. This class was to provide a new sort of organised management of industry and its culture was one that put a high value on being educated for the role. The values and lifestyle of this class, specifically in relation to the shows of Broadway, are described by Michael Schwartz in his account of the emergence of a 'Professional-Managerial Class' (PMC). The definition of this he takes from Barbara and John Ehrenreich: 'salaried mental workers who do not own the means of production and whose major function in the social division of labor may be described broadly as the reproduction of capitalist culture and capitalist class relations' (in Schwartz 2009: 2). Although he questions whether it was a class formation as such, he is clear that the members of the PMC 'owe the existence of their position to the demand for their expertise – to the boom in technology and service, the increasing centralization of business and industry, and the need to address the issues of the poor and immigrants' (Schwartz 2009: 7). The phenomenon of PMC went beyond the United States, however: a more general account is formulated by Scott Lash and John Urry. Their model of what they see as a 'service class' is helpful to us because it contributes to a story of the emergence of directors and in doing so helps us to think about the attributes of the director.

Lash and Urry specify five main points about the service class. First is that it occupies a dominant position in the division of labour without owning buildings, capital or land. Second, it is situated within a series of social institutions that as it were service capital by meeting 'three functions: to conceptualize the labour process; to control the entry and exercise of labour-power within the workplace; and to orchestrate the non-household forms under which labour-power is produced and regulated'. Third, they 'enjoy superior work and market situations: incumbents thus exercise authority within each institution'. Fourth, 'Entry... is generally regulated by the differential possession of credentials, which are either organization-specific or are general. Such credentials serve as the main demarcation between the service class and "deskilled white-collar workers" ' (Lash and Urry 1996: 162). Already perhaps we might recognise some features associated with directors – they select the actors for a show, they have views on the process of rehearsing, they exercise authority in the company or theatre, they have distinct credentials (as opposed, perhaps, to skill-sets).

The rise of this service class is a part of 'an absolutely central development in twentieth century capitalism', namely 'the growth of modern, scientific, rational "management" ' (Lash and Urry 1996: 162). This development was most obvious in the United States. One of its most famous theorists there was F.W. Taylor. His solution to the problem of workers' tendency to restrict output was 'to create the separate category of "management", which had until then enjoyed only a somewhat protean existence, based upon a necessary "mental revolution" ' (Lash and Urry 1996: 164). In *The Principles of Scientific Management* (1911) Taylor explained how his system differed from the current best form of management, which he characterised as 'initiative and incentive', whereby managers tried to persuade workers to use their best initiative by incentivising it. Under the new system managers would take more upon themselves, for example:

> gathering together all of the traditional knowledge which in the past has been possessed by the workmen and then... classifying, tabulating, and reducing this knowledge to rules, laws, and formulæ which are immensely helpful to the workmen in doing their daily work. In addition to developing a *science* in this way, the management take on three other types of duties which involve new and heavy burdens on themselves.

These new duties are grouped under four heads:

> *First.* As explained above, they develop a science for each element of a man's work, which replaces the old rule-of-thumb method.
> *Second.* They scientifically select and then train, teach and develop the workman, where in the past he chose his own work and trained himself as best he could.
> *Third.* They heartily cooperate with the men so as to insure all of the work being done in accordance with the principles of the science which has been developed.
> *Fourth.* There is an almost equal division of the work and the responsibility between the management and the workmen. The management take over all

work for which they are better fitted than the workman, while in the past almost all of the work and the greater part of the responsibility were thrown upon the men.

(Taylor 1911: 21–2)

Taylor clarifies the implications of that fourth heading, which bears specifically on the task of planning: 'all of the planning which under the old system was done by the workman, as a result of his personal experience, must of necessity under the new system be done by the management in accordance with the laws of the science'. This amounts to more than shifting the burden of the task. It creates a new discursive order, which has a new material presence in the form of books and dedicated offices:

The development of a science . . . involves the establishment of many rules, laws, and formulæ which replace the judgment of the individual workman and which can be effectively used only after having been systematically recorded, indexed, etc. The practical use of scientific data also calls for a room in which to keep the books, records, etc., and a desk for the planner to work at.

The discursive and spatial discriminations attach themselves to, possibly even construct – although Taylor doesn't say this – different sorts of people: 'It is also clear that in most cases one type of man is needed to plan ahead and an entirely different type to execute the work' (Taylor 1911: 22).

In his account of Broadway Schwartz (2009) notes that the PMC established new 'manager-experts' alongside theatre managers and actor-managers. The activities he names specifically are those of booking agencies, following the lead of Bernheim's account from 1932, and theatre critics. He also observes that theatre business became increasingly 'corporate', with the listing of 'executive' theatre staff in play programmes. But he doesn't, by contrast, have much to say about the emergence of the director. This, however, seems to be the major result of the PMC's emergence. And it is presumably within the spirit of this emergence that Brander Matthews suggested that the actor, however 'strong in execution', 'needs guidance and cannot steer himself, altho he is certain to make a swift trip if only his course is directed by a wiser head' (Matthews 1914: 38).

That guidance might derive from the general basic principles of Taylor's 'scientific management' which 'included the centralized planning and integrating of the successive stages of production; the systematic analysis of each distinct operation; the detailed instruction and supervision of each worker in the performance of each discrete task; and the designing of wage payments to induce workers to do what they were told' (Lash and Urry 1996: 165). These principles seem to have gained wide currency during the 1920s. It was of course during this period, from the beginning of the century through to the mid-1930s, that the figure of the theatre director became more clearly defined. Almost all of those directors may be said to have engaged, through rehearsal, in the detailed 'supervision' of each actor, using techniques which Taylor may have found familiar. I am thinking here of that conspicuous sign of advanced planning the Regiebuch and the classifying of the arts of acting into something that was indeed described as a 'system'. So too when the experience of the celebrity actor is subjected to the same preparation, or indeed training process, as the whole company one is reminded of the levelling and unifying effect of Taylor's science. The principles of planning were also given physically heroic enactment by some of the new directors. There was Reinhardt with his troops of sub-directors and production staff, himself atop a platform directing the hundreds below him at London's Olympia, but more domestically Stanislavski at a table talking the company through the show.

Within this context it seems natural that Reinhardt and Granville Barker should have pioneered and polemicised for the organisational model of the repertory system which was so closely connected into the mechanisms of planning the sequence of production. So too Barker, and his co-author William Archer, made a point of discussing wage levels in their proposal for a National Theatre of 1904. These directors may not have read their Taylor but they could still be seen to be part of a new class in the theatre. The account of the Soviet Russian theatre by the director André van Gyseghem (1906–1979) from 1943 described the men at the top of the Moscow Art Theatre in these terms:

> Nemirovich-Danchenko from the intelligentsia and Stanislavsky from Trade Capitalism were heart and soul with the rising tide of the bourgeoisie. It naturally follows that their theatre, when it opened in the autumn, reflected their tendencies and expressed the point of view of the Liberal intelligentsia although it declared itself to be free from all political influence.
>
> (1943: 48)

And it could be argued that many directors elsewhere inhabited a culture in which Taylorism 'became an important component of the philosophical outlook of modern industrial civilization, defining virtue as efficiency, establishing a new role for experts in production, and setting parameters for new patterns of social distribution' (Merkle in Lash and Urry 1996: 165).

That philosophical outlook was characteristic of the United States and Germany, but not Britain which, say Lash and Urry, was 'almost the exact opposite of these developments' (Lash and Urry 1996: 178). They quote Charles Maier's summary of the different industrial culture of Britain: 'an underlying satisfaction with decentralized production, with the premises of a liberal regime in a country where the middle classes felt little anxiety about the social order, postponed real interest until the economic difficulties of the 1920s and 1930s'. So there was opposition to American ideas of scientific management, and a failure to understand them: 'too much science . . . is likely to lead to a decrease of efficiency rather than an increase' (in Lash and Urry 1996: 178, 179). This context, when considered in relation to the theatre in particular, provokes a re-invigorated sense of the modernity of that theatre. For while the emergence of theatre directors in the United States and Germany may be said to be of a piece with the general philosophic outlook of scientific management, in Britain it bucked the national trend. We have noted already that Barker had views on the organisation of theatrical production, and now we should bring back another observation made earlier. Barker and Archer suggested there should be a training school for their proposed national theatre, and they did so in a context where others in the theatre were thinking about training. This tends to echo the mind-set of the scientific management of the United States:

> Both the industrial managers and engineers provided a model of how education and industry should be integrated over the course of the twentieth century. One occupation after another sought to strengthen its market-power by connecting together the production of knowledge with the production of the producers via the modern university. There was a structural linkage effected between two sets of elements, specific bodies of theoretical knowledge, on the one hand, and markets for skilled services or labour, on the other.
>
> (Lash and Urry 1996: 173)

This use of higher education to professionalise industry contrasts, say Lash and Urry, with Britain. But while Britain in general may have resisted this outlook, it might be argued that in the theatre – and with the emergence of theatre directors in particular – there was being formed an approach to production processes which was very thoroughly modern and indeed ahead of its time.

Indeed so far ahead of their time were the likes of Barker that older habits persisted. And they persisted for a long time. Lash and Urry note that the British scepticism about 'science' and rejection of American management becomes embodied in 'two preferred "agents of management" within British industry': 'These two agents were the "educated amateur" or the "gentleman", and the "practical man".' For people who subscribed to the cult of the second, 'training on the job was central and they disparaged the value of education or formal training for their work' (Lash and Urry 1996: 184). If we recall the consideration of training of directors in Chapter 2 we shall probably find both of these two figures, the educated amateur and the practical man, haunting the various quotations. Certainly even into the twenty-first century there are those in the British theatre who oppose formal education in favour of learning on the job. And we should not leave this without noting one further characteristically British feature: 'British professions followed the gentry model of "status professionalism" rather than the bourgeois one of "occupational professionalism"' (Lash and Urry 1996: 184). In Craig's definition in

1905 'the director of a theatre must be a man apart from any of the crafts. He must be a man who knows but no longer handles the ropes' (Craig 1980: 173). When directors entered the profession with no more specific training than their having been at the universities of Oxford or Cambridge, they are in a sense acting out what in class terms is a 'gentry' model. So it is ironic that, despite its rather unBritish modernity in the earliest years of the twentieth century, by mid-century theatre directing had become more fully controlled by a British mindset, and of course the class system which shadows it.

There is one further irony to observe before we leave this account of scientific management. 'The Taylor system', Lash and Urry tell us, 'involved an enormous expansion in what Taylor himself called "non-producers" ' (1996: 165). These are the bureaucrats who deal with the planning of the industry. Or, we might say, these are those who run the process but don't act, don't design and don't make things. If I am correct in suggesting that the emergence of the theatre director is a specific and small part of the general philosophical outlook that embraced scientific management, and that, hence, the emergence of the theatre director belongs with that group which Taylor calls 'non-producers', then it is a delightful irony that the theatre, in all its vigorous self-proclaimed modernity, called these people 'producers'. For these, the non-producers, were in effect going to modernise the production of theatre.

THE AURA OF DIRECTING

As we have seen, the famous early twentieth-century producers – or directors – brought into theatre a specifically intellectual engagement, a rationale for making work that was not governed by the simple motive as to what would sell. Indeed it is precisely the early directors' opposition to commercial theatre that stages them clearly as ideologues, in that they are motivated by a set of ideas and principles that go against the mainstream.

In general terms the common features seen in work done by key early directors such as Stanislavski, Antoine and Reinhardt include:

- a form of staging that presents the activity onstage as a collective entity, a group of people all governed by the same discipline, as opposed to the presentation of the difference between star and crowd;
- a project not simply to stage shows within the regular theatre houses but spatially to extend the domain of theatre by stepping outside the assumed topographic boundaries around theatre;
- an implicit contesting of the current working practice of putting on shows for the benefit of those who own the building by instead setting out to purchase and build theatres appropriate to the autonomous project of the directors.

Clearly there are social, if not explicitly political, implications in all this. The opposition to commercial theatre is very clear in the rhetoric, as too is the transition of these new figures from being those who merely offer a service to those who own the building. But alongside these emergent economic changes there were aesthetic ones. When directors were trying out unpopular or experimental dramatists, they were making work that consciously set itself apart from mainstream ideas and expectations. This persisted even when they tackled Shakespeare, who was offered with bodies and designs that linked into work of the experimental avant-gardes: indeed, as I suggest in Chapter 7, the Shakespeare work was possibly more noticeable for the modernising touch of the director. And that gap between the traditional text and its mode of staging was also sometimes played out spatially, in the relationship between the architecture of the building and/or its habitual use and the new show in it. Both were enactments of what was also an ideological and aesthetic gap. In staging that gap the directors replayed the polemical gesture of the Modernist avant-garde.

To make that assertion here is to bring my own narrative into line with that told by Schneider and Cody, if not also by Cole and Chinoy. Recall that these sorts of narrative are characterised by Kennedy as 'modernist', where the manifestoes of theatre directors themselves inform the approach. Schneider and Cody explicitly associate the director with visual organisation in the context of a Modernist emphasis on visuality. Similarly Cole and Chinoy note that Appia, Craig and Meyerhold tried consciously to be 'artists' of the theatre, with a typically Modernist interest in the primitive origins of the form, which Meyerhold expresses thus: 'The new theatre gravitates toward the dynamic beginning, for the latest theatrical experiments approach the theatre of antiquity' (in Cole and Chinoy 1963: 57). Typically these Modernist narratives tend, as Kennedy says, to ignore the commercial in order to concentrate on the avant-garde artist. Further, the theatre director seems not only to have emerged coincidentally with Modernism but to be also one of its primary exemplars as an artist. By contrast my own narrative, while still taking account of a self-conscious avant-garde, wants to do so in order to highlight a slightly different emphasis.

There was, I think, something more substantial going on than simply a sharing in Modernism's interest in visuality or primitivist community. The early theatre directors were 'Modernist' in that they made work governed by a concept that separated itself from, or was irreconcilable with, the mainstream; their project was to purify the theatre of its commercially induced ornamentation and waste; and they brought into theatre an aesthetic based on intellectual focus and physical organisation. P.P. Howe's sense of it at the time, in 1910, was this:

> The art of producing is a part of the art of the theatre which, if it is not altogether the outcome of the new spirit abroad, has developed contemporaneously. The

function of the producer is to give artistic unity to the representation upon the stage. The artistic conscience of the theatre is in his keeping.

(Howe 1910: 182–3)

Note that the task of giving 'unity' is not narrowly conceived as the production of realism's illusory world. Instead it has to do with artistic ethics, by contrast perhaps with commercialism and its dissipation of theatre art. And then, of course, though Howe doesn't say this, there was the practice of being 'scientific'.

The early directors and those close to them had a language of their own for what we might call 'aura'. Let's recall from Chapter 1 Howe's distinction between the 'stage manager' and that new thing, the 'producer':

The producer is the new supplementary authority who assumes responsibility for the artistic unity of the whole. It is a simple matter of allotment of function. The dramatist supplies both letter and spirit. The stage-manager is competent to deal with the letter, and the producer's business is to interpret the spirit.

(Howe 1910: 185)

Howe's sense of the producer's obligations with regard to 'spirit' are a close version of the views of the German director and literary critic Otto Brahm (1956–1912), who said the director must be 'sensitive to the inner spirit of the work' (in Cole and Chinoy 1963: 30). In France Copeau expressed a similar sentiment but instead of 'spirit' he called it 'life'. 'Nothing is easier than to relate artistically the dimension, the decoration, the lighting, etc., of the stage to the character and requirements of each play we produce.' 'That is not my ambition ... It will never bring about a renovation or transformation of the scenic *life*' (in Cole and Chinoy 1963: 46). In this context we might note Stanislavski's description of his early motivations: 'I tried to be natural, to discover the truth, and outlawed in particular spurious, theatrical tricks of the trade. I began to hate theatre in the theatre' (Stanislavski 2008: 118).

Brahm and Copeau and the rest saw themselves not simply creating a coherent work of art but also, crucially, preserving the 'spirit' or 'life' of theatre. The effect of their choice of language was that it established a clearer distinction between the new serious producer and the actor-managers or impresarios and commercial directors who concentrated merely on getting the show on. The actor-manager produced the show supposedly in a way which suited the actor-manager (sustaining the image, being commercially viable). The modern 'director' produces according to something larger than the person (supposedly) – this might be called the 'spirit' of the piece, or the discipline of the process, or a desire to reform theatre, or an opposition to commercialism. The modern director occupies the role of an agent of something hitherto lacking (supposedly), and that thing is an idea or a vision or an ideal which is separable from craft knowledge and experience – indeed it is like the science of scientific management. The principled new director was not doing something which 'works' (the thing that will sell) but which is 'necessary'. This is very different from the Naturalist narrative, which sees the director simply as the agent of a new art movement, because that narrative doesn't require the director to be anything other than a metteur en scène or stage manager, the person capable of organising complicated elements. Such an image is rather different from the 'scientific manager' in its fullest sense, as the guardian of the 'spirit'. In 1913 Otto Brahm seemed clear about the distinction between the two sorts of agency that got the play on stage, between the organiser and the guardian of the spirit. Commenting on the arrangements for a new production of *Antigone* he asks: 'are all our innovations, as conceived or executed, valid? Are they in keeping with the spirit of ancient Greece? Is the performance on the stage of the Deutsches Theater "genuinely" classical? That is the big question that is being asked' (in Cole and Chinoy 1963: 104–5).

Brahm's big question hitches together the point of epistemological break to the moment of structural break, where the first makes the second come more visibly into being. While there had always been organisational figures in theatre, what marks the change at the turn into the twentieth century is the emergence of cultures in different societies that promoted a system of values of which the director could become an embodiment. This is much more than a cultural organisation around visuality or indeed innovation. It had to do, I suggest, with thinking about professional management, with the cultural emergence of a new service class. The Modernist artists felt themselves to be making change if not revolution. The early directors set about creating a changed theatre. As avant-garde artists they tended to position themselves outside traditional practices but nevertheless acted as the only agents, intellectually and aesthetically, for a change in those practices. That activity in part gave the new role its identity.

THE AGE OF THE DIRECTOR

Looking back from the 1990s, Giorgio Strehler identified what he saw as a problem:

> Styles have changed, but very often, too often, this is only a change of mannerisms or of fashion. The work of the director remains the same as ever. This is not the problem. The problem is the excessive emphasis given to the director's role, which has in the last few decades gone far beyond that which has been placed upon the actor since the eighteenth century.
>
> (in Delgado and Heritage 1996: 272)

That problem, if problem it is, had a name. In his 1972 book *On Directing* Harold Clurman (1901–1980), one of the founders of New York's Group Theatre, observed that American theatre had been described as 'director's theatre' (Clurman 1972: 3). The date of the origin of this phenomenon is, of course, pretty slippery, depending as it does on perceptions. Jonathan Miller notes that he did his first production in 1962, 'around the time that the director is generally assumed to have seized theatrical power' (Miller 1986: 76). By 1982 David Selbourne could speak of 'director's theatre' as something he wished to avoid when he began observing Brook's rehearsals for *A Midsummer Night's Dream* (Selbourne 1982: xxxi). Selbourne was particularly sensitive perhaps in that he was an author. Authors seemed to feel from quite early on that directors were a threat. Somerset Maugham said in 1938 that the best directors were those who did the least, believing that 'very often an author's purport is misrepresented by the director's stupid obstinacy' (Maugham 1961: 146). The English dramatist Arnold Wesker raged fifty years later against the 'madness...sweeping through European theatre...which has elevated the role of director above the role of writer. The stage has become shrill with the sounds of the director's vanity; it has become cluttered with his tricks and visual effects' (in Rae 1989: 144).

And possibly the authors raged with reason. Here is Michel Saint-Denis in 1960: 'It has been said that during the first half of the present century directors have made a more creative contribution to the theatre than the dramatists.' Claiming that the greatest theatrical work in Britain in that period had been made by directors rather than authors, he noted that authors merely dealt in ideas while directors worked 'amidst scenic realities' (Saint-Denis 1960: 72, 73). That concern with scenic realities led to legal battles between companies and authors in the United States in 1984: Gerald Rabkin argues that the rise of 'director's theatre' runs parallel to developments in literary studies in producing a new attitude to what a text is (Rabkin 2002: 329).

What had happened over these years was in fact less that the role of director claimed for itself the creativity but more that, pre-eminently, as Saint-Denis says, it dealt with 'realities', and as such was entitled to the supreme power in the processes of theatre. And its new power, often not being used simply for the purposes of putting on shows, seemed to be exercised in ways that mimicked non-theatrical authority. What was at stake, and the contest over it, can be illustrated from two stories from the British theatre close in time to each other.

The first was not a building-based operation but a company without a building. That company was Joint Stock. Early in their existence they did a production of *Fanshen* (1974), a play about Chinese peasants learning and embracing the values of the communist revolution. It grew from a book which formed the basis of research done by the whole company. The director William Gaskill set up the research and making process by establishing a workshop run on democratic lines. This adjustment to the more regular working conditions led to what Rob Ritchie calls 'a process of self-enquiry':

In studying the social existence of the Chinese peasants, the group equipped themselves the better to understand their own. Actors directed, directors acted, all were entitled to question and criticise: pockets were emptied, earnings revealed, status and authority broken down and analysed.

(Ritchie 1987: 17)

As one result the company resolved to organise itself on collective lines. This was not quite what Gaskill intended: for him 'the superior goal was fashioning a common method of work' (Ritchie 1987: 21). The actor Simon Callow views this as a symptom of the company being a 'directocracy' which always 'stood for the taste of its directors' (Callow 2004: 70–7). Gaskill in turn dismisses Callow's account.

The second story concerns, in part, the establishment of a building. Peter Hall became a co-director of the National Theatre company in 1973, first working alongside then replacing the other director, Laurence Olivier. Hall had already, as founder of the Royal Shakespeare Company (RSC), been 'pitchforked' into politics – which he enjoyed. He learnt to work politicians, getting from James Callaghan as Shadow Chancellor a statement that Labour when in power would fund the RSC (Hall 2000: 107). As this sort of political operator he arrived at the National Theatre. The accounts of the transition from the rule of the existing director, Olivier, to the new man Hall vary according to the teller's view of the different management cultures. In their history of the National Theatre Elsom and Tomalin (1978) see it as a removal of a paternalist regime under a traditional actor-manager. Hall's own version has Olivier as somewhat more treacherous, being apparently agreeable to his face while behind the scenes provoking 'a huge ferment, indicating to a full meeting of the National Theatre Company that he hadn't been consulted.' In Hall's eyes it was a straightforward clash between an old order and a new one:

Larry was rightly worshipped by the profession. He returned that love by flirting with his company, sometimes giving favours, sometimes withdrawing them. He was an old-style monarch who could be inspiring but also awesome and wilful ... But it wouldn't be like that any more. For one thing, the organisation I had to run was more than three times the size of the Vic, and we had to do many more productions. For another, I hadn't the great actor's extraordinary magic, which was so much a part of Larry's personality. I hoped, however, that my style was more democratic; it was certainly more open.

(Hall 2000: 270, 273)

Jonathan Miller, who was a director at the National when Hall got there, soon resigned: 'I came up against a form of executive ambition on the part of Peter Hall which I found totally impossible' (Miller 1986: 89).

What makes the ambition particularly unpalatable is that it is 'executive'. It echoes the flavour of Callow's 'directocracy'. And that sentiment, from an actor, was acknowledged by Max Stafford-Clark in 1989: 'at present, the term is discredited. Actors think directors have too much control. Any group of actors in their first tea-break delight each other with horror stories of directorial incompetence' (Stafford-Clark 2004: 3). Having emerged as an artistic leader, indeed visionary, in the service of theatre the director now seemed to be threatening a re-organisation of theatre on non-artistic lines.

It is ironical, therefore, that in 1980 John Miles-Brown noted that there had been criticism of 'directors' theatre', with a suggestion that what was needed was a return to dominance of the actor: the person making the suggestion was Peter Hall. But directors' theatre was not going to be shifted easily. It was only just acquiring a literature for itself. That literature was in part generated by the directors, as it had always been. It was Brook himself who suggested that Selbourne watch his rehearsals. But books were now also coming out of the academy. Edward Braun's *Director and the Stage* appeared in 1982. In 1988 came Bradby and Williams' *Directors' Theatre*. Braun's book positioned the director as a product, and enabler, of new art movements. Bradby and Williams surveyed the individual outputs of what was by then becoming the canon of great directors. In 1989 Judith Cook published *Directors' Theatre*, a collection of interviews building on a book published in 1974, and in the United States Louis Catron published *The Director's Vision*, a how-to-do-it book which said bluntly that the 'vision' was more important than craftsmanship. Also in 1989 appeared Kenneth Rae's report for the Gulbenkian Calouste Foundation on the state of training for directors in the UK, revealing that it wasn't in a good state. So even while students in the UK were being given the apparatus to study the art of the director, with a focus on past directors as the visionaries of theatre, it was very much less possible easily to train for it. The phase of directors' theatre seemed to be about new modes of organisation where the director posed an apparent threat to the art. This was accompanied by a gradual increase in academic publishing that viewed directing within the framework of a sort of art critique, like describing the great poets or painters, but did not have much to say about the future development of an artistic practice.

THE IRRELEVANCE OF DIRECTING

When it started, Antoine was not right in saying that directors came from nowhere. But that sort of rhetoric was typical of the time that gave definition to directors. The articulation of the director role was a function of some of the national, cultural and ideological changes associated with Modernism. And from that Modernist context the role of director got its power, ideological justification and indeed glamour. But that is not to say that they emerged out of some sort of natural evolution or functional necessity.

Indeed, in the longer history they are not necessary. Theatre had for centuries managed quite well without directors. As we saw at the start of Chapter 2, Mnouchkine argued that directing is a 'minor art' because you can't have a play without a dramatist but you can have theatre without a director. Put this way the director becomes something extra to what is really necessary. Indeed Peter Stein suggests that: 'The director came into the business of the theatre at a time of and as a sign of decline' (in Delgado and Heritage 1996: 253).

What Stein is gesturing to is a lengthy process in which theatre work develops for itself a whole set of new roles. Specialisms proliferate. Stein remarks that now (in the mid-1990s) 'you even need somebody to teach you to breathe. More and more positions are created' (in Delgado and Heritage 1996: 253). This development is described by Cohen as a 'collective "directorate"': a veritable assembly line of specialized directors that might include ... a music director, a dance director, a movement director, a combat director, a text director, a vocal director', etc. (Cohen 2011: 59–60). While Cohen sees this proliferation as a healthy move away from the more autocratic director, Stein sees it as a mark of decline because it is dissipating the very thing which gives theatre its strength, namely the culture of ensemble. Remember in his aforementioned account of the origin of directors Stein invokes the German civic theatres with their ensemble companies as the exponents of a form of local, high-standard theatre that was part of the civil fabric. The proliferation of roles destroys that ensemble from inside. So too, on the outside, the ethos of localism, of specific civic ownership, is destroyed by the apparent requirement that, in order to survive economically, directors and their productions should move from one festival to another, ranging across the globe. This is a point with which Robert Lepage agreed: 'the only way to survive is to do co-productions with big international events, and once you've done that you're stuck with the rules of these festivals' (in Delgado and Heritage 1996: 142).

Those specific structural and economic factors contributing to a change in theatre, and thus perhaps directors, may be seen to be most forceful in the later decades of the twentieth century. By then the demise of the director had already been announced several times. Marshall declared in 1957: 'The era of the producer is over' (Marshall 1962: 279). The reason for the demise, as he saw it, was economic. The producers who had been influential and experimental had 'worked under their own management, owning their own theatres with their own permanent companies' (280). Saint-Denis made a similar observation in 1960, but with a different rationale. He observed that the 'period of the director's supremacy is beginning to pass':

> The tendency in Europe, and very particularly in France, is now to deny that the director is what is called a creative artist. I can see the same tendency in London. The policy of an active theatrical organisation in London, the Royal Court Theatre, which shelters the English Stage Company, is resolutely to give first place to the dramatist.
>
> (Saint-Denis 1960: 73–4)

In a sense Saint-Denis's argument was also economic in that new plays were in demand. By contrast with both these economic analyses, Marshall quotes the theatre critic Kenneth Tynan: 'Many of them are affable, intelligent men;

but none measures up to the continental definition – a dynamic compound of confessor, inquisitor and sage ... Apart from Granville-Barker and, intermittently, Guthrie, no English director has had much perceptible influence on English acting' (Marshall 1962: 281). Tynan's location of the problem as one of temperament is a way of thinking characteristic of his own circumstances, and somewhat trivial, but it does take us to one of the grounds on which directing was challenged.

Tynan got it upside-down. The issue, as a number of people saw it, wasn't too much affability but not enough. Looking back in 1989, from the other side of the fence as it were, Declan Donnellan reflected:

> I think at an early stage many of us suffer from a lot of sentimental ideas about all being pals together. Now I feel that attitude has brought about something of a crisis in directing, which is also sentimental – people are frightened of directing because it's bad, right-wing, authoritarian. [new paragraph] 'Director' has almost become a dirty word in theatre and that's wrong.
>
> (in Cook 1989: 92–3)

As Donnellan knew by 1989, 'director' had in many places indeed become a dirty word. In the early 1970s there were experiments with disposing of the director role in groups such as the Danish Christianshavnsgruppen (1966–1972) which operated collectively and had an interest in the effects of creative process on its participants. In groups where shows were directed, the director didn't necessarily have structural authority. For example, the English company Red Ladder (founded in 1968) operated a model in which each member of the company acted as 'chair' for the day, with the authority to run discussions and formulate decisions. These polemical positions became naturalised over ensuing decades, when directors began to stress repeatedly their commitment to collaboration: 'Directors are really just manipulators of people, and their manipulation can be more or less subtle or aggressive .... The art of direction is a process, a kind of collage of people and ideas' (Ian Spink in Giannachi and Luckhurst 1999: 123). What helped the naturalisation was a particular version of directing's history. Even before Christianshavnsgruppen the story of Stanislavski had been told as an object lesson in the importance of moving away from the role of producer autocrat to that of producer instructor. The ideological thrust of this version of events can be revealed by setting it against van Gyseghem's view from 1943:

> In the Theatre of Meyerhold a very vital principle in the Soviet theatre becomes clear – the aim of drawing the majority into an active relationship with the art of the theatre where they shall participate emotionally not in isolated instances but in unified inspection. Such an aim is in absolute opposition to those theories which activated the naturalistic school of the Moscow Art Theatre.
>
> (van Gyseghem 1943: 44)

In turn Meyerhold had been described by Norris Houghton as himself an autocrat: 'Meierhold is not searching for a reading that will satisfy the actor, as was Stanislavski' (Houghton 1938: 127).

The purpose of contrasting these views of Stanislavski and Meyerhold is not to decide which director was an autocrat or not, but instead to note the regular tendency to praise participation and teamwork almost as soon as a role emerges that is given all the power in the theatrical process. That structural allocation of authority had, it seems, to be accompanied by a denial of its autonomy, possibly because the new director had to be separated from the old actor-manager. The director had power but learnt, apparently, to wield it differently from the impresario or actor-manager. This is an argument made in one of the earliest books about directing, Huntly Carter's account of Reinhardt from 1914. In his book Carter celebrates the model of directing which he saw as being initiated by Reinhardt. It was a model which contrasted with the rather more public, and more polemically stated, position adopted by Edward Gordon Craig. Craig was highly critical of the number of departmental 'heads' that tended to operate in contemporary theatre processes. He suggested that these need to be replaced by a single role. This is the person that Appia had already called for, in 1895: the director of 'poetic drama' would need to be 'a despotic drillmaster' (in Cole and Chinoy 1963: 41). To this position Carter then puts the counter argument:

> All the talk about ruler-art and ruler-artist is drivel. If producers really desire to make an advance, let them study Reinhardt, not Nietzsche, and learn how to think in terms of a circle, not of a pyramid. Reinhardt's contribution to the problem of the theatre is co-directorship. Except to the theatre, co-directorship is not a new thing to this mighty booby world, but outside the theatre dull persons are expounding it in the form of co-management and guild-socialism as *the* idea of the century. The new and significant thing in the theatre is the expression of the Will of the Theatre by co-ordinated minds, each artist taking the keenest interest in presenting the artistic work of the theatre.
>
> (Carter 1914: 20)

It is worth noting that Carter clearly had a sense that models of management in the theatre do have a relationship to systems of management beyond theatre. This goes some way to support the parallels with scientific management which I drew in an earlier section. In approaching directors from within the frame of management models Carter's argument articulates the difficulty around authority, autocracy and democracy that we have noted earlier, a difficulty which seems to relate to the new role of director needing to separate itself from the actor-manager while retaining all the power of the actor-manager.

This structural ambivalence within the role of director connects with other uncertainties that seem to be built in from the start. These have a paradoxical effect in that as a particular aspect of direction develops so the role of director begins to disappear. Take, for example, the relationship between director and actors. In the narratives by directors about their own developing technique, from Stanislavski onwards, there is a repeated statement that directors learn not to be autocratic. Peter Brook says that he used to start rehearsals by telling actors how he was going to approach the play, but 'I eventually found out that's a rotten way of starting' (Brook 1988: 3). Learning not to be autocratic is to do with growing up as a director: 'As I have grown older, and I hope more mature, I leave more and more of the discoveries to be made by the actors themselves' (Miller 1986: 100). The assumption in this narrative is that a properly mature practice of direction is one that begins to efface the power of the director. A twist is given to this in the cases where directors take on the job of training.

As is noted elsewhere (p. 55), Stanislavski said that there was a gap between what a director imagines and what they can get, so actors have to be trained for the director's ends. If it is to work such training must take seriously the subject of the training, recognising individual feelings and difficulties. But the project of enabling actors to do what is required slides quite easily into a form of deference towards the dominating importance of the actor's 'reality', as Strasberg has it. At this moment the rehearsal process can be described, albeit sceptically, as 'having strong parallels with psychoanalysis, in that the director (analyst) must penetrate the actor's (analysand's) unconscious so far as to bring into open the actor's hidden choices' (Marowitz 1986: 67). In these circumstances the director/trainer relationship with the actor is of primary importance, potentially more so than the project of creating a show. Back in 1914 Brander Matthews observed that trainers had an influence on actors and offered them guidance in a way that was as powerful as the instruction of authors or managers. From an author's point of view, several decades later, the effect of this sort of work on actors was to diminish the importance of the script or indeed the production itself. Arthur Miller said that Strasberg's training made actors into 'secret' people with the effect that, in a production, the actor was more interested in 'working out his own private fate' than 'communicating the meaning of the play' (see p. 62) (in Roudané 1987: 96). A logical next step is that the production disappears entirely from anybody's concerns, leaving the director/trainer's project as something simply focussed on the development of other individuals, more or less like a therapist.

From a similar starting-point, that focus on enabling actors, by means of a slightly different route we arrive at a very similar outcome, namely the disappearance of the production from the activities of a director. That route can be sketched in by means of a series of quotations. Here is Lee Strasberg: 'It's important for directors to understand the actors' problems and what they may be experiencing.' 'Only a reality that's the actor's reality – not mine, or yours, or the playwright's – can be relied on' (Cohen 2010: 87). Here is a fairly standard how-to-do-it book regurgitating the Strasbergian ethos: an interviewee suggests 'it might be helpful to think of your work with actors in the following way: first as being a facilitator who helps to establish the given circumstances . . . second, as being someone who allows the actors to explore their responses . . . and only then being someone who helps shape those responses' (in Swain 2011: 70). And from all that caution about helping and allowing, here is another how-to-do-it book, this time for practitioners of 'community' theatre: 'community performance practitioners' . . . 'have to facilitate an exchange, bring people together, enable ways for the group to find its ways of working, and allow a group to value all its members' (Kuppers 2007: 10).

It is fairly normal practice for a conventional (if such there be) theatre director to establish the parameters within which actors will work, creating the frame within which they can engage with the material and have their ideas. This is described as 'facilitation'. Lepage describes himself as a facilitator and so too the director for The Builders Association, Marianne Weems, is described this way: 'After a run of a scene that's been rehearsed, Weems asks, "Thoughts, feelings? Want to try anything, look at anything different?" She runs the rehearsal room as a facilitator' (Lavender 2010: 21). The work of facilitating performers takes a new edge in a collaborative company because every member of the company is encouraged to contribute to the creative process, so the facilitation is a primary method of generating material. As a mechanism this is barely different from situations where the emphasis is as much on the involvement and development of the participants as it is on the creation of a final aesthetic performance. These situations are familiar from the activities described as community arts: with their particular aims the verbs of 'helping', 'enabling' and 'allowing' rise into dominance. The process of facilitating comfortably settles into a role called 'facilitator' and this then begins to efface the word, and concept, of 'director'.

Another such word, though used less often, is conductor. The principle behind it is similar. Lepage makes its rationale clear: 'I try to be a kind of conductor in all of this, and not really an author or a director. All the actors improvise and write their own text' (in Delgado and Heritage 1996: 139). So too John Fox, co-founder of Welfare State International, describes his directing practice as like that of a 'band leader' who offers people tunes and harmonies to play with. Although it is uncertain how far people always write their own tunes, the model of conductor is useful because, by definition, it is not the conductor who actually makes the sounds of the music. A conductor is wholly dependent on the ensemble which is the band. For this reason, just like 'facilitator', the word is attractive in community theatre projects. Playback Theatre, who specialise in working with groups and their memories, run sessions where a 'conductor' elicits the stories from the participants. The revealing of material which is already in the person, the 'drawing out' of images and ideas, is very different in metaphoric thrust from the person who tells you where to go, 'directs' you. The model is that of being led rather than sent and indeed one of the most favoured community performance words for the person who facilitates or conducts is 'leader' – the workshop leader, the project leader. Petra Kuppers' introduction to community performance identifies three 'leadership styles', ranging from that which 'tends' towards autocratic through 'group-led' to democratic (Kuppers 2007: 95–6). The leader may well have arrived in this role not because of an aim to make artworks but because they are a teacher (although clearly these two are not incompatible). A number of community projects grow out of educational courses. With that as a point of origin it is easier to understand how the emphasis falls so significantly on the process of making the work rather than on the finished project. Indeed the participants of a community project may decide not to have a final performance. When directing modulates, via its interests in facilitation, into leading, the importance of the finished artwork diminishes.

But even where the commitment to finished artwork remains, the remit and definition of the director seem to be evolving, if not disappearing. In part that is an optical illusion created by the emergence of new terms for what directors once did. The 'band-leader' John Fox describes himself as something different when he heads up Welfare State's shows with thousands of performers. In *Glasgow All Lit Up* the main things the company provided were inspiration, workshop leaders, management structure, materials and funding. In *Shipyard Tales* 'I was more of an impresario leading from the back' (in Giannachi and Luckhurst 1999: 32). In this mutation of the director role it is the tight grip on the artistic creativity which is slackened, while the organisational aspect of the role grows in its size and remit. That shift of emphasis was always potentially there in someone such as Reinhardt with his massive shows. But Reinhardt had planned it all out in his direction book. Where invention of structure and organisation, finding of site and finance, are part of the process, the director may have had the original idea but the main work is in bringing together and managing the elements. Seen in this way the role begins to slide into correspondence with what might now be called creative producing in that the crucial part of the work is to assemble the team, funds and structure to make the event happen: as the teachers of it define it, 'The entrepreneurially skilled and culturally literate producer works in dialogue with artists to create performances and festivals, run venues and companies, manage projects, raise funds and investment and negotiate commissions' (www.cssd.ac.uk/study/postgraduate/masters/ma-creative-producing). Where the focus is not so much on one event but on a company that develops a series of productions within one overall vision, then the director also becomes, to use Fox's word, an impresario.

Some of these mutations, existing simultaneously, can be illustrated from four companies working in southern England in early 2012. Many more models could be found, but the attempt here is simply to exemplify the general argument as to the evolution of the directing role in contemporary aesthetic practice.

First, Little Bulb Theatre formed in 2008, are based in Farnham and do a wide range of work from large-scale to intimate. Their arrangements with regard to direction are described by company member Clare Beresford:

> although we are a devising theatre company, we do have a director figure among us and that tends to be Alexander Scott, who is also the overall artistic director of the company. Though we have a couple of models of show that we make ... for the full length, character based narrative pieces Alex directs. However we make all the material together and 'write' as we go (though it is rare we write things down) so Alex is directing devisers rather than from written material. We also make shows that for want of a better term I'll refer to as 'bish bash bosh cabarets', which we all create together and where there is no one director in the making process; we just all chip in, and often these pieces hang more on improvisation and looser 'characters'. And then there's our shows which are entirely music gigs, which again we all have a say in, but which Dominic Conway tends to take a lead on. I suppose ultimately we all have an opinion and have been directors in our own right, but ultimately came together to create something that was Alex's vision. As well as exploring those visions, we also want to make sure that there is room to explore everyone else's visions.
>
> (personal communication: 7 February 2012)

Shunt are a company who seek to operate as a genuine, rather than director-led, collective – presenting their work as 'designed, directed and performed by Shunt'. There is therefore no artistic hierarchy at the top of which a director would conventionally sit. It is the case, however, that members of the group bring different specialisms to the collaboration, including one, David Rosenberg, whose role is as 'director'. He does not recognise himself in the regularly accepted model of director, however, nor is he expected to work as such. When he does activity which might appropriately be described as directing, it is because that is what is needed at that juncture of the process. Other members of the company may be said to facilitate his operation as director in order to take forward the overall process. Precisely what that directing activity might be would depend on the nature of the project. It is the project which gives rise to the organisational mode of its own process. The organisational arrangements and their roles do not necessarily precede the project. The making of the aesthetic work may therefore be said to be simultaneously a making of the arrangements which produce it. There is no fixed practice of direction which predetermines the work, despite this practice occurring in a consistent role across different projects.

This model operates what might be thought of as dispersed directing. In a collective where everyone contributes ideas there is no one role which has the authoritative vision. Nor indeed does it have an omniscient viewing position. In a show which might take place simultaneously in five rooms, the director figure, like the audience, can only ever be in one room. So performer feedback, as it were 'notes', has to come from other company members who offer an 'outside eye', as well as from the performers themselves. But while within the company directing activity no longer necessarily finds itself located only in one role, outsiders to the company still carry an expectation that they can talk to 'the director' of a project. The business of theatre needs discursively, and institutionally, to invent what Shunt disperse. That dispersal doesn't, however, amount to a devaluing of the activity of directing. When observations or comments are made from the position of director, they are valued and trusted. This trust flows from joint participation in the collective project, rather than from an externally sustained 'authority'. Directing as activity continues to have value, but that activity has been dislocated from a given role, with its supposed identity and power.

Chris Goode, of Chris Goode and Company, describes himself as a maker, rather than director, and his work falls into two parts. The directing he does for others and the staging of himself in his own shows. The process of directing, or making, work for others falls into three stages: an invitation or offering, which might consist of a physical act or reading or discussion; observing the group responding to that invitation; reporting back with some simple questions. Although Goode begins with few expectations, he has an editorial role in relation to the material generated and a casting vote as to what is finally included. Rather more importantly perhaps, he sees his role as the custodian of the structure of the process and its atmosphere. He regards the main part of his work as setting a tone, which is done through the protocols of his own behaviour and the sort of room that he defines. The emphasis in the making activity, then, is on enabling others while also setting rules as a pre-condition of having anything at all to direct. That emerges from the situation. Goode describes the specific stimulus to the work – whatever it is – as the 'campfire' that they are all sitting round. In that image the traditionally assumed relationship between director and text or idea or plan is broken. Where the directing happens is perhaps at the beginning of the process, organising space, cueing behaviour and creating a feeling for the sort of room it is. Once again it is the process which is dominant, the modelling of social space which in turn produces kinds of reflection. Rehearsal, and having audience at rehearsal, is felt to be as interesting as the finished work.

This model of making, or directing, both consolidates and troubles some traditional aspects of direction. Goode regards his work as 'managing what we imagine'. The emphasis is not on director as visionary but as organiser. Against that, however, Goode speaks of a radical uncertainty as to how he has come to be there in the process, a worry about being found out. So his role comes to be that of the one who doesn't know, who, indeed, might stand up and declare himself as a not-knower. So while this might be a re-statement, at some level, of direction as organisation (see Chapter 10), it also productively dissociates the director's role from any authority in respect of truth and purpose.

Punchdrunk was founded by Felix Barrett, who remains overall artistic director. A number of shows have, however, been directed by two people, Barrett and associate director Maxine Doyle. They each have differ-ent interests in the artwork: on the one hand site, light and sound, on the other bodies, performer process and movement. Doyle describes it not as co-directing but parallel directing, where two directors, working within a shared vision – Barrett's – research and cast together but then each tackle different aspects of the production. The shape of the rest of the company is a collaborative team around Barrett, where designers are key collaborators and performers, especially regular ones, are co-creators within the process of actualisation.

What has increasingly happened as the company has developed is that the company has diversified with different projects happening simultaneously. Each project then has its own director. But all of the projects are initiated from, and take place within, the conceptual universe which has Barrett's ideas at its centre. Among those projects might be 'corporate' events specifically tai-lored for a company. For the artistic director there is no separation between what might be called 'aesthetic' and 'corporate' performances. And of course, given that both sorts are generated within the same conceptual universe, there will be no separation. The artistic director overseeing a company which is diversifying its activities becomes also the director of the brand. The man-agement of the brand and its characteristic activities and images is part of the art of direction.

Formulated like that we seem a long way from those early directors who set their faces against commercial theatre. But in all four of the examples a distance seems to have been travelled in the evolution of the director role, with its assumed features being challenged or re-assembled in relation to one another. And the context of these challenges is not, here, the development of community engagement but the specific creation of aesthetic performance. In the case of Shunt it is the artistic project which establishes the roles. For Chris Goode it is the unsettling of the director role which initiates the aes-thetic creation. For these and a host of other instances we might say that, whereas once the director was the force that ensured the coherence of the art, now the art is made in large part by de-cohering the director.

ACTOR-MANAGERS

There is another position, however. We noted, earlier in this chapter, that the actor-managers of the late nineteenth century busily set about labelling them-selves as 'producers', adapting themselves dextrously to the newly emerging role. But name apart, in function and effect they remained actor-managers. And their way of functioning, far from being brought to an end by the arrival of the director, seems to have persisted.

From the beginning it seems that the new role of director was some-times simultaneously inhabited by the old role of actor-manager. Stanislavski was impressed by the Meiningen company because of their discipline. He immediately set about imitating the methods of their Regisseur Chronegk. At the same time, however, he continued to act in his own productions, apparently not always very well. He was followed by a long line of those who are associated with the emergence of the new role of director – Antoine, Copeau, Jouvet, Dullin, Barrault – all of whom acted in their own productions, even though they may not have done much acting before. And if Stanislavski admired the Regisseur Chronegk he also admired the work of Henry Irving, the great actor-manager of late nineteenth-century England.

Genealogies and networks persist across the age of directors (see pp. 25–6), but within them the director slides in and out of view. Take, for example, the performer and director Jean-Louis Barrault: his ideas and practice look back to that great champion of the power of the Regisseur, Edward Gordon Craig, but then forward to Lecoq, a performer who trained performers. Among those influenced by Lecoq are the directors Robert Lepage and Simon McBurney, who often star in their own shows. Indeed McBurney is clear about his primary affiliation: 'It makes it very difficult for everyone else. But it's something I've always done. I'm an actor first and foremost. And I'm a director by chance rather than design . . . I think of a director as a kind of fake job in any case' (in Shevtsova and Innes 2009: 165).

If it is seen as appearing with early twentieth-century Modernism and then dissolving into a series of related functions in the latter end of the century, directing as a role might seem to have had a relatively short life, a temporary blip in the long history of theatre.

That history, as we know, has seen a range of roles that take responsibility for putting on shows. And of those roles there is one that seems now to have a significant persistence, stretching out across a span of time well beyond that of the brief moment of the director. This role, still there, is the actor-manager.

Chapter
5
The Pre-history of Directors

There comes a point in western theatre history when the role that oversees the staging of the work gets separated out and regarded as a role in its own right. As we have seen it is given various names but what remains in common is the idea that it is both involved with the artistry and yet a separate role. There are various rhetorical claims in support of this but together, at base, they amount to the argument that the new role is necessary because it is a guardian of the seriousness of the art, and only able to be that guardian because it is structurally separate from the others involved, the pair of eyes out front.

This claim for the role effectively distinguishes it, on one hand, from the actor or author who is already involved with the creation of the art through their role as actor or author and, and on the other, from the manager whose responsibility it is to run the theatre successfully by ensuring that popular shows are staged but who has no artistic competence in making those shows. As Chapter 1 notes, however, there are many examples of these other roles that oversee the putting on of the show before the emergence of the directing role. This section offers some examples of a range of such practices which could be seen as part of the pre-history of direction. The effort here is neither to draw a fixed line between before and after, since such lines are artificial, nor to attempt total coverage of all of this pre-history, since that would not be wholly relevant, but simply to exemplify some of the sorts of previous practice. The extracts have been taken from non-dramatic material. Obviously there are renderings of rehearsals in various plays – for example, Shakespeare's *Midsummer Night's Dream, Hamlet*; Brome's *Antipodes*; Molière's *L'Impromptu de Versailles*; Buckingham's *The Rehearsal*; Sheridan's *The Critic*; Pinero's *Trelawny of the 'Wells'*; Pirandello's *Six Characters*. But all this sort of material presents slightly more difficulty in that one has to allow for the fact that what is represented is a mediation designed to function for particular dramatic effect within the specific purposes of a whole text.

Each subsection below should be self-explanatory as to its date and immediate context.

PROPERTY PLAYERS

The extracts below are taken from John C. Coldewey's 1977 essay 'That Enterprising Property Player: Semi-professional drama in sixteenth-century England', in *Theatre Notebook* 31, pages 5–12.

In the essay Coldewey argues that in the counties surrounding London, there existed a tradition of 'semi-professional' theatre which began earlier than the establishment of the first formal theatre buildings in London. He calls it semi-professional because, although it was staffed and performed by amateur townsmen, it was 'professional' insofar as 'directors were imported from London to oversee the productions, and they were paid handsome sums for their services' (p. 5).

The most extensive, though not the earliest, references mentioning a property player occur at Chelmsford, the county town of Essex. Here during the summer of 1562, a series of four plays and shows was produced and other shows were taken to nearby Braintree and Maldon. Two plays—the first two—were managed or served by a man named Burles. To convey some sense of this property player's accomplishments, I think might for a moment rehearse what we know of the Chelmsford performances. Significantly, they conform to no known model of sixteenth-century 'amateur' drama. Information about them is found in the Chelmsford Churchwardens' Accounts, which detail for us on four consecutive closely writen [sic] folios, the elaborate properties, extensive preparations and extraordinary sums involved.

The plays began apparently, on Midsummer Day and ran through the summer, ending sometime in August. The enterprise, though, had been under way for some four or five weeks before the plays started. Burles and a helper, his 'boye', were given room and board during this time and while the first two plays were being staged. The performances were financed by loans from nine prominent townsmen, and their initial capital investment was considerable: more than £21. These loans were no doubt tinged with some hope of profit for the church if not for the individuals, and they demonstrate one way in which ambitious towns might have hoped to foster drama on home ground.

The time scheme of the plays was approximately as follows: sometime in early or mid-May, about five weeks before Midsummer Day, Burles came to Chelmsford to oversee the scaffold building and make other preparations for the first play. On a Saturday afternoon (probably Midsummer Day), minstrels arrived. Sunday was the first 'showday', and Monday the 'playday'; Tuesday was another 'showday' in Braintree, involving perhaps fifteen players from Chelmsford. At this point, Burles apparently went to Maldon, where he was boarded for two weeks, along with one William

Withers (a Chelmsford man) and fifteen men under his control. Burles arranged for the show to be presented there; then he returned to Chelmsford and stayed three more weeks, preparing for the second play. With its production he ended his duties. The accounts for the last two plays give no indication whatsoever of time. They may have been similar to the first two though, with activities for each play covering a total of about three weeks. In any case they were managed by local men.

. . .

. . . by now one thing should be clear: what we are examining in Chelmsford in 1562 was a summer dramatic festival, unlike anything mentioned in the histories of sixteenth-century drama. Burles' involvement in all the above activity was extensive. He supervised the scaffold building and was personally responsible for such things as the ironwork on the hell stage. Other entries indicate that he had a hand in keeping the accounts, in designing scenery and ordering props. And he was well paid for his pains: he received 53s. 4d. for 'serving' the first play and 42s. for the second. Certainly the size and scope of these Chelmsford plays and the presence of a professional manager are noteworthy; if this were an isolated instance we might view it as, at best, an interesting anomaly. It is not.

In Essex, records have survived from four major centres of local drama during the sixteenth century: Chelmsford, Maldon, Heybridge, and Great Dunmow. Three of these towns availed themselves of the services of property players. Let us, for our next example, follow Burles from Chelmsford to Maldon, where the Chamberlains' Accounts pick up the story the Chelmsford Churchwardens' Accounts started. Although far less detailed, these accounts provide an outline of the play Burles oversaw in that town.

The preparations for the Maldon performance took about two weeks—at least this is how long Burles was given board and room. Explicitly called 'property player' here, he seems to have served in the same capacity as at Chelmsford. Maldon's share in the dramatic activities was simply to provide costumes for the players, and most of the entries in the accounts refer to scouring armour, brushing up and mending gowns, or carrying costumes to and from the tower where they were stored.

. . .

But this was not the first time the town had made use of a property player's services. In the Chamberlains' Accounts of 1540 a tantalizing item appears near the bottom of the page: 'payde to ffelstede of Londone for servynge the play that yere kepte on Relyke sondaye and for other expencs and chargs in and abowte the same playe as yt appereth pertycularly in a boke thereof made and to this acownte annexede, vj£ viij s. jx d. ob.' By a stroke of fortune, this 'boke' still survives 'annexede' to the accounts. It consists of three very closely written pages itemizing receipts and expenses incurred at a large production that year. We thus have fairly detailed information about what took place in Maldon on that Relic Sunday (the third Sunday after Midsummer Day), and part of this information is evidently the copy of an expense account made by the property player himself.

From the receipts we learn that this play was financed in a different way than the Chelmsford plays. Here, the Maldon bailiff was in charge of all monies coming in, and twenty-four men from Maldon and other towns worked under him as collectors or gatherers. It is noteworthy that among the towns supporting the venture, Chelmsford shows up. From the expenditures we learn that our earlier surmises about the property player's duties and the extent of his control were correct. Felsted made payment for items used to build and decorate the scaffolds, and for other items having to do with props, scenery and costumes, so he was clearly responsible for all the 'gross mechanics' of the play. He, like Burles, had a helper, and they were given board and room together. Like Burles too, Felsted was well paid: he received 25s. 4d. for his services.

Further entries indicate that, besides the play, the Maldon festivities included games and a good deal of drinking. One hundred and forty-four gallons of beer and ale were sold in various sizes of 'yerthen potts' purchased especially for the occasion. One of the most suggestive entries records that fifteen hundred 'lyveries' — apparently badges, ribbons, or some other kind of personal decoration — were bought, along with one thousand pins. These point to a huge audience, even if only a half or two-thirds of the anticipated crowd appeared. From the entries concerning costumes we get some idea of what the play was about. Two calfskins were bought and dressed for 'hym that pleid John Baptyste', and three more skins were dyed for 'Crist's cote', so we may reasonably conclude that it dealt with a New Testament subject. Two 'harnesses' or coats of mail were cleaned up for the production, so the cast also included soldiers. Gunpowder was used for some spectacular effect, though we are not told what.

. . .

At Lydd, the Chamberlains' Accounts indicate that five plays were performed between 1526 and 1534. Although sparse in detail, the Lydd accounts mention again and again the services of a 'Mr Gybson' of London in connection with four of these plays. During the years of the plays, the town paid for special trips into London to consult with Gybson, for bringing him the playbook, for boarding him and his horse while at Lydd, and for beer and bread consumed apparently by men working under him. Though nowhere referred to as a property player, clearly his duties at Lydd correspond to those of property players elsewhere. Certainly Gybson was more than a reviser, since in one year the town spent 35s. on presents for him and for his travel to and from London.

. . .

In New Romney, court records and Chamberlains' Accounts from 1560 combine to give us, again, another full picture of dramatic activity. It started on Whitsunday and lasted until sometime after August 4. Four plays were produced there under the direction of a man named Gover Martyn. He is called a 'Devysor' in the accounts, and seems to have hailed from London — like Burles, Felsted and Gybson. That is to say, he was not a local man, and much of his materials, costuming and play gear was bought in London or brought from there. For his services, Martyn received the considerable reward of £5 6s. 8d. The Devysor, though, worked hard for his money. While he may not have supervised the building of the seven stages used that year, he did decorate them. He also coordinated the fabrication of costumes from start to finish, took charge of rehearsals and handled the advertisements—the proclaiming and 'crying' of the play in nearby towns.

. . .

The evidence we have, though it comes from three counties and covers half a century, is not conclusive—though it is suggestive. Were we to draw a profile, a composite picture of the 'archetypal' property player from the performances we have examined, he might be described as follows: a highly paid professional who flourished between 1515 and 1565, whose services included supervising the physical staging and sometimes the economic organization of local plays. He probably directed players, and certainly saw to the orderly marshalling of costumes, props and other play gear.

At the beginning of this paper, I mentioned that the appearance of these property players in the sixteenth century is strange and interesting. It is strange in the sense that we do not usually think of the theatre as having achieved quite the industry these men exhibit. It is interesting because of what their activities imply. First of all, it is clear that we need to reassess our attitudes towards local plays. The productions we have been examining are not simply the bumbling work of 'rude mechanicals'.

MASTER OF THE REVELS

The extracts below are taken from W.R. Streitberger's 1994 book *Court Revels, 1485–1559*. This is a detailed study of all the occasions and contexts of court revels, together with their organisational arrangements and persons involved. One of the crucial offices that came into being was that of Master of the Revels, the role that formally oversaw all arrangements, including aesthetic ones, and which is thus a sort of precursor to both producer and director.

Revels at the English Tudor court of the late fifteenth and sixteenth centuries were entertainments and spectacles consisting of various combinations of a range of elements which might include 'costuming, music, poetry, dance, visual spectacle, barriers, tourneys, and dialogue'. (p. 4)

Revels were used to signal two separate yet related functions, for the royal household was at the same time a domestic and an administrative organization. As a domestic organization, the household was concerned with the lodging and feeding of the sovereign and his retainers. Around these functions developed the ceremonies and entertainments associated with the traditional religious and secular feasts. As an administrative organization the household was concerned with the means and methods of governing the realm. Around these functions developed the ceremonies and entertainments associated with dynastic and state occasions. The domestic and administrative functions of the household were closely interwoven in the Tudor period, and the same individuals often served the sovereign in both capacities. (p. 5)

Since by their very nature they reflected the character of the sovereign and the state, revels were planned by the king or the council... The council planned wars and defence, oversaw finances and government bureaucracy, issued proclamations, sent and received ambassadors, and administered justice from the court of the Star Chamber. (p. 5)

... the core of the early Tudor council was composed of the chief officers of state and of the royal household. In addition to the heads of writ-issuing departments, such as the Chancellor, the Treasurer, and Privy Seal, it usually included the Admiral, the Steward, the Chamberlain, the Master of the Horse, often the Treasurer of the Chamber, the Treasurer of and Comptroller of the household. (p. 6)

Essentially, the council included the heads of state and the household acting collectively on everything that affected the sovereign, court, and government, and was therefore prepared to give advice in all matters. Since revels were fêtes given by the sovereign not only to his important retainers and to his household but also to foreign ambassadors, the order for such gatherings did more than confirm the hierarchy at court. Revels served as a means by which monarchs could project an image of themselves and of their courts to foreign princes. (p. 6)

When tournaments were planned, the council appointed a supervisor to organize them. And when revels were needed, the council appointed a supervisor to produce them. Initially, the appointment of a supervisor to produce revels was no different from any of the other appointments of supervisors to manage temporary projects, and none are called by special titles. Beginning in Henry VIII's reign, the appointed supervisor was called Master of the Revels, and, in 1545, the title was confirmed by patent for life. (p. 7)

Revels were the result of collaboration by artists, costume designers, writers, composers, choreographers, artisans, and labourers in relation to whom the supervisor stood as producer and director who had financial, administrative, and aesthetic control under the king and council. The responsibility of the earlier supervisors for the content of their particular revels became a standing duty of the Masters by the early 1570s, and it is likely that this also influenced the decision in 1581 to appoint the Master as censor of plays and licenser of public theatres and acting companies. (p. 7)

The early supervisors of revels were appointed for specific feasts or diplomatic occasions. When they completed their projects they returned to their ordinary posts in the household. (p. 8)

Late in Henry VIII's reign, when the Master was appointed to his position by patent for life, his duties expanded to devising or selecting and to producing or supporting the production of virtually every entertainment and spectacle at court. This was a permanent appointment to a specialist who did not return to other duties after his productions; rather he was made Master of several household offices and so gave full attention to these duties throughout the year. He was assisted with ordinary production details by a staff in a complex of offices which became by mid-century a fairly extensive organization of compatible functions. (p. 8)

Henry Guildford, son of Sir Richard Guildford (d. 1506) – Master of the Armoury, Comptroller of the Household, and half-brother of Edward Guildford, also Master of the Armoury – was twenty years old at the accession of Henry VIII and one of the king's close, personal friends who rose rapidly in public service . . . He was a member of the council who participated in the negotiations and signed most of the treaties of the reign . . .

Guildford participated in many of the revels at Henry's court during the first eighteen years of the reign, and certainly was the most distinguished public figure to hold the Mastership of the Revels on a regular basis. His appointment not only elevated the status of revels at court, but also was an important practical innovation. As a personal friend of the king's, he could participate not only in planning revels but also in the informal discussions about them and would know at first-hand the sometimes changing aims and preferences of the king and council. He could also more easily coordinate his revels with other court activities. His constant association with officers at high levels of administration in the household and in the government provided an appropriate complement to Gibson's coordination of business at a more practical level, and integrated the production of revels into the structure of the household in a way which it had never been at Henry VII's court. (p. 70)

Guildford's title was not ceremonial, nor was his supervision, early on, relegated to high-level administration. He is credited with devising or supervising most of the major entertainments from 1511 to 1517, in 1522, and in 1527. He signed Revels and other accounts relating to them, and was paid on occasion for his personal attendance on business related to the production of revels. Further, there is evidence to show that his duties extended beyond the production of disguisings and masks. He was in charge of the construction of the banqueting house at Greenwich in 1527, and in a letter from Brussels on 4 February 1516, Knight wrote to Wolsey that Guildford had sent letters to Hans Nagel, the actor, to come to England with his company to play before the king at Christmas. (pp. 70–71)

Guildford was to have as his deputy the man who had been actively helping to produce revels and tournaments from at least January 1510. From the time his name shows up in the Revels accounts in 1510 until his death in 1534 Richard Gibson was actively involved in the production of every major tournament and revel at court of which we have record . . .

[Under Henry VII] he had received two grants during pleasure, one on 22 January 1501 of the office of Yeoman Tailor of the Great Wardrobe . . . and another on 22 May 1504 of the office of the Porter of the Great Wardrobe. (p. 71)

At the opening of the reign, Gibson received his instructions and his material from high-ranking courtiers. Within a year he was receiving material and instructions in the presence of the king or ordering material himself from the Wardrobe. Early on, his accounts were declared for him, but by 1 June 1512 Gibson was receiving direct payments from the Chamber. Thus recognition by the king, his receipt of payment from the Chamber and material from the Wardrobe, and his charge of the storehouse containing properties for the revels all put an official stamp on his position as 'deputy' to the Master of the Revels. It remained only to find a place in the household for the developing organization.

By February 1513, Gibson became 'deputy' to the Sergeant of the Tents. The methods used to construct and to maintain the equipment for the Tents were similar to those used to construct pageants and to maintain revels costumes, as were the procedures for contracting the services of artists and artisans and for airing, repairing, and storing material. Perhaps as important, the period during which the workload was heaviest was reversed. Except when the army was in the field – and it was usually not in winter – the Tents were busiest in the spring, summer, and early fall. While there are exceptions, revels were produced mainly from December through February or March. Attaching the production of revels to the Tents was an intelligent administrative innovation. A permanent officer with the proper background could handle both offices, eliminating the need for separate appointments and the inefficiency that inevitably resulted from the need to coordinate services. Gibson was just such a man. His offices in the Great Wardrobe, his fifteen years of acting experience with the King's Players, his experience in costume design, and his obvious accounting skills, made him an ideal choice.

Gibson filed an account in October 1513 as 'deputy' to Sir Christopher Garnesche, 'Sergeant of the Tents', and he is styled 'Yeoman' in a book of payments dated 29 October of that year. (pp. 72–73)

The appointment of a Yeoman as a mid-level supervisor who functioned as deputy to the Sergeant of the Tents as well as the Master of the Revels was a key step in reorganizing these compatible functions and led to their formal combination in 1545. While Tents and production of revels were functionally and administratively compatible, their status at court was different. The Sergeant of the Tents was not a courtier.... Revels, on the other hand, ordinarily reflected – in fact, helped to create – the king's image, and Henry was anxious to exploit revels for this purpose. The thrust of the changes initiated at the opening of the reign was precisely to elevate the status of revels by appointing a Master who attended on the king and sat on the council and to relegate production duties to a household office.

Gibson ordinarily received his instructions from the king or from Guildford, his issues of material from one of the wardrobes by the king's warrant, and his imprests from the Chamber. All of the practical aspects of production were under his supervision. He rented houses large enough to serve as workshops, contracted the services of the Works and other household departments, hired artists and artisans to fabricate costumes, pageants, and properties, arranged for transportation, attended the productions, cleaned, stored, and cared for the inventory; kept records; and filed the most descriptive set of accounts to have survived from the early Tudor period. He was responsible for making the jousting apparel for the king and his companions, the trappers and bards for their horses, and the pageants for martial exhibitions. He also decorated banqueting houses, made costumes and properties for certain plays performed before the king, and, of course, supervised the construction of all of the pageants, costumes, and properties for the revels. His position in the Tents made him responsible for housing the army in the field, for setting up pavilions for tournaments, receptions, and conferences, and for helping to construct banqueting houses.

(pp. 73–74)

. . . .

THE EIGHTEENTH-CENTURY ACTOR-MANAGER: GARRICK

Garrick (1717–1779) was a star actor and manager of Drury Lane Theatre. In this joint role, as actor and manager, he chose the plays and adapted them as necessary, he engaged the company and cast the plays, and he oversaw the work of getting the plays onto the stage. Some of the work was simply that of a theatre manager, more or less disconnected from the activity of performing. Thus, as Stone and Kahrl tell us, he managed audience behaviour both within the theatre and outside it: he placed restrictions on the servants' gallery and the lounging of gallants on stage; he made arrangements with the City authorities (1766–1767) that the 'passage-way from the Strand up Catherine Street to Drury Lane be clear for carriages'. He also dealt with the press in that he 'consolidated regular notice of performances in the *Public Advertiser*, and for this monopoly the paper paid Drury Lane £100 annually' (Stone and Kahrl 1979: 333, 340).

He was assisted by his brother George and by the prompter (first Richard Cross, then William Hopkins); the prompter wrote out the parts, obtained licences, heard line rehearsals and had 'complete charge of the stage during performances' (Burnim 1961: 39). Garrick himself instituted and observed a code of discipline for the performers: Dibden was fined for neglecting rehearsals; Aicken was sacked for retorting when Garrick reprimanded him for wearing his hat behind the scenes. For our purposes, in tracing the pre-history of directors, it is perhaps the actual work done towards getting the play into performance that is interesting. It was at that time regular for authors to oversee the staging of their works but at Drury Lane the job was done by Garrick, thereby occupying a role which was neither author nor simply actor, although his authority came from the fact that he was both a star and a manager. In his 'directing' role he fixed what parts the actors should play and attended to the detail of stage business. But it is not clear that he systematically oversaw anything which we might recognise as a rehearsal process, let alone having a 'vision' or plan for the show. New plays might have been given a few weeks preparation but a familiar piece would rely on the actors to do what they normally did: he told

Mrs Cibber that a play would require 'four or five regular Rehearsals at least' (Burnim 1961 47). And even though he nominally oversaw those rehearsals, one actor is on record complaining that Garrick was not often in attendance:

> When the play was in Rehearsal & we got it rough hew'd, I expected Mr Garrick would have given his promis'd attendance, but he was so extremely remiss that some of the performers could not forbear complaining of the neglect. I only saw him at two rehearsals: he hardly staid half an hour at either.
>
> (in Burnim 1961: 42)

The detailed descriptions of Garrick in rehearsal are given in Kalman Burnim's full-length study, published in 1961, *David Garrick: Director*. The extracts below describe further directorial activity and are taken from pages 50–56 of Burnim's book, with minor omissions in order to maintain the focus on this specific sort of activity.

The rehearsing of a new play usually commenced with Garrick reading the script to the cast in the greenroom. From the very outset he conveyed his concept of the characters and their interpretations by acting out all the roles with the appropriate facial expressions, vocal intonations and feelings. 'As no man more perfectly knew the various characters of the drama than himself,' writes Davies, 'his reading of a new or revived piece was a matter of instruction. He generally seasoned the dry part of the lecture with acute remarks, shrewd applications to the company present, or some gay jokes.'

Although Garrick respected the varied talents of his company, he seems to have fashioned each character to his own interpretation. During rehearsals he paced the actor through his role, often acting out the scenes for him—including the female roles—with convincing realism. Helfrich Peter Sturz, traveling in England in 1768, saw him at work during the preparation of Bickerstaffe's *The Padlock* and marvelled that his delicate health could endure the constant strain which he subjected it to as he turned from one actor and character to another, attempting to kindle a fire where often no spark existed. Garrick once described his labors at 'plot and practice' as a school for underlings where the teacher was required to transform parrots into scholars and orators. Unlike most of his predecessors, however, he was convinced that only by 'Rehearsals before ye Person you may think capable of instructing you' could the actor ever achieve a true proficiency in 'the tones and actions.' . . .

As the director took infinite pains to inform, he demanded according to Davies an implicit submission to his instruction.

. . .

At the beginning of his directing career, when his company was populated with actors who had already established substantial reputations in their own right, but were rather case-hardened in their manners and techniques, it is probable that whatever 'beating in' of his own ideas Garrick could achieve must have been accomplished by the exertion of a great patience and effort. Indeed, from 1660 right through most of the period under consideration almost all discussion relative to acting centered upon the degree of excellence which an actor displayed in following the accepted traditions for portraying a particular character. The closer each succeeding actor approached imitating the preceding distinguished player of the part, the finer his performance was acclaimed. Especially prior to 1741, the year Garrick and Macklin finally asserted the actor's right to re-interpret a role according to his own peculiar genius, the tradition of fixed interpretation passed down from actor to actor naturally tended in most cases to reduce the art of acting to a matter of mere study, very often mere mimicry...

When Garrick took over Drury Lane one of his main artistic challenges was to convince the performers that a good voice, graceful manner of delivery, and easy treading of the stage were not the only qualifications essential to acting; nor was it enough to be the parrots of the poet's words without having any idea of their true meaning. Confiding in his private papers, Garrick lamented a breed of 'automaton Players, who are literally such mere Machines that they require winding up almost every time before they act, to put them into motion and make them able to afford any pleasure to an audience'.

The new actors, however, who broke-in under his management were, for better or for worse, the products of their master's making. From the moment an applicant auditioned the shaping of the mold began. Garrick's custom was to hear the hopeful read or recite before him: he would then immediately correct him by rendering the bit himself. If the student improved by Garrick's instruction, on the next reading he was accepted. It was Garrick's practice to have his more promising apprentices travel up to his Hampton villa during the summer months to receive instruction in the roles they were to play the coming season. When John Palmer joined Drury Lane, after sacrificing a more attractive contract with Beard at Covent Garden, he was relegated to attendants and messenger parts for the first season, but then made the pilgrimage to Hampton as often as possible to rehearse the roles 'the little monarch had there in study.' Certainly one of the most profitable summer semesters held at Hampton was the one just prior to Garrick's departure for the Continent in 1763. The star pupil, William Powell—whom Garrick had discovered in a Wood Street spouting club—went on that season to become in Garrick's absence the rave of London. His string of rapid triumphs set him up in the town as the successor to Roscius himself. In the midst of all his prosperity Powell modestly wrote the itinerant manager to express his gratitude for 'the foundation of all, [laid] by your kind care of me during the course of last summer' (*Private Correspondence*, I, 169). In Garrick's gracious yet temperate response will be found a lecture from a theatrical master by which any apprentice scholar might profit. He warned the young sensation that the hard work and sacrifice to his profession was now only beginning:

> You must, therefore, give to study, and an accurate consideration of your characters, those hours which young men too generally give to their friends and flatterers... When the public has marked you a favourite, (and their favour must

be purchased with sweat and labour) and you may choose what company you please, and none but the best can be of service to you ... Study hard, my friend, for seven years, and you may play the rest of your life. I would advise you to read at your leisure other books besides plays in which you are concerned ... But above all, never let your *Shakespeare* out of your hands, or your pocket; keep him about you as a charm ... One thing more, and then I finish my preaching: guard against *the splitting of the ears of the groundlings* ... do not sacrifice your taste and feelings to the applause of the multitude; a true genius will convert an audience to his manner, rather than be converted by [sic] to what is false and unnatural: *—be not too tame either*.

[Priv. Cor., I, 177–78]

Powell unfortunately did not live long enough to develop the full flow of his potential talent (he died 1769), so there is no telling how individualistic a style may have emerged from his own creativity. Many of Garrick's other students, lacking any special spark which might allow them to transcend imitation, remained mere shadows of their teacher. Garrick's method produced many excellent copyists but few artists. Charles Holland, who constantly endeavored 'to conform his Gait, his Voice, and Look, to those of the much admired Manager,' was generally dismissed as a happy but uninspired mimic 'that meanly servile in his walks of parts ... strives to shine by imitative arts'. In his satirical ode which seized upon each Drury Lane actor and actress in turn, Nicolas Nipclose (p. 41) wondered that Garrick did not costume the performers with clothes of his own size – 'they would most fit as well as his manner.' The production of *Romeo and Juliet* will suggest how his interpretations manifested themselves in the characterizations of his actors. Among the many actors he had trained in Romeo was the younger Charles Fleetwood, son of the former patentee, whose performance on September 25, 1758, was 'receiv'd with a great & deserv'd applause.' The *London Chronicle* (October 3–5) pointed out that Fleetwood's moments of greatest excellence were those scenes wherein Garrick himself had appeared to greatest advantage: ...

V

The degree to which Garrick pre-plotted the business and movements during rehearsals is not readily ascertained.

. . .

The directions that are in the promptbooks, and in some of the especially complete printed editions of such plays as *The Alchemist, Every Man in his Humour, Bon Ton*, and *The Guardian*, will suggest that Garrick moved his productions along at a very brisk pace. In *The Alchemist*, for example, he adds five directional cues for entrances or exits where Jonson does not have them, which are designed to remove characters from the stage when they are no part of the present action. *Bon Ton, Neck or Nothing*, and other farces achieve a rapidity through interjected bits of stage business. The multiple directions for entrances and exits in the promptbook of *The Provok'd Wife* (played in two hours and twenty-three minutes) give the impression of an exceptionally fast moving pace. This rapid pace was facilitated, as we shall soon see, by a scenic production technique which by its relative simplicity and plasticity afforded easy transitions of location and supplied many places of access and egress for the playing area. Even after allowing for cutting, the fact that a play of such notorious length as *Hamlet* could be performed in about two and a half hours will testify to the fluidity of the action. Surely Garrick never amalgamated the movements, gestures, and the attitudes of the stage pictures with the attention to the details of ensemble playing which directors now lavish upon their productions. On the other hand, neither did chaos exist. In a play like *Every Man in his Humour*, so eminently successful in Garrick's version which required at least 110 entrances and exits and the arrangement of up to seventeen speaking characters on the stage at one time, someone had, at least, to direct the traffic in an intelligent and effective manner.

. . .

In the confines of the traditions . . . Garrick animated his plays with a considerable amount of action. Indeed, he was sometimes attacked for supplying his actors with stage tricks and gestures which were 'often essential, but oftener used as a take in, to those who have more eyes than understanding.' In his direction, as well as in his own acting, there was reflected a 'quick and amazing art of magnifying trifles, which is sometimes the force of trick: not always taste and nature.' The success of *The Wonder* and *Bon Ton* (which with its many hidings, discoveries, disguises, double-takes and comedy groupings is almost all stage business) may be attributed to the animation that Garrick had provided. In innumerable instances the high points of the action, the very 'moments' that the audience anticipated with delight and applauded with rapture, owed their excitement and attraction to Garrick's inventiveness, both as an actor and director. So much of *The Alchemist*'s business never found its way into the printed version, but the famous scenes where Drugger dropped the urinal bottle and when, finding himself duped, he 'stripped off his cloaths, rubbed his hands, clenched his fists, and threw himself into all the attitudes of a modern Broughtonian bruiser,' certainly must have been admirably staged.

THE NINETEENTH-CENTURY ACTOR-MANAGER: IRVING

Like Garrick, Henry Irving (1838–1905) was an actor who eventually managed a theatre. Also like Garrick he was a celebrity figure who cultivated the effect of his persona and could be said always to perform even when offstage. While Irving had views on the art of acting, and published them, it is his role as the overseer of the production of plays that concerns us here.

As a leading actor it was normal practice for Irving to instruct the other actors. Here is the general picture as seen by the dramatist Dion Boucicault: 'You know that in Paris acting is taught. You are aware also that actors and authors are in the habit on the stage of teaching the actors how the characters they have drawn should be played.' Here he mentions the example of the dramatist T.W. Robertson:

> That man was in the habit of teaching and conveying his ideas to actors on the stage, and as to how the parts should be rendered. I may also refer to M. Sardou in Paris, who, it is notorious, does the same thing, as well as many of the stage-managers of the present day. Alexandre Dumas is known to be constantly doing the same thing. I may refer also to Mr. Gilbert, the author, who does the same thing, and so stamps the character that that character is entirely new, and one that you had never seen before. You know that all active managers, such as Mr. Irving, Mr. Wilson Barrett, Mr. Bancroft, Mr. Hare, Mr. Kendall, all teach the younger actors and actresses how to play their parts.
>
> (Boucicault 1926: 22)

In his account of Irving's practice, his assistant Bram Stoker has this to say:

> The play as a whole is a matter of prime consideration for the actor, though it only comes into his province *quâ* actor in a secondary way. In the working of a theatre it is the province of the stage manager to arrange the play as an entity; the actor has to deal with it only with reference to his own scenes. But the actor must understand the whole scheme so as to realise the ultimate purpose; otherwise his limitations may become hindrances to this. Irving who was manager as well as actor, puts the matter plainly from the comprehensive point of view:
>> It is most important that an actor should learn that he is a figure in a picture, and that the least exaggeration destroys the harmony of the composition. All the members of the company should work toward a common end, with the nicest subordination of their individuality to the general purpose.
>
> (Stoker 1906: vol. 2, 14)

In a lecture given in March 1885, Irving defended his practice: 'There have always been critics who regarded care and elaboration in the mounting of plays as destructive of the real spirit of the actor's art'; Betterton, he notes, was attacked for introducing scenery. But acting is inextricably bound up with the making of stage pictures:

> Now all that can be said of the necessity of a close regard for nature in acting applies with equal or greater force to the presentation of plays. You want, above all things, to have a truthful picture which shall appeal to the eye without distracting the imagination from the purpose of the drama.

The appeal, though, is of a particular sort: 'To-day we are employing all our means to heighten the picturesque effects of the drama.' These presumably include 'harmony of colour and grace of outline', but, on the other hand, 'Nor do I think that servility to archaeology on the stage is an unmixed good' (Irving 1893: 62–8).

The stage picture, however picturesque, was, of course, under the sole control of Irving who as manager imposed the disciplinary regime and as actor kept careful guard on his interpretation of the play and his part within it.

Madeleine Bingham (1978) gives an account of his preparations for a production:

Approach to rehearsals

...in his theatre Irving demanded obedience, sparing no one, not even himself. Rehearsals would last all day and sometimes half the night. There were no lunch breaks or tea breaks; actors could nibble a sandwich as and when they could. The driving will demanded sacrifice, human sacrifice, in the temple of the theatre. Here everything was held in reverence, there was to be no facetiousness. The theatre was a serious matter. Ellen sliding down the banisters had shocked him – how could an Ophelia or Portia show such a lack of dignity?

This total dedication of Irving amused Ellen. 'Yes, yes, were I to be run over by a steam-roller tomorrow, Henry would be deeply grieved; and would say quietly 'What a pity!' and then add after a moment or two's reflection 'Who is there – er – to go on for her tonight?''

The infinite patience of his productions was like the old way of painting – first the drawing, then the sepia paint, and finally the careful painting of the colours, layer by layer. First he studied the play to be produced, by himself for three months, until every detail of it was imprinted on his mind. A Shakespearian scholar once asked him some abstruse question about Titus Andronicus and Irving answered, 'God bless my soul, I've never read it, so how should I know?', shocking the questioner. Later he said, 'But when I *am* going to do Titus Andronicus, or any other play, I shall know more about it than any other student!'

When he called the first rehearsal, the play was set in his mind. He knew what he was going to do on the first night. Ellen remarked that the company would have done well to notice how he read his own part, for he never again, until the first night, showed his conception so fully and completely. It was as if he were constrained to keep his views secret lest anyone should choose to out-dazzle him.

The first reading of the play was carried out solely by Irving. He read all the parts, never faltering or allowing the company to confuse the characters. He acted every part in the piece as he read, and in his mind the tones of his actors' voices, the moves of the characters, the processions, and the order of the crowd scenes were already set. All the actors had to do was to come up to the expectations which lay in his mind. He spent no time on the women in the play. Occasionally he asked Ellen to suggest a move or two for them, or to coach them as he coached the men. To the modern mind, it was a curious way of proceeding.

Possibly Irving regarded the women in the play solely as decorations, like flowers to be placed here and there once the room was furnished. He lived in a male-dominated society and the action of most of the plays he produced was concerned with male passions. Such few plays as he produced where the female element predominated usually had Ellen as their guiding star, and he knew that she could sew the material of her part into suitably glittering raiment.

The men, the 'table legs', as Gordon Craig called them, were coached in the most intricate detail. On one occasion he wanted one actor's voice to ring out like a pistol shot with the words 'Who's there?' Fatigued by the constant repetition, Ellen finally told Irving, 'It's no better.' He said, 'Yes, it is a *little* better, and so it's worth doing.'

On and on, day after day, year after year, the iron will drove his motley company as near to perfection as he and they could reasonably reach. Scene painters, designers, gas men, stage carpenters – all were harnessed to the chariot driving towards the dream. The cost of the dream was considerable. For there were 600 people employed at the Lyceum itself. These included 40 musicians, 60 gas and limelight men, 60 carpenters, 250 extras and supers, and 40 artists and artisans in the property room under the property master, Mr Arnott. The permanent core of 600 did not include outside specialists, technicians and experts like wigmakers, dressmakers, or armourers. A report dated 1881 stated that Fox (the theatrical wigmakers and costumiers) of Russell Street 'thatched' the Irving company, making them 347 wigs. This was presumably for one season.

Nothing escaped the attention of Irving. Unsuitable scenery was turned down with the contemptuous words: 'Is *that* what you think you are going to give my public?' Dressmakers were reduced to tears or despair or both, and made to re-dress Ellen, or anyone else whose costume did not fit into the general picture of the play.

(pp. 158–9)

Preparations for *Faust*

The other cost to Irving was the nervous energy needed to control such a vast cast, which required subtle orchestration if the right effects were to be achieved. Alice Comyns Carr complained that when she saw Irving at rehearsals she realised that there were two different Irvings. The debonair holiday companion had been put off with his holiday hat, and in his place was a ruthless autocrat, 'rough in his handling of everything in the theatre – except Nell'.

No one was allowed to watch him at work, and he was ever ready with a flood of bitter satire if anyone accidentally strayed into his vision. This view of him contrasted with his kindness to his small-part actors, and the infinite patience with fools which Ellen had so often remarked upon. He was under a strain and had obviously no time to spare for artistic ladies who strayed into rehearsals to see how their party dresses looked.

The backstage complications were immense, for it was the most expensive and complex of all the Lyceum productions. There were 400 ropes to be used by the scene shifters – and each rope was blessed with a name to avoid confusion. The list of properties and instructions to the carpenters was so long that it became a joke.

(p. 216)

. . . .

The patience attributed to Irving seems to be a quality of which he himself was aware. The lengthy preparation and its requisite patience evidenced the seriousness, measurable by the effort involved, of the art to which he was devoted. It was an art which he felt should be supported by the state. Stoker quotes him:

> The mere study of the necessities and resources of theatre art – the art of illusion – should give the theatre as an educational medium a place in State economy. Just think for a moment: a comprehensive art effort which consolidates into one entity which has an end and object and purpose of its own, all the elements of which any or all of the arts and industries take cognisance – thought, speech, passion, humour, pathos, emotion, distance, substance, form, size, colour, time, force, light, illusion to each or all of the senses, sound, tone, rhythm, music, motion. Can such a work be undertaken lightly or with inadequate preparation? Why, the mere patience necessary for the production of a play might take a high place in the marvels of human effort.
>
> (Stoker 1906: vol. 2, 15)

This belief in the public status of his art ran alongside, indeed was possibly a part of, his production of himself as a public personality. Bingham tells the story of the celebrations at the hundredth night of *The Merchant of Venice*: the scenery was struck and the stage was turned into a canvas-covered banqueting hall 'for 350 gentlemen'. The guests entered through 'Irving's and Ellen's private doorway' – this was Ellen Terry, who had to vanish of course once she had performed her welcome. From the first room, the 'armoury', 'they went into the reception room which was the old room of the original eighteenth-century Beefsteak Club. This had been enlarged and its oak-panelled walls were decorated with portraits, notably one by Long of Irving himself as Richard III.' At midnight they then went into the supper room, which was the marquee on stage: 'The house lights had been kept full on and they shone dimly through the canvas like starlight upon a summer sea'. Unfortunately the celebrities present used the occasion to attack Irving (Bingham 1978: 149–50).

Brockett and Findlay (1973: 41) call Irving 'the first English director to make an art of stage lighting'. While it is true that he was very interested in lighting and historically accurate stage pictures, as an actor he was in effect lighting himself. There was no separate role of director. When the manager hosts a banquet on the same stage on which he acts, it seems clear that the role of manager is dominated by, and subsumed into, the person of the actor. For all his insistence on patient preparation of productions, and for all his emphasis on the actor submitting to the whole picture, Irving was pre-eminently the actor at the centre of the show, the actor in control of the picture to which other actors had to submit.

CONCLUSION: THE SAXE-MEININGEN COMPANY

Very close in time to Henry Irving's activities as actor-manager, the Meiningen company were touring productions which were to have a deep impact on the first generation of acknowledged modern theatre directors. Yet in some ways this company also belongs to the pre-history of directing. For the company was owned by a German aristocrat, the Duke of Saxe-Meiningen. Theatre was his hobby and he had a particular interest in scenography. As Osborne (1988) says, he was principally a visual artist, but his observations on staging, published in 1909, show an awareness of the actor's body in relation to the scene and, by extension, the arrangements for and difficulties of crowd scenes. But, in structural terms, he employed an agent to help him carry out his hobby, the ex-actor Ludwig Chronegk. Chronegk was not even a civil servant as was Goethe. He was employed solely to oversee the implementation of the Duke's ideas, to deal with the human material, somewhat like a Yeoman of the Revels (see Richard Gibson above). It was a late nineteenth-century version of a fairly old aristocratic practice. Chronegk's role with regard to the production was similar to that known often as stage manager and sometimes Regisseur. In carrying out the Duke's instructions he was operating in a role which had grown out of Garrick's prompter and was to metamorphose into the stage director who, early in the process, rehearsed actors for Belasco. Chronegk seems to have had more local power than either of those roles, but he was nevertheless not the guardian of the vision of the piece. At the same time the Duke seems to have been less involved with the operation of the process than was, say, Belasco or Stanislavski – or indeed Irving.

What impressed those who liked the Meiningen company, and there were those such as Ostrovsky who did not, was the quality of performing. The acting was apparently not very good but it was different from what was the norm in commercial theatres. Komisarjevsky tells us that the actors 'did not rant, pose, or give exhibitions of simulated temperament'. He attributes this to the fact that they were not 'playing for themselves, as was customary under the "star" system' but were instead more mutually dependent (Komisarjevsky 1929: 58). For directors fighting battles against the wilfulness, and cost, of star actors, this demonstration of a company freed from the commercial system and its temperaments was inviting. Of course the Meiningen actors could not behave as if they were in commercial theatre because they were not. They were employees of an aristocrat and, through the agency of his Regisseur, they were kept in that place. The same was true of the court orchestra. Its conductor, Hans von Bülow, aspired to make the orchestra as good as the theatre: rehearsals were intensive and the orchestra was treated as an ensemble. He was a fierce disciplinarian and he compelled the orchestra, for example, to play standing up.

Meiningen was a fairly old-fashioned model of theatre whereby the players were wholly subservient to the aristocratic patron. Such a model pre-dated the time when players could independently negotiate their own status by means of their popularity in the commercial marketplace. For the new directors ushering in their new vision of reformed theatre, this old-fashioned model, from a time when actors were servants, was attractive.

Indeed it might be argued that, since the acting wasn't very watchable, the main thing staged by the company, its main aesthetic effect, was the beneficial operation of discipline.

It is an interesting irony then that at the heart of the emergence of new theatre was a very old, and far from egalitarian, model. The early directors took the model but without the aristocrat. They were in urban theatres which they had often founded or acquired for themselves. So it could be said that the aesthetic effects of Meiningen which resulted from disciplined preparation in ducal service in turn inspired, and justified, the new – and perhaps radical – directors' exercise of power.

The Meiningen company sits then on the edge of the pre-history of directing but ends up belonging with the first moments of modern directors – not perhaps because of its old-fashioned structural arrangements as a company but because its aesthetic effects were acknowledged by the first directors, and in particular Reinhardt. It is as if their acknowledgement of its artistic influence, different as it was, positions it, necessarily, as their predecessor.

Chapter 6

Christophe Alix: A Brief History of the Publicly Funded Director in France

This essay aims to analyse developments in the status of the director in relation to the State, from the influence of German political theatre on formation of theatrical policies to the relationships between the State and the publicly funded network of directors in France. I shall demonstrate in particular that the stance taken by the director tended to influence French State authorities in establishing theatrical policy. This led government and director to adopt similar institutional and organisational structures in France, while creating tension with regards to the director as both artistic and administrative executive of a publicly funded theatre.

Directing relates primarily to the *making of the performance* guided by a director, a single figure charged with the authority to make binding artistic decisions. Each director has her/his own personal approaches to the process of preparation prior to a show. This is exemplified by the variety of terms used to describe the role and function of directing, from *producer* to *facilitator* or *outside eye*. However, it is essential at the outset to make two observations, each of which contributes to a justification for a generic and historical analysis of the role of director. Firstly, a director does not work alone, and cooperation with others is involved at all stages of the process. Secondly, beyond individual variation, the role of director remains two-fold. The first is to guide the actors (meneur de jeu, acting coach); the second is to make a visual representation in the performance space (set designer, stage designer, costume designer, lighting designer, scénographe). The increasing place of scenography has led contemporary directors such as Robert Wilson, Romeo Castellucci, Robert Lepage or Jan Fabre to produce shows where the performance space becomes a semiotic entity that displaces the primacy of the text. The play is not, therefore, the sole artistic vehicle for directing. This definition of directing obviously calls for a definition of what the *making of the performance* might be.

The *making of the performance* is the activity of bringing a social event, by at least one performer, providing visual and/or textual meaning, to a performance space. This definition enables us to evaluate four consistent parameters throughout theatre history: first, the social and organisational aspect associated with the performance event; second, the devising process which may be based on visual and/or textual elements; third, the presence of at least one performer in the show; fourth, the performance space (not simply related to the theatre stage). Although this essay focuses primarily on theatre practice, such definition blurs the boundaries between theatre and other collaborative performing arts (opera, music and dance).

The rise of the director in the Modernist era must be considered as an evolving and historical phenomenon rather than a mere invention at the end of the nineteenth century. It has been mainly identified with the influence of Naturalism (illustrated by the Meiningen company, André Antoine and Konstantin Stanislavski) and the invention of electric lighting. The influence of the Naturalist movement on the emergence of the modern director in the late nineteenth century is often considered a radical factor in the history of theatre practice, mostly because the texts describe the psychological condition of people, and reinstate, as Erwin Piscator wrote, 'a proper relationship between literature and the state of society' (Piscator 1980: 32–34). Most noticeably Naturalism contributed to changes in staging, costume and lighting design, and to a more rigorous commitment to the harmonisation and visualisation of the overall production. Although the art of theatre was dependent on the dramatic text, scholars have demonstrated that Naturalist directors did not strictly follow the playwright's written indications in the late nineteenth century (Osborne 1988). The main characteristic of directing in Naturalism at that time depended on a comprehensive understanding of scenography, which had to respond to the requirements of verisimilitude. Electric lighting contributed to this by allowing for the construction of a visual narrative on stage. However, it was a master technician, rather than a director, who was responsible for key operational decisions on how to use this emerging technology in venues such as the new Bayreuth theatre in 1876. Although electric lighting reflects a natural technological evolution and cannot be considered as a main cause of the emergence of the director, Naturalism as an artistic movement cannot solely explain the rise of modern staging.

Two further causes of the rise of the director, rarely considered in previous studies, are the Symbolist movement (Aurélien Lugné-Poë, Vsevolod Meyerhold) and the invention of cinema. The Symbolist director's approach was to expose the spirit, movement, colour and rhythm of the text. Therefore the Symbolists disengaged themselves from the material aspect of the production, and contributed to giving greater artistic autonomy to the role of the director. So although the emergence of the director has its roots in the Naturalist practitioners (through a rigorous attempt to provide a strict visual interpretation of the text on stage), the Symbolist director heralded a modern perspective on the making of performance based on the two previously mentioned elements working together to define the director's overall function: the guidance of actors and the materialisation of visual space. As for the cinema, it had an important technological influence on the practitioners of the Naturalist movement. In order to achieve a photographic truth on the stage (tableau, image), Naturalist directors strove to decorate it with the detailed properties that would be expected if the situation were happening in reality. Film production also had an influence on the work of actors (Benjamin 2008). The film director took a primary role in the making of the film, as the source of the script, the filming process and the editing. This role influenced the perception that theatre directors had of their own work with theatre personnel. It is this concept which influenced the development of the theatre director.

The role of the director became stronger, more prominent and more hierarchical through a more political and didactic approach to theatre, as exemplified by the case of Germany at the end of the nineteenth century and through the First World War. This particular feature of the director's development originates in the midst of significant political and social upheaval throughout Europe at this time. Industrial changes during this period led to a profound transformation in social hierarchy as well as growing secularisation. The role of the theatre director reflects these changes in relation to other practitioners involved in the making of the performance, not only as self-appointed figureheads in the rendering of artistic vision or the conduct of a specific working method, but also as patriarchal and organisational figures in the implementation of the project.

The didactic perspective in theatre has its sources in the development of political theatre, and specifically in the emergence of the German theatre trade union movement (Volksbühne) and the great directors at the end of the century. The Freie Volksbühne (Free People's Theatre) movement, founded by the German trade unions in 1890, allowed workers to express their political and social demands. German workers developed, without a director figure, a theatre dedicated to their political and revolutionary beliefs, as a counterpart to the Naturalistic or Symbolic forms then emerging on the European stage. The German State re-asserted its role, especially after the First World War, by institutionalising a system which emerged among the workers of the Second Reich. As Sylvain Dhomme explains (1959: 202), it gradually became a huge administrative machine, a kind of official public service, made available to a broader audience through a complex system of redistribution of public funding which allowed the government to contribute to theatre productions and to encourage the working class to see shows. There are, of course, past examples of authorities financially involved in the support of productions and public access to institutional theatres: Louis XIV helped Molière to create and show his pieces at the Versailles court. The Volksbühne is, however, the first example of a public institution aiming to give access to the theatre for all, and not only to an elite class.

In Germany, the government, in responding rapidly to union demands for theatre support, consolidated the political initiatives of its leading directors. Indeed, while the notion of political theatre is often framed by scholarship that offers a Marxist interpretation of the great German directors' productions (as with Esslin or Willett), their personal or artistic affiliations should not be ignored: Otto Brahm created the Freie Bühne (Free Theatre) in 1889 in Berlin; Max Reinhardt began his professional career as an actor in Brahm's theatre in 1894, while Erwin Piscator and Bertolt Brecht were both students of Reinhardt at the Deutsches Theater – which was subsequently managed by Brecht from 1905. Piscator and Brecht had a crucial influence on the German political scene during the inter-war period. As John Willett pointed out in his book, *The Theatre of the Weimar Republic* (1988: 209), the Weimar theatre was more a theatre of directors than of playwrights, for the German State had built its theatre policies on renowned directors. Very soon after the First World War, the Weimar government recognised the fervour of the workers' demands, as well as those of political theatre practitioners, and consequently funded an extensive network of public theatres.

In contrast the French government subsidised only the four traditional and major Parisian theatres: the Comédie Française, the Opéra, the Opéra-Comique and the Théâtre de l'Odéon. From the end of the nineteenth century, the people's theatre (or théâtre populaire) was shaped, mainly in Paris, by writers and actors. They included: the author Romain Rolland in *Le théâtre du peuple* (People's Theatre), who aimed, in 1903, to create 'the terms of a new society, its voice, its thought, a war machine against an obsolete and aged society' (Rolland 2003: 45); Louise Michel, who created an early feminist and anarchist revolutionary theatre; and the author Maurice Pottecher, with his Théâtre du Peuple at Bussaing (1895), claiming, without success, that the French State should support a popular theatre in which its members could be paid monthly like any other civil servants or factory workers. Other examples of similar companies include the Théâtre Civique (1897) with the comedian Louis Lumet and the Théâtre Populaire de Belleville (1895) with the author Émile Berny. All these companies survived independent of any form of public funding at a time when theatre remained one of the most popular sources of entertainment or artistic activity in French society. A network of public theatres in France began in the inter-war period, and more significantly after the Second World War, leading French directors to be nominated as both artistic director and executive director of institutionalised theatres.

In 1920, the director and actor Firmin Gémier became the first theatre practitioner to receive State funding. Created in 1910, Gémier's company, the Théâtre National Ambulant, established a network of practitioners and audiences all over France. For almost 20 years – with Antoine and Lugné at first, then on his own – Gémier toured with his company. He had an appetite for showing didactic productions in the French provinces, denouncing the poor conditions of many theatre tours and the poor quality of equipment and comfort in most venues. He was also, as were others, influenced by German political theatre. After attending a mass production directed by Reinhardt, Gémier rented and transformed the Cirque d'Hiver to create a massive show, *Oedipus, King of Thebes*, a free adaptation by Saint-Georges de Bouhélier, in 1919. This production consisted of two hundred athletes and dancers and even a parade of animals.

In Germany political parties subsidised such huge productions for their annual congresses of trades unions, which became the scene for all the major political conflicts in the inter-war period. Gémier, on the other hand, was far more isolated financially than his German counterparts, although he consistently tried to convince French politicians to establish a publicly funded popular national theatre alongside the four subsidised theatres in existence at the time. In 1920, after a show at the Cirque d'Hiver, the French government mooted, for the first time, the idea of implementing a public network of theatres. In theory, this could be seen as the beginning of the Republican idea of the decentralisation of a public theatre service. But, ironically, Gémier received his first public funding when his company settled at the Théâtre du Trocadéro in Paris – and the government, by offering financial aid to Gémier, obliged him to work with the four other subsidised theatres, whose members were a priori quite remote from the idea of a popular theatre.

In the same vein the association in 1927 between the directors Gaston Baty, Charles Dullin, Louis Jouvet and Georges Pitoëff, called the Cartel, was created to 'deplore the indifference of the State to their efforts to advocate the urgent need for a decentralisation of theatres' at the same time as 'to reaffirm, after Antoine, the specificities of directing as an autonomous art form' (de Jomaron 1992: 774–8). By contrast the director Jacques Copeau refused to be supported by the State for fear of losing his freedom of creation. According to Denis Gontard (1973: 53–8), Copeau had the opportunity to lead one of the four major public theatres in Paris before 1940 (the date when he directed the Comédie Française for one year) and even to receive public financial assistance for his company, the Théâtre du Vieux-Colombier, which opened in 1913. His friends tried to convince him to think bigger, to which he responded in 1919: 'No, we must think smaller, try to protect our freedom and to escape from any form of servitude (public funding or commercial exploitation)' (Copeau 1973: 60).

These theatre directors began to be seen by the Popular Front government as an emergent force. The French socialists expressed their strong concerns about the rise of Fascism in Germany, Italy and Spain and provided an opportunity for directors to celebrate the new Socialist government of Léon Blum in the manner of the early German mass rallies. The two biggest shows ever produced were the celebration of the victory of the Popular Front in 1936 and the *Naissance d'une Cité* (The Birth of a City) by Jean-Richard Bloch at the Vélodrome d'Hiver stadium in 1937. Jean Zay, Minister of National Education and Fine Arts from 1936 to 1939, tried to help a few directors who were becoming key negotiators between the theatre companies and the public authorities. Despite the Budget Minister's refusal to provide a new budget for theatre, Jean Zay managed to obtain a budget from the Minister of Posts and Telecommunications. The debate in parliament was virulent. At one point Anatole de Monzy allegedly called out to Jean Zay: 'Why are you looking after the theatre? A Minister of Education should not care about the theatre. What's that, the theatre?' (in Lang 1968: 105). The idea of public funding for theatre was not fully accepted by politicians. But it may be that the activities of a number of directors such as Jean Vilar, Jean Dasté, Hubert Gignoux,

Gabriel Garran and Guy Rétoré, who played a major role in the resistance to the German occupation, could have helped numerous French politicians after the war to justify and promote to the public a vision of theatre as an influential didactic tool that should, hence, be state-supported.

After the Second World War, as Bernard Dort says (1988: 283–4), the status of the director rose as a result of the State's mission to contribute culturally to the educational life of the French people. Jeanne Laurent was the first French official in charge of theatrical affairs, appointed as Deputy Director of the Directorate of Theatre and Music at the Ministry of National Education in November 1944. Her first strategy, despite a limited budget, was to reaffirm the decentralisation of theatre structures promulgated by theatre directors before and during the Second World War. This emergence of the patriarchal and institutional figure of the director also stems in part from the disciplinary methods used in the devising process. For instance, Jean Vilar, one of the most eminent French directors, who created, with the help of Jeanne Laurent, the International Festival of Theatre in Avignon in 1946, describes his role as a 'servant of the playwright' (Vilar 1955). He was also a very strong-minded director, making unchallengeable decisions on the visual and acting outcomes of the dramatic text in performance. This was attacked in the late 1950s by Roland Barthes: 'Now there is a figure called Vilar representing a set of aesthetic and ideological standards ... leading to a particular cohesion which stifles any personal development of the actor' (Barthes 1958: 80–83).

But the status of the director as public figure continued to rise through the cultural strategy put in place by André Malraux, appointed in 1959 as the first Minister of Culture by Général de Gaulle, who returned to power with a significant government reform (the Constitution of the Fifth Republic). Emile Biasini, a senior official at the Ministry of Culture from 1959 to 1966, said on French radio that Malraux was 'the carrier of French culture, the holder of a philosophy of action ... he did not really care about the function of his ministry, aware that he was in post only to legitimate De Gaulle's power' (Attoun 1999). Malraux's theatrical policy was based on the idea that France needed to put in place institutional theatres in regions which were considered to be cultural deserts. However, the ministry only acknowledged about fifty directors (out of one hundred as originally planned) who had already established a robust reputation in their regions and who created the image of public figures representing the strong power of De Gaulle's State. From the late 1960s onwards, the French authorities, while still including the patriarchal figures of the great directors of the public theatre services, appeared to struggle to integrate and promote, within their network of public theatres, a new generation of young practitioners. This decline of the didactic function of the director has various causes. These include diminishing audiences in public theatres, criticism of the management at the Ministry of Culture, a lack of transparency in the nomination of directors, the outdated repertoire of plays and complaints from renowned playwrights that their work was not being performed in the institutionalised theatres. On this last point, the iconic first production of Samuel Beckett's *Waiting for Godot*, directed by Roger Blin in 1953, was refused by all the institutional theatres before being produced in a small commercial theatre in Paris, the Théâtre de Babylone.

The State and theatre institutions were seriously shaken by the social and political turmoil of 1968. Students stormed the great symbols of the French public theatres such as the Théâtre de l'Odéon (May 1968) and, to some extent, the International Festival of Theatre in Avignon (July 1968). Jean-Louis Barrault was the director of the Odéon while Jean Vilar was at Avignon. They were both key representatives of the public service theatre, in the foot-steps of the Cartel before the Second World War. During the events of 1968, both Vilar and Barrault failed to channel the young people's expectations. In the case of Avignon, Vilar, fearing clashes with the demonstrators, tried to prevent the American company the Living Theater from performing in the public venue. Nonetheless, the show, *Paradise Now*, was freely improvised by the company (and the audience) in the street. Barrault's attempts to get the students out of the Odéon ended with himself being excluded from his own theatre by the crowd (Abirached 1995). The events of 1968 demonstrate the complexities of one person trying to combine the artistic activities of the director with the administrative and executive role as head of a theatrical institution.

The link between the State and the institution in which established direc-tors were entangled was also challenged in the 1960s by young emerging directors (such as Peter Brook, Ariane Mnouchkine, Julian Beck and Judith Malina, Jerzy Grotowski, Augusto Boal, Eugenio Barba) who rejected institu-tionalised responsibility in favour of the autonomy of the performance artist (director or actor) as author. These practitioners had a strong commitment to giving an equal voice to all participants, and specifically the actor, in the devising process of a theatre production. For instance, Grotowski considered that he was

> not a director or producer or *spiritual instructor*. In the first place, my relation to the work is certainly not one-way or didactic ... This is not instruction of a pupil but utter [sic] opening to another person, in which the phenomenon of *shared or double birth* becomes possible. The actor is reborn – not only as an actor but as a man – and with him, I am reborn.
>
> (Grotowski 1968: 24–5)

Nevertheless, the director essentially continued as a strong figure. What was initially new, experimental, collective creation turned into a series of struc-tured, planned and conventionally accepted working methods guided by the director. Such practitioners sought support from French public funding, which became a fundamental means for sustaining their activities from the 1980s onwards.

But the change in the nature of creative work had an impact on the role of director. The fierce controversy surrounding the official programme of the

Avignon Festival in 2005 illustrates the distinctive nature of contemporary performance. Jan Fabre, nominated as associate artist of the festival, chose to invite Romeo Castellucci (Societas Raffaello Sanzio), Thomas Ostermeier, Marina Abramovic, Wim Vandekeybus and Pascal Rambert. The festival directors supported the programme because 'it questioned the limits and boundaries of theatre' (Darge and Salino 2005), but many critics showed their artistic disorientation, with regard to productions based on the body and visual representations, revealing assumptions founded on attending theatrical events based on written dramatic text. As a result, the festival attracted many more young spectators in 2005 than previously (Banu and Tackels 2005). However, the role of the institutionalised directors may continue to follow, yet more strongly, the hierarchical conventions of their predecessors. Kinetic images are more prominent on the contemporary stage, but this also implies a developing requirement that participants respond to the will of an autocratic director, in the same vein as the overseeing role of the stage designer in the nineteenth century. Jan Fabre writes that he is 'a dictator and a manipulator', adding 'I have always been. Once I hid it. Today, I claim it openly' (Van den Dries 2005: 338–9). The status of the institutional director seems to depend strongly on the visibility of their artistic leadership in the company. Many French institutional theatres find it difficult to consider the collaborative creation of a piece without clearly establishing the name of one artistic director.

The role of the theatre director has, however, begun to decline as a result of the rise of alternative art practices, such as live art, cyber-theatre, trans-disciplinary performance art or autobiographical performance. These new art practices, mediated through individual rather than collective experience, have gradually dominated the art scene since the 1990s. On the one hand, it becomes more difficult for the authorities to allocate subsidy to individuals as opposed to a public theatre with a recognisable hierarchical structure. On the other hand, the artistic nature of most institutionalised theatres' productions remains solidly anchored in the well-established figure of the director and, to a certain extent, in the representation of the dramatic text. French theatre is still dominated by a strong state-funded network of institutionalised directors. Recently Stanislas Nordey, theatre director and former executive director of the Théâtre de Nanterre and the Théâtre Gérard Philippe (Saint-Denis), has complained about the difficulties of navigating a two-tier system that consists of responsibilities for both institutional administration and artistic vision. More worryingly, he also admits (Anderson 2003) that he took fewer risks artistically on stage as an institutional director: '[Nordey] equated being metteur en scène with artistic freedom, and the role of director with organisation, protocol and obligation ... describes his initial desire to change the institution "from the inside", and the difficulty of achieving this'. For the French critic Jean-Pierre Thibaudat, the public theatre director acts as 'a monarch, sometimes in a despotic manner, who commands his subjects: actors, writers, designers' (Thibaudat 1994: 12–13). The institutional theatres have missions to acknowledge innovative theatre practices and to provide an educational resource for France's younger generations. Recent criticism has, however, centred on the need to modernise theatrical policy in the light of new practices and reform the publicly funded theatres, starting with the status of the director, without any reductions in public funding.

The French public theatre director, as executive manager and artistic director, is deep-rooted in the historical convergence of a State hierarchical scheme since the Modernist era. An interdisciplinary perspective on this role would therefore include a socio-political analysis of the relationship between the director, her/his institutionalisation, her/his theatre productions and the political realm. This would help us comprehend the implicit decline of the role of director today.

Christophe Alix lectures in theatre and performance at the University of Hull.

7 How Shakespeare Shaped Direction

It is early February 1931. At Cambridge's Festival Theatre, the setting for the show consists of aluminium sheeting and a metal ramp curving across the stage. On walk two actors carrying cardboard figures. These are placed on either side of the stage. Labels are hung around their necks, one saying Norfolk, the other Abergavenny. The actors take up positions to the side of the stage and, through megaphones, speak the lines of Norfolk and Abergavenny. Shakespeare and Fletcher's play *Henry VIII* is beginning. As the play goes on the stage will fill with characters dressed as playing cards, looking very similar to something from *Alice in Wonderland*.

In considering the emergence of directing and the shaping of its remit, the question when confronted by something such as this at the Festival Theatre is not about whether the production was any good, nor about how other directors did *Henry VIII*. The question instead is: how was it that Shakespeare's works became such an efficient vehicle for defining the power and remit of that new thing, the director?

Many accounts of the emergence of direction cite the need to deal with Naturalism as the key challenge which brought it into being. The director role, it's asserted regularly (see Chapter 4), became necessary in order to deal with the range of elements required by the Naturalist text. In asking my question about Shakespeare I am suggesting another story that might sit alongside that of Naturalism. And the outcome of that story, we should note, has established a minor industry devoted to describing how Shakespeare has been directed (see, for example, Lavender 2001; Brown 2008; Hortmann 2009).

MAKING SHAKESPEARE MODERN

That production in February at Cambridge was done by Terence Gray. It sat alongside productions of works by the likes of Toller, Kaiser, O'Neill, Rice – German and American avant-garde dramatists. Shakespeare was in

Modernist company. In putting him there Gray expressed his attitude to the historical text:

> In the modern drama history may be taken seriously, that is to say a dramatist may set out to create a pageant that brings before the eyes of a modern audience a new representation of the outward semblance of a past epoch of the human race, or he may take it satirically, that is to say as a means of poking fun at, or otherwise bringing into light relief aspects of the modern world by contrast with a caricature of an age that is past.
>
> (in Shaughnessy 2002: 70)

This is a considerably different sense of historical method than that advocated by William Poel in the 1890s. Poel's was an antiquarian project driven by the assumption that one could get close to the truth of the original Shakespeare productions by faithfully reconstructing their staging arrangements. This project had already been anticipated in Germany: in 1836 Ludwig Tieck had collaborated with the architect Gottfried Semper to reconstruct the Elizabethan Fortune theatre (Condee and Irmer 2008: 249). That reconstruction grew logically out of Tieck's research into Shakespeare's texts. As a textual scholar he supervised verse translations into German and as a dramaturg in Dresden and Berlin he explored modes of staging. It became clear to him that the comedies could only do their real work on an audience if done in Elizabethan stage conditions (Williams 2008: 137). This combination of elements – the textual work and the questioning of theatrical practice – was what re-appeared in the British theatre. But in Poel's case, as perhaps with Tieck, it was limited because it was conceived as a return to something which was lost. Both Tieck and Poel may have challenged contemporary practices – for example, the activities of the actor-managers and their lavish pictorial stagings of heavily edited texts, but the intervening years since Shakespeare could not be effaced. Gray's approach assumed a relationship to Shakespeare that could never be organically close, never a seamless return to a recoverable truth. The relationship of modernity to Shakespeare had always to be negotiated by a third party, the director. In handling that negotiation the director becomes a form of author. Gray said his Henry VIII 'will act in a completely stylised manner, for his object is not to persuade people that he is Henry VIII, but to express, in a stylised manner, the emotions and ideas which Shakespeare intended to convey' (in Shaughnessy 2002: 74). It is the director who knows what Shakespeare intended, and as such the director can assist that intention, by drawing on another director. When he did *Richard II* there was not only the hand of Shakespeare in the work but also that of the German Modernist director Jessner.

The attitude to direction held by Gray comes into being in Britain with Harley Granville Barker, who did three Shakespeare productions beginning in 1912. By the time he did them he had already staged modern realist plays together with Greek classics at the home of serious new drama, the Court Theatre. He had learnt from Poel, for whom he also acted, with respect to the use of the plain platform stage, but he was also critical of Poel's anti-quarianism and indeed his historical mystifications: 'We shall not save our souls by being Elizabethan... To be Elizabethan one must be strictly, log-ically or quite ineffectively so' (Barker 1913: iv). That caution about being able to return to Elizabethanism is not, we should note, of relevance only to the early days of directing classics. John Caird says of his relationship with Jonson's texts:

> I get such a strong feeling of the man while I'm working on his plays. I almost get the feeling that he moves in during rehearsals. There he is, this spiky colossus, a highly intelligent, vain, but approachable man, who begins to haunt the rehearsal room, as he must actually have done for the original productions of his work.
>
> (in Cook 1989: 45)

As against this sort of mystification, the key issue for Barker was not an imaginary sloughing off of the present to sink into the past but an explicit negotiation of the pastness of the past. This also involved a sense of, in Barker's phrase, 'intimacy of contact'. Both past and very close: for his first Shakespeare show he chose an unpopular play, *The Winter's Tale*, regarded as difficult, and then played it close up to the audience, opening it up, giving it the feel of clarity. The modern director as it were rescues the Shakespeare text and re-establishes its dramatic fullness. No longer the actor-manager's elaborate pictures nor an austere antiquarianism, this was a new form. It was a felt contact that simultaneously questioned assumptions.

As Barker saw it, one of the key issues to be faced when trying to estab-lish intimacy of contact was the soliloquy: 'A producer of Shakespeare will find no more important and no more difficult task than the restoring of this intimacy of contact, without which the soliloquy must fail of its full emo-tional effect' (Barker 1923: xviii). This was closely followed by other prickly matters – the aside, the settings, the relationship between scenes, the verse. In fact the whole dramaturgy was rebarbatively different from contemporary play writing. Which is why the actor-managers simply cut out whole swathes of intractable early-modern art. Granville Barker's solution was instead to analyse very closely the dramatic form that he had in front of him:

> To hold an audience to the end entranced with the play's beauty one depends much upon the right changing of tune and time, and the shifting of key from scene to scene... All the time it must be delightful to listen to, musical.
>
> (Barker 1922: 225)

> We hear the name sounded – sounded rather than spoken – seven times in twenty-four lines. The very name is to dominate.
>
> (Barker 1927: 94)

The effect was like being, pleasurably, in the presence of a piece of crit-ical writing, as Masefield noted: 'The performance seemed to me to be a riper and juster piece of Shakespeare criticism... than I have seen hitherto

in print' (in Styan 1977: 90). This effect coincides with the gradual movement of English away from being a 'women's subject', on the model of
general cultural studies, into a 'masculine' academic discipline in its own
right, with the status of the 'text', scientifically examined, being a crucial element (Doyle 1982: 24–5). The association of directors and literary academics
was close: Granville Barker and Bradley; Gray and Dover Wilson. The project
of dealing with Shakespeare reveals the director as, necessarily, the critic in
the theatre.

The terms of that intimacy of contact needed to be negotiated, however. This involved managing not just the audience but the place of the old
artwork in a contemporary world. Barry Jackson famously experimented
with modern-dress Shakespeare, handling Hamlet and Gertrude in 1925
much like Noël Coward's Nicky and Florence in *The Vortex* (1924). The
designs Norman Wilkinson produced for Granville Barker made reference
to a geometric Modernism and played with the relationship between stage
depth and flattened, decorated surface. Barker's actors in, for example, the
fainting scene in *The Winter's Tale* did gestures that could have come out of
German Expressionism.

So the work of the critic-manager was aiming to do two things at once:
to analyse the play and to negotiate its place in the contemporary world.
The means by which he sought to do both of these, simultaneously, was
through engaging in a close relationship with the written text. In his productions he restored most of the lines that had previously been cut. This made
for a fuller version of the plays Shakespeare wrote but at the same time he
refused to enter the assumed world of the play, its Elizabethanism. So he
rejected both the Shakespearean fictional spaces and the supposed archaeological reconstructions of Poel: 'precise knowledge of the structure and
usages of Shakespeare's own theatre will be as useful as a philosophic study
of Hamlet's character may be inspiring' (Barker 1923: xii). This approach is
analogous to that other relatively new role, the orchestral conductor – indeed,
Granville Barker speaks of the text as a music. If the conductor gets large
emotional effects by attending to the basic shapes of artistic organisation –
form, rhythm or sequence – Barker's approach to the play works in a similar way. Take, for example, this series of observations he makes of various
characters in *Macbeth*:

> It is a negative figure. But that is its significance
>
> We should see her even physically weighed down with the crown and robes that
> she struck for.
>
> the rest of the dialogue is often but a mask
>
> the unwritten motion of the play.
>
> (Barker 1984: 104, 95, 98)

The analysis made in the Preface to *Macbeth* attends not only to musical
and structural elements but also to the material elements (the sounds and

costumes). These latter elements provide a way of approaching character-isation which avoids non-Shakespearean assumptions about character as psychic entity. And in saying that we can realise that we have come to a place where the director doesn't need the stage presence or the imagina-tive empathy of the actor; and that instead of these arts directors can enter the play by using arts of their own. By challenging the director to come up with an approach which addresses both its early-modern specificity and its position in the contemporary world, the Shakespeare text created the conditions for, indeed the necessity of, a craft of direction separable from that of acting or design. Which, in successful productions, demonstrated its usefulness.

This new analytic and overseeing presence in the theatre produces a text alongside the original author's text. That new text mobilises elements over which the original author does not necessarily have full control, given chang-ing spaces and techniques, and in so doing establishes a new aesthetic. This may be seen in both the speaking of the play and the way it inhabited its spaces.

Speaking

An author's text can exert pressure on, even sometimes control, where actors breathe and it can instruct as to volume and pitch. The return to the Shakespeare text, as opposed to the convenient ditching of uncomfortable bits, opened up a new need for being able to speak it. The director is the role that addressed this need.

Barker saw verse-speaking as a way of controlling the audience. It was not to be done through characterisation but through techniques of voice and rhythm. The issue of verse delivery had previously arisen with the revivals of classical Greek plays, in Murray's translation, but there the attention was mainly to chorus work. In the Shakespeare text the verse shaped, and embod-ied, a more conversational interaction. This meant that, in order to render it appropriately the actors had to attend to the techniques of the art, requiring, principally, a voice that could speak verse. Such a voice required training. While an actor-manager such as Irving said that acting was best learnt by doing it, the new director such as Barker embraced a world in which training came to be of importance. Just like Stanislavski and Meyerhold in their dif-ferent ways, the new director shows his difference by being concerned with modelling of the materials of theatre.

When the actors' voices were properly trained, modelled, what they would arrive at was not so much expression as control. This control is effectual as music rather more than exposition or story-telling. The sound of Shakespeare is recognised as being as important as, if not more impor-tant than, the sense. Thus Barker had this to say of one moment in that 'difficult' play *The Winter's Tale*: 'Though they are certainly wild and whirling words, they are . . . the more indicative of Leontes' quiet pathological state of mind. An intentional obscurity surely, and a quite legitimate dramatic effect' (in Kennedy 2008: 132). That approach in turn influenced Tyrone Guthrie, of whom Anthony Quayle said:

> He regarded the play as a musical score: its changes of pace, its modifications, its climaxes, crescendos and decrescendos were treated very much as a piece of music. He was keenly aware of rhythm – the overall rhythm of a scene rather than the clear carving of syllables. So there were passages where he didn't care if the audience heard exactly what was said.
>
> (in Rossi 1977: 19)

Guthrie's approach, from Barker, turns up again decades later with Simon McBurney: 'Don't act in Shakespeare. Find the music. Find the musical rhythm of it, first and foremost. If you can find the musical rhythm, then you can find the shape, the dramatic shape and the emotion at the heart of it' (in Shevtsova and Innes 2009: 169). McBurney might argue that he is focussed on that new form, physical theatre, but his views here come straight out of the thinking that consolidated his role as director in the first place. For the director, Barker, Guthrie, McBurney, as the creator of a new text, the theatrical text, it is the overall music, the dramaturgic structures and rhythms, which appear to matter more than the 'meaning' of Shakespeare's words. Or, to put it the other way, the meaning is found to reside in the music, in the theatrical effect.

Based in its analysis of patterns and rhythms, with its foregrounded sense of techne, this new directors' aesthetic was part of a much wider movement. In the visual arts, in the work of Léger or Le Corbusier, there was an emphasis on a purity of 'style', a form uncluttered by human emotion. A similar sentiment is articulated in the Modernist British theatre: Granville Barker said of *Love's Labour's Lost*: 'It asks for style in the acting. The whole play, first and last, demands style' (Barker 1927: 14). This makes it sound rather like the new comedy of the 1920s. Noël Coward remarked of his own play *Hay Fever* (1925): 'it has no plot at all, and remarkably little action. Its general effectiveness therefore depends on expert technique' (Coward 1979: xvi). Its commonalty of discourse with other contemporary avant-garde forms possibly gave more substance to the new role of direction. Indeed, in a world of artworks by Léger or Malevich, 'direction' itself becomes an appropriately loaded name for an artistic concern.

Inhabiting space

Shakespeare's texts were performed in a theatre which did not imitate the appearance of a life lived in rooms; it didn't show the textures and furnishings of everyday living. They were done on a 'platform'. But Barker, as we have seen, rejected attempts to return to that platform as faulty antiquarianism. So Shakespeare's work presents a problem to those who would stage it in a modern world as to what sort of space it happens in, and therefore how the space is inhabited, and thus how the bodies work.

Barker did *Winter's Tale* and *Twelfth Night* in front of decorated drapes. The pictorial stage of Irving and Tree was conspicuously stripped back, as it were, to use a Corbusier word, purified. But it was also composed, ordered according to abstract principles, in much the same way as the spoken text was organised, with its attention to rhythms and structures. The actors were arranged into architectonic groups, balanced masses. They were put into profile against the abstractly patterned backgrounds, made balletic, as it were flattened and diagrammatic even. Here exhibited is the hand of the new director plotting movements and positioning on the stage, and conspicuously doing so. We hear of Chronegk with the Meiningen company closely working out the moves of the actors, but that was done within the framework of what was often offered as historical realism. Barker's stage pictures seem to have been responsive neither to actors' needs nor to the revelation of character. They were instead, accompanied as they were by those flat decorated drapes, a declaration of the effectiveness and pleasure of compositional technique: 'To invent a new hieroglyphic language of scenery, that, in a phrase, is the problem' (Barker 1913: iv). This was not the actor-manager's pictorial space nor was it Shakespeare's historical space: it was directed composition.

In the hands of the new directors the material elements of Shakespearean theatre became translated into dramaturgic rhythm and music. Nugent Monck described his spatial arrangements at the Maddermarket Theatre thus:

> part of the action takes place on the staircase, welding the two levels together. There are curtains across the balcony and the under-balcony, and a large pair to shut out the middle stage from the forestage. These are used for punctuation, the actors closing (or opening) first one, and then, after a few words, the other.
>
> (Monck 2002: 73)

A similar sort of compositional device can be seen in Guthrie's favoured technique of banners which visually call attention to the dramaturgic flow. Such composition can also be sonic, in a way which has nothing to do with the expression of character. Spectators noted the plop of each new drape that fell in Barker's productions.

The foregrounded abstraction and patterning of the stage were, according to Barker's designer, a deliberate attempt to produce a particular sort of audience engagement: 'at the Savoy there was no attempt to convince the eye against the judgement of the mind that one was out-of-doors looking at clipped yew hedges and marble canopies' (Norman Wilkinson in Styan 1977: 95). What was being offered was a new way of looking at the stage. It may have been Shakespeare's text but it was always mediated by something almost as powerful, the director's vision. The hedges of the *Twelfth Night* garden were almost like mechanical structures set in a relationship of balance, not just framing the human activity but in partnership with it. A reviewer of Barker's *Midsummer Night's Dream* described it as the 'dream of a poet' (in Styan 1977: 103): the poet was, of course, not the dramatist but the director.

What, then, came into being to meet the challenge of staging Shakespeare in the early twentieth century was not simply the new role of the person who gives direction, but also a new felt presence on the stage, the director's aesthetic. After Barker directors would go through a period of announcing their presence with increasing polemical glee. There were Barry Jackson's serious modern dress productions (*Cymbeline* in 1923, *Hamlet* in 1925), Gray's witty allusions and borrowings from avant-garde forms, Komisarjevsky's wild jokiness. But it all comes into being on a stage stripped down and made faster. This is rationalised as a return to the realities of Shakespearean theatre but it is also, at the same time, a placing of Shakespeare in the modern. Barker's statue scene in *The Winter's Tale* disallowed Victorian specular fullness and depth. It was flattened, refused to use shadows and perspective, even refused to do full-face address to the audience. This is both a statement of the new director's compositional space but also an engagement with a modernity which denied the centrality, fullness and illusory completeness of the human being.

We might see the Shakespearean text as the passive vehicle for bringing this modernity into being. If so, we need to see, as an analogy, the discovery by Parisian artists from about 1907 onwards of African artefacts. This was the first phase of Cubism. The discovery of the African mask revealed to a modern audience a rich heritage of neglected – supposedly primitive – art. It also enabled a new art to come into being which could break with representationality and the dominance of a bourgeois way of looking. In a similar way the Shakespearean text provoked and apparently required innovations in theatrical thinking and thus allowed to come into being the new art of the director. Much as for African masks, we might say that the emergence into the Modernist western world of Shakespeare's plays depended on the new art that they had provoked. This new art, in the theatre, had at its heart a new role, the director.

INTERPRETATION, RELEVANCE AND REFUNCTIONING

Even after its emergence, however, the role of director continued to be shaped by demands apparently put upon it by the Shakespearean text.

Terence Gray's work on Shakespeare in Cambridge was in large part a polemical challenge to a deeply English tradition. Even though the actor-managers had thrown away large chunks of the Shakespearean text, they had done so in order to produce conventionally beautiful pictures. Gray retained the text but put it into a different relationship with convention and tradition. And that was the point.

By the time he did this there had not only been full-scale recovery of hitherto ignored Shakespearean lines and texts, through the explorations of such as Granville Barker, but there had also been Poel's work in relation to the potential of original staging arrangements. So the sense of 'return' to Shakespeare had brought its theatrical excitements. These led to the self-conscious and polemical modernity of Gray or Komisarjevsky. At this point Shakespeare production now stood poised to go down two broad avenues, one that aimed to reveal the art and meaning felt to be contained in the original text and the other that found meaning by bringing the original text into explicitly abrasive relationship with contemporary reality. This led to that reality being made to break in on, and break up, the hitherto protected text. Crudely speaking one avenue of production may be said to try to interpret what is there and the other to re-function it. Both did what they did in the interest of discovering Shakespeare's relevance to contemporary audiences.

That division between interpretation and re-functioning affects more dramatists than Shakespeare. It is potentially present when directors deal with any 'old' plays. Bradby and Sparks suggest that in France after 1968 some directors rejected the impulse to make the classics 'relevant' and 'began to lay claim to a different status: that of restorer.' This brings with it an ideological promise, that such directors can 'rediscover the impact of the work' (Bradby and Sparks 1997: 49). Clearly rediscovery and restoring are one side of an ideological fence; making relevant is the other. The 'old' play thus poses a challenge to directors which drives them back to their basic definition of their role in relation to written text (see pp. 159–60). Is the director an interpreter of the already written or the master-author who shapes the theatrical event of which the play is merely one element?

This question comes to be articulated with particular force in relation to Shakespeare's work because the Shakespeare heritage has placed this particular author in such high cultural standing. That is not only the case in Britain but also in those parts of Europe which have the Romantic movement in their cultural history: Duke Georg of Saxe-Meiningen, for example, had a particular interest in the plays of Shakespeare. Shakespeare's special status means that the work of the interpreter is often couched in language which has to do with showing 'respect' for the art of the text, or being 'true' to its point of origin. When these ideologically loaded terms enter, the argument becomes fiercer. It becomes an argument about truth and art and tradition and even nation. The director's definition of her or his role in these circumstances becomes obvious, provocative and often politically loaded.

Changing the theatre

As I noted above, the scholar William Poel, and before him Ludwig Tieck, wanted to test, in practice, the theatrical implications of what they assumed to have been original Shakespearean practice. From Poel onwards, the staging of Shakespeare potentially raised questions about current conventions of theatrical spaces. It was this that led to Tyrone Guthrie's series of experiments. These began in practice more or less by accident when Guthrie was doing *Hamlet* at Elsinore in 1937. Heavy rain prevented the planned outdoor performance so Guthrie, who knew of the experiments with platforms, decided to play in the middle of the hotel ballroom, 'with the audience seated all around as in a circus'. It was, he notes, an arrangement that would later be called theatre in the round. The strength of the response motivated him to do his famous production of *Three Estates* at the Edinburgh Assembly Hall in 1948, with the audience on three sides of the stage, no longer lost in illusion but ' "assisting" as the French very properly express it, in a performance, a participant in a ritual'. From here, in 1952, he was asked to advise on a planned new Shakespeare festival in Ontario, Canada. Determined to observe Elizabethan modes of theatre practice, without being 'olde worlde', and with no appropriate spaces available, Guthrie and his team did the first productions in a very large tent with 'a stage which closely conformed to what is known of the stage for which Shakespeare wrote, and by relating the audience to the stage in a manner which approximated to the Elizabethan manner'. Over five successful years the tent was replaced by a theatre building. On this stage 'no illusionary scenery is possible', yet actors can be grouped expressively. An audience of nearly 2,000 'can be accommodated so near the actors that the farthest spectators are only thirteen rows from the front' (Guthrie 1961: 170, 279, 284, 300). The Ontario theatre was in turn to have its influence on other theatres.

That theatre, which Guthrie says wasn't perfect, grew out of his understanding of, and commitment to, principles of Elizabethan staging. Since 1936, he says, he had been convinced that there could be 'no radical improvement in Shakespearean production until we could achieve two things'. These were, first, a background with 'no concessions whatever to pictorial realism' and, second, an arrangement of the actors 'in choreographic patterns, in the sort of relation both to one another and to the audience which the Elizabethan stage demanded' (Guthrie 1961: 186). Guthrie, thus, offers an example of a case where the Shakespeare director's role comes to assume, through its respect for the 'original' text, a legitimate responsibility for the architectural arrangements of playing spaces. This is a different matter from simply finding appropriate venues for different sorts of show, as, say, Reinhardt did. If Granville Barker was led towards a new sort of lighting arrangement Guthrie pioneered his new sort of playing space. This in turn for the audiences at Ontario produced, as he saw it, a new sort of watching, 'a ritual in which actors and spectators are alike taking part' (Guthrie 1961: 301). The director, wholly in keeping with the need properly – effectively and indeed, sometimes, 'truthfully' – to stage Shakespeare, can extend his or her remit to the actual shape and construction of the theatre. The address to the 'demands' of Shakespeare legitimates this extension of the director's role and can produce a change in the expectation as to what a theatre performance is.

The proper way with text

This debate surrounding the director's role with regard to already written text is focussed in particular on the relationship to 'old' plays. The issue, crudely put, is about the degree of responsibility that the director has towards a dead dramatist. In the early days the establishment of the remit of his role meant that, as Jean Chothia says, 'in order to define his own imaginative space as director, Antoine needed to be absolutely clear that the dramatist's prerogative was located in the dialogue' (Chothia 1991: 14). Granville Barker seems to follow this line when he modernises the staging but restores hitherto cut text. But there remains a problem. Although Barker restored the text, the delivery of that text was initially felt to be inappropriately fast. Poel, the archaeological scholar, happily cut lines but required a musical mode of delivery that actors had to learn. So although the dramatist supplies the 'dialogue' the onus is still on the interpreter to get it delivered. Barker's choices in this were justified, as we've seen, by detailed analysis of the written material, rather than by reference to current practices or idealised models of what it should be like. The director's authority came, then, from the strength and precision of the analysis.

This was the model followed by the campaign, once again, to bring Shakespeare into the modern world of the 1960s, led by Peter Hall and his Royal Shakespeare Company. It was based in a detailed understanding of the mechanics of the written language. As he put it many years later, 'If we understand the author's formal demands, we have some chance of representing them in modern terms.' Those formal demands, as he sees it, are contained in the words. The analogy is with musical performance: 'an iambic beat is still an iambic beat; a legato phrase in Mozart is still a legato phrase'. The director who respects, and who is competent at, close verbal analysis becomes the guardian of the true theatrical effect of Shakespeare's work: 'if Shakespeare's form is observed, an audience is still held; if it is not observed, the audience's attention strays and strays very quickly' (Hall 2009: 10–11). Of course it could be argued that there are other formal demands – the rhythms of the dramaturgy, the modes of presenting the persons of the drama – but the RSC approach favoured verbal form. This privileging was consolidated in the early days when Hall asked a Cambridge University academic, John Barton, to join the company.

It may have strengthened a certain sort of analysis, but in those days the engagement of literary academics with Shakespeare's text had next to nothing to say about such things as the bodies of performers. The work led, in some instances, to some rather silly acting out of verbal imagery arrived at by doing the then fashionable image analysis: I seem to remember a pot or two sitting about on stage so that at the appropriate moment Richard II could dip in his hands and let 'earth' trickle through his fingers. And it seems on occasion that the analysis has been driven by an already existing assumption about atmosphere and emotion. Hall says that Time in *Winter's Tale* speaks in 'strange, archaic verse' which has a 'deliberate chilling effect' (Hall 2009: 175), although there is no inherent reason why the archaic should be chilling as opposed to funny, as in *Hamlet*. When working for the RSC in the late 1960s, Peter Brook was asked by David Selbourne whether he believed there was an 'objective rhythm' in the lines to be uncovered by actors. Brook denied this, saying it was an idea 'peddled' in the 'academic notion' of subtext and the RSC's own practice where it was believed there are 'correct and incorrect ways of speaking Shakespeare'. This, said Brook, leads to an 'emphasis on a "realistic stress" to communicate a practical and prosaic meaning'. The alternative is that there is a rhythm to be found by each particular actor, so that what emerges will be diverse, each actor's own rhythm 'married to the words' rhythm, as he or she finds it'. This leads to further questioning in which it turns out that the process of 'finding the rhythm' is a sort of metaphysical quest, looking for a 'truth' (Selbourne 1982: 19, 21). One feels the presence of Grotowski sternly pointing at the triviality of the mere analysis of the material words on the page. So, on a number of counts, the directorial approach to, and guardianship of, the truth of Shakespeare's words had its limits.

There is, however, another way of discovering how the form of the text might produce a staging. This is done not by identifying form merely with words, not by close analysis simply of verse or prose but of dramaturgy. One of the model examples is that of Brecht, who wrote a 'Study' of the first scene of *Coriolanus*. It is in dialogue form and opens with the question as to how the play begins. Immediately an omission of a detail is noted, and from this a discussion follows as to the unity or otherwise of the plebeians who open the play. They seem united but 'neither we nor the audience must be allowed to overlook the contradictions that are bridged over, suppressed, ruled out, now that sheer hunger makes a conflict with the patricians unavoidable.' Another speaker objects that this can't be found in the text. 'Quite right. You have got to have read the whole play.' After this Menenius Agrippa enters and delivers his political parable. One speaker says he or she isn't convinced by it, but 'It's a world-famous parable. Oughtn't you to be objective?' Another says that the plebeians complain about a series of issues, including the war. It is pointed out that actually they say nothing against the war. The description of the sequence continues until it is pointed out that they have forgotten the entry of the People's Tribunes: 'No doubt you forgot them because they got no welcome or greeting.' 'Altogether the plebeians get very little further attention.' Towards the close of the exposition someone notes that the end of the scene is 'a little unsatisfactory': 'We'll note that sense of discomfort.' They then conclude this part of the analysis by celebrating the rich diversity of the text: the wit of the plebeians, the language of the parable, the clarity of Marcius' harangue; and they note 'great and small conflicts all thrown on the scene at once'. By contrast most productions make the opening scene work as an exposition of the character of Marcius, aligning with the patricians' cause rather than the plebeians (Brecht 1964: 252–5). From here the conversation moves into considering how to stage the analysis, which in turn makes the analysis even more detailed.

Brecht's overall attention here is to an accurate description of the sequences and modes of writing of the text, even where – or especially where – there are difficulties and contradictions. A similar approach was taken by Strehler, who was much influenced by Brecht: he

> refused to restrict the meaning of the work by presenting either the story of a tragic hero narrated within a political context, or the story of a society in which the fate of the individual is relatively unimportant. His method — whether in analysing the play or in staging it — was, he argues, neither 'romantic' nor 'idealistic', but 'dialectical'.

This led to a particular sort of acting: 'a constant awareness of the ambiguities of situation, and a performance style which meant acting in the third person, maintaining an objective distance from the role rather than being immersed in the character in a naturalistic Stanislavskian way' (Hirst 2006: 68, 69). It is important to note that this dramaturgic analysis can produce, or require, a different mode of acting, in a way which might be more radical than verse analysis does. Furthermore, while verse analysis can tend to suggest a route into finding out what the text really says, it tends to imagine that this is singular – a truth that can be found. The dramaturgic analysis, in the hands of Brecht and Strehler, admittedly familiar with Marxist dialectics, tends to reveal, and then play, ambiguity and contradiction. So the different ways of analysing text can lead, without altering one word of it, into very different modes of acting and staging.

Re-functioning

But not altering one word of it might be the problem. If you are dealing with a text that has high cultural status and is imbued with national tradition, and if you are in a society where terrible things have been done in the name of culture or nation, then to leave such a text intact is to imply compliance with the things that have been done on its behalf.

There are several positions that demand tough scrutiny of the viability of the dramatist's text. All of them would begin by challenging Antoine's view of the extent to which the dialogue does indeed remain the dramatist's prerogative. For too much respect for that prerogative might restrict directors in areas which fall to their own responsibility. The French director Roger Planchon separated himself from the position of his contemporary Jean Vilar who saw his role as interpreting and diligently servicing the author's text. Planchon by contrast, as we shall see in more detail in Chapter 8, suggested that 'stage language', as he defined the whole visual apparatus of the stage, 'has a *responsibility* equal to that of the written text' (Daoust 1981: 15). There is something more to this responsibility than merely looking after the visuals with as much care as the words.

In one of his regular experiments with Goldoni, one of the classics in the Italian tradition, Giorgio Strehler put three Goldoni plays together into one show. This required a considerable amount of cutting. In a number of places, apparently, long soliloquy or aside was replaced by dumbshow. For example, in one play a husband-to-be is not allowed to see his wife and, alone, expresses his feelings in soliloquy. Hirst describes Strehler's change: 'this was reduced to one line — "Yes, it's no more than I deserve; I deserve worse" — the rest being expressed in terms of action.' In silence the man shows the stages of his reaction until his final immobility is interrupted by his servant 'carrying a wet umbrella' (Hirst 2006: 56–7). Hirst comments that Strehler's cuts 'achieved an alteration of emphasis, a shift of dramatic values which amounts to a significant modemisation of the plays'. But he adds that this shift of values was acceptable: 'Strehler excised what he felt to be an outmoded convention [asides] in favour of a gestic technique more appropriate to epic theatre. This is the main reason why critics felt that he had made Goldoni so contemporary. Without doing violence to the basic structure of the original, he had found a way of investing eighteenth-century dramatic method with a vital new life' (Hirst 2006: 56, 57).

Strehler was, then, being responsible, to use Planchon's word, because his careful visual text replaced an outmoded convention, thereby allowing Goldoni to work in the contemporary theatre, but at the same time, likewise responsibly, he was showing respect for the original text, not doing it violence. The problem with this tactful negotiation of positions, as some might see it, is that it keeps in place the status of that original. Even where a director is exercising power over the visual language there are ethical or political reasons why respect for the written may be problematic. Historically, for example, the written has been associated with a dominant class, and children have been separately streamed in some systems of schooling on the grounds of their capacity to deal with the written (as Balibar's analysis of French schooling observed). In more extreme circumstances, as I noted at the top, where the original text carries meaning or indeed has a cultural status which is oppressive, then it might be necessary, ethically and politically, to do it violence.

Thus, while Peter Hall was leading a return to the verse, in the German theatre from the mid-1960s onwards Shakespeare was dragged with more brutality into a contemporary world. This world was coming to terms with the trauma of the ethos, and its murders, of the National Socialist regime. Shakespeare, as a 'classical' dramatist, becomes important to it, as Wilhelm Hortmann argues, for several reasons. The first was a widespread sense that theatre's role should be that of Aufklärung, promoting an attack on middle-class society, for this society and its values had been powerless to prevent Fascism. This coincided with, and was enabled by, the development of new models of organisation in theatres. A vogue for Brecht in the mid-1960s led to interrogation of theatre practices and the theatrical canon, which in turn led to a critique of the classics and their cultural place. In the case of Shakespeare in particular the publication of Jan Kott's *Shakespeare Our Contemporary* in German in 1964 opened the door to re-thinking this particular classic, a project energised by the split the previous year in the German Shakespeare Association, fissuring the institutional coherence of Shakespeare studies.

But among the regularly respectful treatments of high culture only one unorthodox production actually appeared in 1964. This was Peter Zadek's production of *Henry V*, which juxtaposed Shakespeare's text with more contemporary images: for example, 'A screen at the back showed Hitler's troops marching into Paris and "Harry" taking the salute' (Hortmann 2009: 222). The choice of a history play anticipated what was to come, in that the histories pre-eminently allowed for reflection on the absence of order, logic, or intention in the process of history. Assumptions about the persistence of liberal and humanist values, enshrined in traditional theatrical and critical readings of the classics, had to be demolished. And the demolition went further than the mere juxtaposition of Shakespearean texts with uncomfortable modern contexts. Following various dramatists in the English-speaking world German directors set about adapting the Shakespearean text. Hans Hollmann's *Titus Titus – 50 theatralische Vorgänge* (1969) 'showed a gang of hippies chancing upon costumes on a stage and being conducted by a narrator/director through the stages of the action terminating in an orgy of killing' (Hortmann 2009: 244). While many plays could be used to take their audiences through the relatively recent historical trauma of irrational but unstoppable violence, one play in particular allowed for a probing of a very specific issue. *The Merchant of Venice* potentially mobilises anti-Semitism, and requires careful deconstruction. Yet Zadek, a Jewish émigré, presented a Shylock who was treacherous and offensive, and confirmed anti-Jewish caricature. But for all that cultural abrasiveness some of the basic conventions of theatrical representation remained in place. These conventions were then torn up in George Tabori's *Improvisations on Shakespeare's Shylock* (1978). This, says Hortmann, was 'not meant to be an adaptation or actualization of the play but a combination of anamnesis, diagnosis and therapy'. Originally due to be done at Dachau, where Tabori's father was killed, it was shown in a 'former assembly room of the Munich SS', with an audience of less than one hundred on three sides. 'All thirteen actors played Shylock and doubled for other parts. The performance comprised eighteen scenes'. These mingled episodes from the play with those from Nazi history (Hortmann 2009: 260).

The felt pressure of a very particular history, with its accusation of guilty complicity, gave an urgency to the German adaptations of Shakespeare, in order not only to make the Shakespeare texts confront the contemporary world but also to show that the revered classic can be, and must be, removed from high status. When Hollmann's *Titus* invents a narrator/director figure leading the other players through the action, it is hard not to think of this as a generalised image. The ferocity with which the Shakespeare texts were adapted and re-worked can be seen as a sort of staging of the power of the director, who becomes the agency which forces Shakespeare to be newly relevant.

Part

IV Directors as Authors

Chapter

8 Authoring Authority

Some directors are authors in the most obvious sense in that they create the script for the show. This might be a pre-written script as when Bernard Shaw directed his own work or it might emerge from the editing of material generated by company workshops as, say, with Tim Etchells. Once you accept that a theatre text need not be defined simply as a written medium, then all the other authorings done by directors swim into view. These include the arrangement of the stage, the shapes and rhythms of the bodies on stage, the idiom and texture of the performance. This chapter will begin by looking at the range of material directors author and from there move to thinking about directors as authors – or, even, auteurs – and the assumptions bound up in that sort of thinking.

DIRECTORS SCRIPTING WORDS

In order to keep tight the focus on the role of the director this section will aim to steer clear of those instances where playwrights direct their own work, even though that might be one of the oldest mechanisms whereby plays got onto the stage. So too it will glide around choreographers since that role involves a range of specific knowledge that does not pertain to directing in general.

We should begin by observing a deep division between directors. Some see the director as the instrument of the playwright while others see the director as responsible for scripting something more than, beyond, the written play. Some would argue that this difference is also embedded in national cultures with the director in Germany much more conspicuously taking on the role of author (this process is noted in the account of Shakespeare productions on pp. 147–9). The result of this has acquired its own descriptive term: the 'concept' production. In a concept production the director's creative vision is understood to have replaced – or driven out – that of the author. As the playwright Arnold Wesker saw it in 1989, 'The playwright's vision of the human condition has become secondary to the director's bombastic striving for personal impact' (in Rae 1989: 144). What's not clear, however, is where one draws the line. Like a number of discriminations it depends on some uninspected assumptions, such as how far 'intellectual' activity is a proper part of the process and how the author really 'should' be done; or why a director's concept is nastily personal whereas an author's is disinterested.

We shall encounter some of this mess later, but let's begin somewhere simple, with the director who straightforwardly re-models the play. David Belasco, although also a playwright himself, was, as a director, committed to the expressivity of all aspects of the theatrical means. He commented that he could increase the persuasiveness of a speech simply by increasing the value of the light on the actor. Thus it is no surprise to find him describing, in 1907, a moment at rehearsal:

> The dialogue is cut, whole pages being ruthlessly blue-pencilled, because so much talk at this point impedes the action and spoils the intended effect.... Or, again, this particular actor may not be able to bring out the value of the lines, and new expressions must be substituted which are better suited to his personality.
>
> (quoted in Marker 1975: 75–6)

And at the end of the process one run of the show was set aside so that he could concentrate entirely on the play, as opposed to its performance. With a stenographer at his side to take notes, he looked out for repetitions, 'unduly emphatic speeches and climaxes that have not been consistently approached', and altered them (Belasco 1919: 79).

We begin therefore with the products written or developed as part of the activity of directing. Chief among those is the Regiebuch, one of the earliest forms of which is associated with the methods of Max Reinhardt. In his 'direction book', Reinhardt assembled a mass of notes and diagrams which effectively mapped out the entire production in every detail. His contemporary in the United States, David Belasco, also began with a pre-planned mise en scène. The Regiebuch subsumes into itself the dramatist's text insofar as it elaborates on that text, showing how the stage will look and how the lines should be delivered. Open Reinhardt's Regiebuch and you see the typewritten author-text struggling for air beneath layer upon layer of annotation.

The Regiebuch is not like the prompt copy, the stage manager's book, which records all decisions taken. Instead it is the initiation of the process, the place where the early thinking is done, the site of envisaging and creation. As such it is not the writer's play but the director's book which becomes the master text of the idea. And following on from Reinhardt, many directors set about their task by developing a form of Regiebuch, even if only to throw it away (as does Lepage). The development of Regiebuch materials is a persistent activity even though they might not be formalised between the covers of a book. It is the director's process known as 'research' (see Chapter 3).

A variant on Reinhardt's Regiebuch were the records of thinking, analysis and indeed creation published by his British contemporary Harley Granville Barker. When he did his Shakespeare productions at London's Savoy Theatre the audience could buy scripts of the plays accompanied by 'Producer's Prefaces' in which Barker laid out his approach, director's text accompanying playwright's text. Later on he was to publish more formal and extended analytic 'Prefaces' to Shakespeare, free-standing pieces of Shakespeare criticism but thoroughly imbued by a director's intelligence (see also Chapter 7).

Yet another sort of book was developed by Bertolt Brecht and Ruth Berlau. Their Modelbuch was a way of preserving the special effects, and rationale, of an epic-theatre work. While it offered a formula for the re-staging of the work, it was something much more than a prompt copy. It was also something much more than an author's script. Brecht as playwright created the playtext of *Mother Courage*; Brecht as director collaborated in the creation of the *Mother Courage* Modelbuch. The difference between the two texts – and, by implication, the difference from a prompt copy – is illustrated by Brecht himself:

> What difference does it make if in the text of the play you find that Courage has given the peasants money for Dumb Kattrin's burial before she goes away, or further that by a study of the model you learn that she has counted the money out in her hand and put a coin back in her leather bag? In fact, you find only the first in the text of the play, the second in the model with Weigel. Should you keep the first and forget the second?
>
> (in Cole and Chinoy 1963: 349)

By attending to the precise details of staging and the work done by – and invented by – the actors, the Modelbuch doesn't simply give supplementary information that comes as an addition to the playtext. Instead, as Brecht notes, it establishes a critical relationship with that playtext. The tension between author's text and Modelbuch, as director's text, is productive in that, as illustrated in the example of Courage and the money above, a reader of the two texts has their attitude to Courage shifted. The relationship between the two texts replays, and locks the reader into, the contradictions embodied by Courage.

In creating two texts of *Courage* Brecht was breaking with the traditional practice of the author-director. That practice commonly treated actors as automata whose only job it was to illustrate and embody precisely what the author had written. The Brechtian Modelbuch records inventions made by actors as well as the specific effects created by exact positioning, muscular work, scenic texture, all those elements which an author's text tends to gloss over. In as it were giving voice to the other elements in the production process the Modelbuch implies that subservience to the author's text is insufficient and that, consequently, the traditional approach of the author-director is limited. But then, in the decades after Brecht, a curious inversion happens.

Technological innovation and, more importantly, its accessibility allowed for the creation of increasingly detailed visual records of shows. Still cameras gave way to video cameras, analogue to digital, while methods of archiving the visual material became easier, cheaper and more reliable. Each director and company could produce a textual record of their show. In the case of devised material, or shows for which there was no full dramatic text as a starting point, the visual record becomes the authoritative text of the show. Such texts, however, don't often have the same cultural status as the author's playtext which has an independent existence, circulating as a book in its own right. A sense of this inequality in status can be seen in one or two specific cases. After Peter Brook did his famous *King Lear* for the Royal Shakespeare Company in 1962, he made a film of the play. The film is clearly based on the production, but it is not a film of the production. It takes place in an environment which is not a theatre. So it works as a film in its own right. As director of the film Brook acquired an authorial status that was not available to him as stage director, for in the film industry the writer takes a clear secondary place to the director: the film is by Brook, the screenplay is by Shakespeare.

In the 1960s, however, there was no easy and cheap circulation of visual texts such as is now possible digitally. The film could be seen to be an effective method of allowing a greater number of people to see what Brook did with *Lear*. Nearly 40 years later Tim Etchells published *Certain Fragments* (1999). The book is a collection of essays, journalism and records of various shows done by the company Forced Entertainment. The company devises its material together, but Etchells' role has tended to be that of editor, reviewing and shaping the devised material: 'I am like an organizer, a filter; but not a neutral filter, because it's ultimately what I like that gets prioritised' (in Giannachi and Luckhurst 1999: 27). In a sense this role is directorial, in that it organises and gives shape to devised material. But it also makes claim to being an authorial role.

The potential tension here is illustrated by Eugenio Barba's account of his own behaviour in relation to what his actors have devised. In recognition of their work he formulates the term 'dramaturgy of the actor'. This 'implied that my results as director did not derive only from my personal creativity and technical know-how, but was [sic] deeply influenced and shaped by my actors' creativity'. His role in relation to that creativity is that he 'elaborates' it: 'I proposed variations, accelerations and decelerations, modified the directions in space, moulded the volume of the actions', etc. But these are more than proposals: 'If my kinaesthetic sense was not persuaded, I insisted on elaborating day after day.' The work is subject to the decisions of the 'non-conceptual part of my brain', 'the feeling', with the result that the bases of his judgement seem 'incomprehensible' to some actors (Barba 2010: 24, 54, 55, 56, 61). Note the slide from what seems to be collaborative process to the authority of individual judgement based on instinct, from, perhaps, director to author – or, as Barba would have it, and his book would title it, 'dramaturg'. But actually one is always imbricated with the other. The 'collaborative' director can assume a more autocratic behaviour by sliding across into the role of author.

A textual mechanism for establishing authorial role, beyond the directorly one, is implicitly evidenced by such texts as *Certain Fragments* where Tim

Etchells describes the company's circumstances and its processes of work. There is a consistency of voice between the prose accounts and the records of the shows. And those records are merely a part of a larger text, as if the work of the company as a whole is assimilated to, and contained within, the overall text which is authored by Etchells. That overall text circulates as a traditional published book, promising access to the work of the company. The director of a devising company in a digital age still wants to disseminate his work as an author published in print format. And as author he comes to have pre-eminence not available to other company members. This is not the production of a Brechtian Modelbuch with its productively tense relationship with authorial production. Instead it may be seen as re-instatement of the authorial role at the expense of the status of the whole company.

That authorial role is shaped within a familiar model of book production. In their various ways all of the examples surveyed above have in common the fact that they can be thought of as, and indeed have a separate existence as, books. But there is much scripting by directors that never emerges in the form of a book. Even where directors would never aim to create the book of the show, the apparently controlling overview contained in a Regiebuch, they accept it as normal practice that they should invent script to be performed by others. For example, when Katie Mitchell did *Iphigenia* she created 'offstage' activity, including a twenty-minute improvisation, which was an addition to the playwright's text. These additions were not simply filling in what was suggested or implied but inserting material where the original playtext opted not to show it: offstage Clytemnestra and Iphigenia 'continued the actions that they would have done – getting changed, nattering to each other or whatever – and these improvisations were relayed through microphones back into the room for the Chorus to react to' (in Shevtsova and Innes 2009: 193).

In part Mitchell's scripting, and that of others before her, takes its logic from the necessity, apparent over many years, of doing something with situations seemingly taken for granted by dramatists, most obviously where unscripted crowds and choruses are expected to have a lively stage presence. From Saxe-Meiningen onwards, through Reinhardt and Granville Barker, there was a well-established practice of giving individuals lines to say in order to animate the crowd as an entity. These lines, not usually supplied by dramatists, were the invention of directors. But this activity is actually a merely superficial version of the most influential writing produced by directors.

This writing emerges in the practice of giving actors motivations for their characters. Katie Mitchell, for example, advises that it is useful at the start of the process for a director to construct a biography for each character. And since actors like to be able to picture what has taken place in between the scenes – that is to say, in the places where the playwright has chosen to write no scenes – a director should write 'a chronology for the action between each scene or act. Then put each chronology on a separate sheet of A4 paper and slip in into your script before the relevant scene.' The director here not only literally adds to the written script but also potentially learns to disregard it: she recommends that a director who is trying to identify character intentions should 'try to see through the surface detail of the words into the thoughts or desires that are motivating those words' (Mitchell 2009: 39, 62). There is a potential question here as to whether a surface detail gains or loses significance in relation to whichever thoughts and desires the director has discovered to be important. At what stage does a new surface detail unsettle the analysis? So, by suggesting a 'motivation', the director may well be either filling in or fixing something on which the dramatist's text is not specific, or they may be selecting or emphasising one of a set of deliberately open possibilities. In this respect the director is acting as author in the sense that they are editing or, more powerfully, silently adapting a primary source.

THE LANGUAGE OF THE SCENE

The instances above are mainly examples of directors working with words. In the case of the work in rehearsal with actors they are placing their own form of words around the words of the primary verbal source, the scripted play. An obvious motivation for producing this 'secondary' verbal text is that directors need to script something about which the written play is usually more reticent, namely the actual spaces imagined by the play and the movement of bodies within those spaces. The need for this scripting was asserted by Craig in 1905, when he was trying to argue for the 'craft' of the new 'stage-director' as against the dominant craft of the author. The difficulty in 1905 was that plays, unlike those written by Shakespeare and his contemporaries, now contained lengthy detailed stage directions as to place and activity. But they are all, says Craig, to be ignored. And this ignoring of the directions is perfectly consistent with the stage-director's faithful promise to the author that he will 'interpret' the play 'as indicated in the text'. For in the first reading of the play by a good stage-director 'the entire colour, tone, movement, and rhythm that the work must assume comes [sic] clearly before him'. The author's stage directions become irrelevant because the objective of the director is that 'his action and scene match the verse or the prose, the beauty of it, the sense of it'. So it is the spoken verse or prose which inspires the design for the scene. And it is also this that controls the actors' movements. For once the 'unified pattern' of the production has been established, the actors cannot be allowed to break this. Even the leading actors cannot be allowed to move as they think fit, for they must be 'the very first to follow the direction of the stage-manager, so often do they become the very centre of the pattern'. With this assertion Craig, having curtailed the power of the dramatist, now draws even the star actors within the disciplinary regime of the director. And his ultimate justification for imposing this new discipline is respect for the play: 'the play, and the right and just interpretation of the play, is the all-important thing in the modern theatre' (Craig 1980: 149, 166).

Of course that parenthesis is all: it is the 'right and just interpretation' over which the director, rather than the author, is the guardian. This is not really an argument about respect for the play but respect for the work of interpreting the play. That work, as Craig sees it, involves supplementing the dramatist's script (and ignoring bits of it) with the designs and patterns developed by the director. But, in the years – and practices – following Craig, 'right and just interpretation' came to be more than just interpretive procedure. From Elia Kazan's point of view there are two intelligences at work, each with their own autonomy: 'It is not necessary that the director's reaction match the author's intention ... the director's first question in approaching a script is not what the author intended, but what is his own response as an independent artist' (Kazan 2009: 7).

The definition of directors' position in relation to the author is of importance because it also potentially defines another crucial relationship, that with the actors. In defending the importance of the director's creative initiative in the rehearsal room, Jonathan Miller says 'it is essential that the director feels provoked by the text rather than responsible for it'. The director has a special relationship with the text which is not available to the actors, for although they may live the lines 'some of their meanings and implications are apparent only to someone who stands outside ... the director' (Miller 1986: 101). So when directors don't defer to the text they show themselves as creative as actors; but in that they know the full meanings of the text they show themselves superior. It is not the play but the status of the author's text that allows this negotiation of position. This is a point Joan Littlewood made in a characteristically forthright gesture when a cast turned up on the first day word-perfect: 'the first thing she did was pick the script up and say "Well, this is a load of fucking rubbish. Isn't it?" And tore it up' (in Leach 2006: 121).

And that negotiation was not necessarily merely a matter of the rehearsal room. In 1984, as Gerald Rabkin (2002) shows, the Wooster Group's *L.S.D.* and the American Repertory Theatre's *Endgame* both ran into legal challenges from the original dramatists as to the use being made of their work. What needed to come discursively into existence was the notion of a 'performance text' or 'theatre text' as opposed to the written text, bringing with it questions as to its status as intellectual property and the protocols to be used in reading it.

Rabkin argues that the challenge to the dominance of the playwright was spearheaded by the radical companies of the 1960s. But there persisted a simultaneous belief, particularly in textbooks for students, that directors who were properly interpreting a dramatist should be in service to the imaginative creation of that dramatist rather than substituting it with their own. As John Fernald said in 1968, 'The director is there first of all to serve his author and second to serve his actors' (Fernald 1968: 30). The notion of serving the written text is at one extreme of the negotiation between the power of the director as against the power of the playwright. Also from 1968 James Roose-Evans has a less submissive position: 'The director's main task is to understand his author, to seek, not to impose a style, but to unearth the form within' (Roose-Evans 1968: 9). Michel Saint-Denis goes a little further than merely unearthing:

> When faced with a great work of style, the director is in a complex position. He must be submissive and creative at the same time. In other words if he is to succeed in being both faithful to the work and efficient in his treatment of it, the director has to substitute himself for the dead dramatist and recreate the play.... Submission should not lead to a ready-made, scholarly, or pedantic attitude ... invention doesn't mean fantasy.
>
> (Saint-Denis 1960: 78)

In that notion of being both 'faithful' and 'efficient', in the balance of qualified submission and creativity, we almost begin to hear Craig's 'right and just' interpretation. The crucial element here, of course, is that duty of recreating. One of the clearest theorisations of this position was put by the French director Roger Planchon.

Polemically opposing himself to the opinion of his contemporary Jean Vilar, who regarded the director as the interpreter of an author, Planchon makes the case that the visual medium, the 'langage scénique', is as important as the written text, and that the director is the author of langage scénique:

> The lesson which we can learn from Brecht the theoretician is that ... stage language ... has a *responsibility* equal to that of the written text and, finally, a movement on stage, the choice of a colour, of a set, of a costume, etc., this involves a complete responsibility.

Every decision made by a director is a form of authoring: 'There is no neutral set ... every object placed on the stage or every absence of an object ... has some kind of significance' (in Daoust 1981: 15).

Alongside langage scénique Planchon sets one other key mechanism by which a play works on its audience: the fable. The fable consists of what actually happens on stage, rather than what is merely said: 'A play progresses only through its events ... Actions can be in flagrant contradiction with the words spoken.' This too is where the director needs to be working as someone who scripts, subsuming the author's text into something larger:

> A *mise en scène* in itself means nothing. What counts is the development of the scenes, their relation to one another, the relation between a character and his language ... It is the situation which counts, its relation to the other situations of the same character.
>
> (in Daoust 1981: 14–15)

While the notion of the langage scènique having responsibility seems to rework Craig's rightness and justness, the idea that spoken words may be in tension with activity or picture is an obvious but crucial point to articulate. The director therefore becomes the ultimate guardian, indeed the author, of the relationship between events.

Richard Foreman is explicit about this – and also explicit that this relationship might not re-affirm any sense of order or norm as to the status of the staged elements. He describes preparation for rehearsals in which he amasses a range of props which might not bear any relation to the written text – but might 'add an interesting second level to the scene'. This 'second level' connects to his overall sense of how the stage works: 'Most directors think of the stage as a platform on which to display action, whereas I consider it a reverberation chamber which amplifies and projects the music of the action so that it can reveal the full range of its overtones.' Such revelation is not, however, anything like a transparent communication between stage and audience. The audience must not be allowed to feel they are 'peeking' through an imaginary fourth wall. To that end between the audience and the playing space Foreman places physical barriers, most famously strings stretched across the stage. The strings 'introduce lines that dissect the picture plane' with the effect that the audience notice the actual act of looking, because there is interference to it. For Foreman, there must be a distance between audience and stage, so that the audience are not able to enter imaginatively what is in front of them. For the same reason he shines light into their eyes. Together the string and the lights 'turn the stage into a participant in the play' (Foreman 1992: 19, 57, 58, 61). The langage scénique exercises its responsibility here by raising questions not only about the mechanism of viewing but about the whole nature of the theatrical event. Indeed it asks questions about the function of both verbal and scenic language.

SCRIPTED BODIES

Authoring is now recognised in the area of the scenic space, and productions have company members dedicated to the work of design. A rather more slippery area, so to speak, is the body of the actor. The positioning of actors and their gestural vocabulary will always have a relationship to the written text and scenic space. This relationship can be one of coherence or critique, with all points between. Decisions about the physical disposition of actors are taken mainly in the bits of rehearsals given over to blocking. Some directors let this happen as it were organically. The blocking emerges in relation to a correctly understood text and sensitive rehearsal-room interrelation. Other directors, such as Brecht or Saint-Denis, script it very deliberately.

Where the blocking is very carefully controlled, it amounts to a choreography. Choreography, as the word implies, is a form of writing, but it is a writing which, in the opinion of the Modernist French poet Mallarmé (1842–1898), can say more than words. In his essay on 'Ballets', first published in 1886, Mallarmé argued that the ballerina's craft put her into a space abstracted from the bodily real: the dancer, he said, is not a woman who dances but a metaphor. And, rather than dancing, by a bodily writing, 'une écriture corporelle', she *'suggests* things which the written word could *express* only in several paragraphs of dialogue or descriptive prose' (Mallarmé 1956: 62). For Mallarmé this écriture corporelle, with its purity of abstraction, was a superior form of writing in that it apparently cancelled the gap between writer (dancer) and reader (audience). This sense of the directness of écriture corporelle seems to inhabit quite a lot of directors' thinking about langage scénique, as if they were not servicing the written play but achieving a form of direct communication of which it was itself incapable. In her account of the Théâtre du Soleil production of *Les Atrides* Susan Bryant-Bertail suggests that 'The historical responsibility taken on by Mnouchkine is an elucidation through theatrical means, above all that of l'écriture corporelle, or writing by the actors' bodies, of the fateful intersection between the discourses of gender and empire in this founding myth of the West' (in Williams 1999: 179). The écriture corporelle allows for an elucidation of something about which Aeschylus' text may be less clear.

Now there are theoretical problems with the idea of ballet's purity of abstraction, since dance is already culturally mediated. At minimum we have to note, for example, that at a very deep level bodies are socialised into value systems which in turn define the beauty of body and gesture. But practical problems also arise with the transposition to theatre of écriture corporelle. While in dance the performer might simply do what the choreography requires, in much theatre something gets in the way of this – the character. Actors will often want to know why their character does what it does at that moment, and sometimes will resist external suggestion because the character wouldn't do that. In forms of theatre where the fictional character has less privileged status, this resistance can be overridden: Houghton tells us that Meyerhold worked with actors as a sculptor works with clay, there was 'no seeking for the underlying meaning, no discussion of the real thought of [sic] emotions which some speech conveyed, no feeling the way' (Houghton 1938: 119, 127). The actors did what was required. In the contrast between this sort of practice and one where there is attention to 'real' emotions, the director's role as author of écriture corporelle – and the abrasiveness of that role – can be revealed.

This becomes most obvious in cases where directors, like Craig's stage-director, see themselves as primarily visual artists. The Polish artist and director Tadeusz Kantor (1915–1990) is a case in point. His approach to the work of art was predicated on the belief that in imagination the 'highest values' lie in a 'poor corner' and neglected objects. Thus he says: 'I can include among my works of art the following objects: a lumber room, a cloakroom like a slaughterhouse, people hanging in a wardrobe, an academic discourse on a heap of coal, a mad woman with teaspoons, a woman with a plank, a woman in a henhouse' (women seem to be particularly objectified). The return to the 'Dead Classroom' includes 'People sprouting objects' (Kantor

1993: 30, 31). The artistic vision also established the mode of directing. For *The Return of Odysseus* (1944) the actors were asked to bring in found objects – a muddy cartwheel, dusty parcels: 'When the room was filled with objects, the text of the play lost its importance. What was important was constructing that environment, and the action of finding, choosing, bringing those objects in' (in Klossowicz 2002: 141). The use of found objects is in part an attempt to escape from a practice controlled by the project of imitating and representing. These are not 'art' objects. Their authenticity as they crowd into the room diminishes the status of that less real thing, the text of the play. And so too they show the way for the performer to become de-theatricalised. Kantor apparently encouraged a sort of non-acting so that actors merely became parts of a visual construction (Witts 2010: 35). The human actor learns to participate in the status of object. As Kobialka comments: 'The concept of the object-actor, which in 1980 acquired the name *bio-object*, signified a new relationship between the object and the actor, both of whom were engaged in a space that created and shaped them both' (Kobialka 1993: 275).

But the director's scripting of the bodies of performers potentially begins well before any blocking is done. When directors train, or at least give exercises to, their casts, they are at the same time placing the actors' bodies within a framework the terms of which are established by the director. Some actors may become habituated to thinking in terms of super-objective, others in terms of gestus, for example. This language develops in relation to concepts which underpin the process, defining, for instance, what the work of acting is, what the relationship of performance and audience should be, what the work of theatre is (we looked at some examples of these in Chapter 3 on Methods). Those concepts then establish the sets of binaries that often run though processes, largely pertaining to the truth or falsity of what is being done. Declan Donnellan, for example, sees his role as imposing laws where necessary, with fewer laws required where there's an 'atmosphere of love' (in Delgado and Heritage 1996: 90). The love-law binary is a version of what 'works' and doesn't 'work', the permissible and the out of order. To this Brook adds a slightly fiercer binary: an actor should know that a 'sympathetic but rigorous director can help him distinguish between intuitions that lead to truth and feelings that are self-indulgent' (Brook 1988: 16). Not all of this always flows from the single figure of the director, of course: companies may share a group ethic and politics. But it is also the case that it is the discourse of directors pre-eminently, as opposed to that of actors or designers, that has historically come to establish, and indeed publish, itself as 'system' or 'method'.

But lest that observation seem rather typical of the self-appointing authority of directors, let's conclude here by looking at the work of an author and director who has done so much to unsettle that which is systematic and methodical. Richard Foreman considers himself primarily a writer but directs his own material. Just as with Brecht, however, when directing he claims to be distanced from his own written text. This text, as with those perhaps of any playwright, is defined as a 'deposit', 'the "tracings" of what obsessed him' (Rabkin 1999: 179). Directing then becomes the primary task – left unfinished by the mere scriptor/depositer – of deciding how the materials relate together. In directing his own work Foreman often chooses the one text out of several that looks least theatrical, since that will present the biggest challenge. Directing exposes itself to risk, but has to abstain from the drive to make order and discipline from the materials: 'I can't emphasize enough how casual all this has to be at the beginning of the process, allowing the mind to float through multiple possibilities' (Foreman 1992: 17). Of course this could be seen as another sort of drive, the necessity to be casual. The fact of its casualness doesn't obscure its origin within an individual driver. That is confirmed by Foreman's view of his role: 'I'm actively engaged in deciding, from moment to moment, whether the staging should reinforce the overt meaning of the text, or if it should contradict it in some way' (Foreman 1992: 50). If it's 'casual', it's very decidedly so. And it's Foreman who does the deciding.

This approach to directing, and to writing, apparently comes from an interest in 'distractions', the suggestion that at any moment life can go off in different directions. So as director he works to stage 'the way the language of each line tries to say something but stumbles a little and implies something else, and the character's response to that is to decide whether to respond to the interruption or to the line' (Rabkin 1999: 139). The interest is in the moment of stumbling, the awkwardness. So in the early days he worked with nonactors, whom he didn't ask to 'act', because he wasn't interested in acting. Instead he was committed to each individual's particular awkwardness, and enjoyed the 'collision' between his precise directions and the idiosyncratic way the performers carried them out. Like the strings stretched across the stage that we noted above, the physical awkwardness insists on the materiality of the bodies in front of the audience, which in turn creates a different sort of viewing:

> In normal theater you tend to empathize with the characters' goals, which makes you look past his or her palpable physical presence and dream instead about what will happen when their projects meet resistance or achieve success. But in my theater, there was no project to dream into. There was only the physical being trying to manipulate his body in the material world.
>
> (Foreman 1992: 37)

For Foreman the work of art is a 'contest between object (or process) and viewer' (Rabkin 1999: 148). The aim is not to make art that audiences fall in love with or that becomes a fantasy extension of themselves. For in that relationship to it, audiences never become aware of their own separation or of the terms of their engagement. Those terms are crucial: 'I refuse to analyze objects and problems using the terms insisted upon by our socially enforced perspectives' (Foreman 1992: 25). Appealing art and empathy often do not create challenges to that which is socially learnt and enforced. For the work of directing generally takes on the job of ensuring that audiences do not become distracted, and continues a tradition that 'still demands you craft the audience's attention toward that specific "important" thing that is supposed to happen inside your preconceived premise' (Rabkin 1999: 139). Apparently normal directing keeps things tucked inside safely preconceived premises. It is a work of enforcement through pleasure. And part of its own pleasure is enforcement. But, as Foreman says, 'every artist finds out that at a certain point mastery can be a prison' (Rabkin 1999: 135).

We should pause and note here that there is a different way of reading what is being said. Foreman's rather easy reference to 'normal' theatre tends to leave hanging the question of what this might be. Instead the adjective takes its place in the thinking that produces a sense of an 'I' that is fairly confident of its ability to be separate from that which is 'socially enforced'. Coming from this point of view we might say that while the art may not offer audiences a fantasy extension of themselves, it may constitute a fantasy extension of the director. So presumably the mastery of casualness can also become a prison.

Foreman's project of unsettling authorship may not so much destroy authorship as reposition its impetus. While 'normal' authoring might be assumed to create order and perspective and limit distraction, it can also appear to evidence itself in the inhabiting of the individual, or indeed individualist, stance against the normative. And in that sense any director opposed to the preceding tradition and its norms is nonetheless an author. In fact the very whiff of lone radicalism can come to constitute a version of authorship that replays an ancient version of romantic heroism.

AUTHORISATION

From here we should note that directors script more than individual productions. When Selbourne watched Brook working on *A Midsummer Night's Dream* he thought he saw that Brook in the process of producing Shakespeare was also producing, as 'chief actor', Brook (Selbourne 1982: 27). Accurate or not in that case, this observation prompts us to think about the ways in which directors may be said to produce themselves and to author a range of constructions beyond individual shows. This range might include their personal image, their 'philosophy', their company, their signature, their relationship to the building they work in. Let's look at some of these, at how they work and at their effects.

We have noted above Kantor's approach to theatre, in which the selection and arrangement of objects were important to his artistic vision as was their relationship to performers. For one production he constructed a pyramid of chairs which had the effect of closing down on the performers and literally pushing them off stage (Witts 2010: 17). In this context we can set a specific feature of the performances from 1967 onwards – Kantor's staging of himself in them. Klossowicz describes what went on:

> He appears on stage wearing his own clothes – but the color of his garments always corresponds to his visual compositions. He moves around the stage reacting in different ways but never saying anything .... The actors know he may interfere in their acting, change the order of scenes, alter their rhythms, or regulate the volume of the music .... Kantor does not conduct so much as he plays the role of the conductor.

Klossowicz rightly asks what the point of this is. He cites Kantor's own statement: 'I am the author. But what brings me happiness is this role of a provocateur' (Klossowicz 2002: 144, 145). Kantor is being provocative in that the director role is customarily hidden. But Klossowicz is not wholly convinced: pointing to Kantor's declaration elsewhere that he is 'the Prime Mover', he concludes that Kantor is only interested in theatre as a staging of his own inner process as artist.

Whether or not Klossowicz is correct, we can note that Kantor takes to himself the role of conductor which alone is entitled to do things which could be highly unsettling to actors in performance. And, while these actors are often participating in the condition of objects, Kantor wears a costume of his own clothes. His literal staging of himself as director/author arrogates to himself an actual power in a spectacle of, we might say, self-authorisation.

If Kantor scripts himself into the show as an individual, it is also possible to present an image of a company, as it were to script the impression created by that company. Famously there are several ensembles and collaborative companies that do not function collaboratively at all. The will of the director dominates either through taking on the role of 'editing' material generated by others – literally as the master-author – or through their presence in the rehearsal room. Max Stafford-Clark (2004: 3) sceptically observes how the 'total theatre' ensembles of the 1960s were often run by autocratic directors. Tim Etchells concedes that he used to be 'a control freak' but now values what performers 'do individually', even though it's what he likes which gets prioritised (in Giannachi and Luckhurst 1999: 27).

While the ensemble director's name is often associated with their company, the figure of the director can appear more prominent not only than individual shows but also their companies. The theatre building comes to be an extension of the director. A celebrated example of this phenomenon is that of Nigel Playfair (1874–1934) at the Lyric Hammersmith in the 1920s. Playfair bought the Lyric as a run-down theatre in late 1918. He built it up by staging a range of work but it was in particular his revivals of late seventeenth- and eighteenth-century work that gave the theatre prominence. The work of revival was in effect a sort of tidying up, making *The Beggar's Opera* less of a satire and more of a delightful entertainment. The theme was set with an early production of *As You Like It*, which was studiously hated in Stratford and by various reviewers, who accused Playfair of treating Shakespeare 'as if he were some modern drawing-room playwright, some dramatist of the colloquial telephone school' (in Playfair 1925: 43). From this point onwards the production of old texts removed their sharpness and replaced it with style. It was a form of modernisation that steered a very wide berth around Modernism. And this production of the eighteenth century as a sort of dressing-up charade was extended to the theatre apparatus, with a bewigged theatre orchestra in one production and footmen regularly attending to onstage candles. The 'style' was encouraged to spread from one production to another so all became gathered up into a theatre style, a cod eighteenth century with its tongue always in its cheek. And all of it flowed from the personal taste of the man who owned the theatre and directed the shows, Playfair. Accused by some of being an amateur, he seems to have built on this in order to differentiate himself from the more earnest side of the profession. He apparently disliked mixing with other theatre people outside work, but instead had a wide range of non-theatre acquaintance and a reputation for giving big parties. Thus many who attended the Lyric personally knew Playfair (even though he would not be present on site during his shows). So there is a sense that through his performed taste and his social network Playfair constructed a presence as director, even though he had no mission with regard to theatre's function and his productions were somewhat trivial. The show he made was the performance of Playfair's Lyric.

Integral to that performance was the persona of the director. In Kantor and Playfair we see a couple of examples of how directors may be said to stage themselves as part of a deliberate performance to an audience. But there is also the case we noted briefly at the top of this section where the director – it was Brook – produces himself as part of the making process. In that instance it was unclear how far that self-creation contributed to the making process. By contrast, however, there are cases where directors take on a particular role in order to assist with the generation of material. Recall that one of the roles Kantor gave himself was that of 'provocateur'. This role doesn't seem bound by particular modes of theatre. Joan Littlewood created a rehearsal persona which, usually with appropriately abusive language, put down and then built up actors (Leach 2006). And, from the viewpoint of one of his performers, Roger Planchon

> places the actor in such a position that he must automatically feel lost. Being lost, the actor asks himself questions. He becomes anxious. He is no longer interested only in his own role but in the whole play. Roger Planchon provokes the actors. A good director must be a *provocateur*.
>
> (Daoust 1981: 21)

An extension of this role is that of the director who facilitates as much as provokes, and does so for the audience as much as the performers, or even where the audience are performers. Such is the case with Augusto Boal's Joker in his Forum Theatre practice. The Joker role grew out of the Arena Theatre in São Paulo where it explicated the forms and themes. In Forum its role is not so much to talk to the audience as to talk with them, to facilitate their involvement but at the same time, importantly, to ensure that the process works according to clear and equitable rules. The Joker is the director turned into an agent for enhancing community problem-solving. While it's clearly part of a thoroughly democratic ideal of process, the Joker position is also that of one who presides above, or outside, the discourses in operation. Not just the source of rehearsal-room discourse (see p. 163), the director can also position her- or himself outside of, or beyond, that language, in a place from which they can question what others are thinking and doing.

The authority to do that questioning, to provoke deeper thought, comes from somewhere deep in the concept of what directing is. Back in 1910, P.P. Howe said the director is the one who discovers, and guides, the 'spirit' of the production. This responsibility declares a separation from the mere 'letter', the superficiality perhaps, of theatricality. In other terminology, the director role is the one which appreciates and preserves the 'truth' of the work. Indeed, in some cases, directors show their commitment to truth and reality by distancing themselves from, or should we say more accurately disavowing, theatricality. Brook goes to Africa 'where we learned to de-intellectualise our work. We learned to play outside theatre conditions without formulated concepts' (in Schneider and Cody 2002: 249). The director needs to move outside theatricality in order the better to guard the truth of the work.

Let's explore this by taking the example of the Polish director Jerzy Grotowski (1933–1999). As a director Grotowski moved from, crudely speaking, a phase in which the emphasis was on actors working hard to refine technique through to a phase in which they had to abandon the security of everything they knew, learning to become subjectively exposed: 'The first item on Grotowski's list of the objects of methodological investigation to be conducted at the Laboratory in 1967 reads "To stimulate a process of self-revelation".' Actors were interrogated not about the character but about their own selves, and taken through exercises designed to estrange the sense of self (Mitter 1992: 83, 85). Interviewed in 1968, Grotowski describes the apparently paradoxical nature of a process that gets to a result by not looking for it: 'If you look for it you will block the natural creative process.' Later on he describes this as not conducting the process but being conducted: 'The process must take us.' The actor has to avoid artificial or easy solutions: 'The problem is always the same: stop the cheating, find the authentic impulses' (in Schechner et al 2002: 237, 239). The word 'authentic' is crucial – an authentic confession, an authentic process. Grotowski as director is the one who can recognise that which is authentic and differentiate it from that which is artificial. His capacity to do this, and to justify the necessary difficulty of the actors' work, derives from a concept which belongs in the same category as 'spirit'. Mitter summarises: 'Grotowski speaks for example of his attempt to recover "the life giving force in the world" through which access may be had to the "complete man" ' (Mitter 1992: 95).

Grotowski's process brings the performers through into a new psychic space. He describes their discovery of what he calls the 'secure partner'. While this cannot be defined precisely it is 'this special being in front of whom [the actor] does everything, in front of whom he plays with the other characters and to whom he reveals his most personal problems and experiences' (in Schechner et al 2002: 238). Testimony of performers suggests that they felt the punishing exercises had brought them somewhere new: 'After two hours of such work, I lay crumpled in a heap on the floor. My voice had begun to awaken in its entirety.' (in Mitter 1992: 96) While the actors struggle with their exercises Grotowski, say Slowiak and Cuesta, 'served as observer and critic' (2007: 19). Their use of the word 'served' is interesting in the context of Grotowski's own language (as commentators quote it): 'One need not define this "secure partner" to the actor, one need only say, "You must give yourself absolutely" ' (in Schechner et al 2002: 238). Grotowski is the one who makes the demand, authorised by his project of connecting with the 'force'. That demand has huge impact on the performers: when Rena Mirecka talked about *Apocalypsis*, 'More than 30 years later, tears still came to her eyes as she remembered the difficulty of this process.' From Grotowski's point of view, 'I loved them so much it sometimes seemed to me that I would die – from despair. Then again I didn't love them and was afraid. Occasionally, there was aggression: since you don't love me, I will hate you' (in Slowiak and Cuesta 2007: 25, 96). But alongside this account of a deeply personal relationship, in a process which requires the actors psychically to expose themselves, Grotowski was carefully managing his own discourse: 'When I work – either during a course or while directing – what I say is never an objective truth. Whatever I say is a stimulus which gives the actor a chance to be creative' (in Schechner et al 2002: 237). The director, then, seems to preside over the discourses within which others work – here the binary division between artificiality and authenticity. He is the source not only of demands, but also of the actor's ability to come through suffering to find a newly awakened 'voice'. He scripts not just discourses but also psychic process. Invoking a mystical force, and in charge of the discovery of authentic being, the self-authorising director is in charge of a truth machine.

Having arrived here, we can make some general observations. First, whether the director is provocateur or visionary, the role seems to govern – as it were to script – the language used by others. Second, part of that scripting works to position the director with regard to those with whom she or he works. That positioning is done by use of language, attitude, appearance, behaviour. As we see in Chapter 3 Robert Wilson's actors learn to work 'within the context of his coordinates'. And these can include not explaining anything:

> Bob's game is to ask 'What does this play mean?' The question was addressed to anybody and everyone, to whoever was in the room at the time or to the waitress in the restaurant. It was like a game and not a game. I think he wanted some answers and he knew there wasn't an answer.
>
> (Shyer 1989: 17)

In this game/not-game the director governs by being in charge of enigma, the source of questions to which there are no answers. It's a manipulation of language about which David Mamet is very cynical:

> You've heard directors and teachers by the gross tell you, 'Come to grips with yourself,' 'Regain your self-esteem,' 'Use the space,' and myriad other pretty phrases which they, and you, were surprised to find difficult to accomplish. They are not difficult. They are impossible. They don't mean anything. They are nonsense syllables, strung together by ourselves and others, and they mean 'Damned if I know, and damned if I can admit it.'
>
> (Mamet 1998: 73)

So just as the individualised 'look' of a production is a result of various materials having been worked on in a particular way, so the persona of a director may be said to be produced. But, in an ideological volte-face, and ideology is good at them, the director's identity comes to be seen not as the product of a set of composed elements, as a product of the work of authoring, but, instead, as the originating point, the fountainhead of vision. And they are not just the author, in the sense of the person from who all (imaginative) vision flows, but the one who thereby has the authority to be different. The overall consequence is that the special status of the director in the organisational machine is made to feel natural. And, like many effects which seem natural, what is concealed is in fact an inversion. Rather than being the one from whom all organisation subtends, the director is actually a function of the organisational machinery.

From the various processes of authoring, then, the cumulative effect is that of a role which doesn't so much give direction to the work done by others but, in its ideological projection, is a role which knows the direction the whole production must go, is indeed possessed by this certainty of needing to travel in a particular direction. Not so much merely leading others' work as articulating the already immanent trajectory ... What directors most profoundly author is the role of the director, as truth-keeper, visionary, the one inhabited by direction.

AUTEURS AND OTHERS

Described that way the theatre director comes close to the phenomenon that film theorists learnt to refer to as 'the Auteur'. Rather than the work of a jobbing director where one simply consumes the narrative, the auteur film is one where the personality of the director seems to be stamped on the film. This, critics once felt, made it a better film because it gained the coherence of having a distinct vision, for want of a better word, behind it. Although the term first surfaced in *L'Écran français* in 1948, it gained polemical pre-eminence in the journal *Cahiers du Cinéma* early in 1954 as the 'politique des auteurs'. It was a frontal attack by François Truffaut on a tradition of criticism in French cinema which privileged the role of the writer as the main creative force, with the director as the person who simply filmed the text. Truffaut's argument was that the director was the creative force and that film should not be simply novelistic but instead be truly cinematic.

The assumptions about the film director as auteur tend to replay a particular version of the emergence of the theatre director. The separation of the auteur director from the mere 'metteur en scène' replicates the distinction between the new theatre director and the old stage manager. The auteur, like the director produced by Naturalism, brings coherence and discipline to the material. The struggle over creative primacy – Truffaut's 'politique des auteurs' – is not so much like a battle between theatre director and playwright as between the director and the actor. And the sense that the auteur insists on the integrity of their personal vision as against the pressures of commercialism replays of course the early theatre directors' opposition to commercial theatre.

Now, as noted in Chapter 4, this version of theatre directors' emergence is but a version. Some of its clearest articulations actually postdate the 'politique des auteurs', almost as if the theatre story is influenced by the film story. Indeed this seems precisely the case of the argument put by Avra Sidiropoulou in which theatre director-auteurs are defined as those whose 'signature' is on the work. That signature supposedly becomes visible in work which is self-reflexive and impressionistic rather than transparently communicative, which is experimental rather than 'normative' or 'naturalistic'; it is hence aligned with that which is anti-commercial. Positioned in this way the activity of the director-auteur can be tracked back to the emergence of a Modernist avant-garde at the beginning of the twentieth century, with Alfred Jarry and, especially, Antonin Artaud as founding fathers. Thus, if Naturalism brought into being the director as coordinator (and Sidiropoulou says it did), then Modernism's experiments with stage language, and in particular its distancing of itself from the literary script, produce the director-auteur. And the natural, so to speak, inheritors of the mantle are those in whose work can be seen 'some of auteurism's key elements', which include 'the celebration of deconstruction, anti-textuality, hybridization, and heterogeneity' (Sidiropoulou 2011: 3). It's a familiar list, for, indeed, the director-auteurs are – and presumably always already have been – postmodernists.

Now in this narrative we can see at work not so much a history, for there are some highly contestable assumptions, but an ideological mechanism. That mechanism has the function of privileging texts that might be described as postmodern, and it gathers them and their auteurs together into a space that is comfortably radical. It is radical insofar as it is on the side of 'performance' and open text and collaboration as against the constraints of the literary and commercial, and it is comfortable insofar as this binary, and Postmodernism in general, are the stock-in-trade of dominant literary criticism. For literary criticism is largely what this sort of account is. It is much more interested in analysis of the end product, the authored work, than the mode of its production. And here, in one of those jolly reversals done by ideological mechanisms, we find that while we were celebrating our radical distance from the literary we're actually in the thrall of its protocols.

This definition of directors as auteurs brings in its train a particular mode of analysis and particular assumptions. Back in 1954 André Bazin noted how: 'The *politique des auteurs* consists, in short, of choosing the personal factor in artistic creation as a standard of reference, and then of assuming that it continues and even progresses from one film to the next.' While some films of quality will be the exception, 'these will systematically be considered inferior to those in which the personal stamp of the auteur, however run-of-the mill [sic] the scenario, can be perceived even minutely' (in Caughie 1981: 45). In a similar way, of course, the products of theatre directors can be so regarded. As Liz LeCompte says of Forsythe, 'there were certain signs that made a Billy piece' (in Shevtsova and Innes 2009: 103).

What the auteur approach enables is the reassurance that 'Billy' is in place as a recognisably consistent creative presence. It suggests that an auteur-based approach is a way of reading productions, of any sort, which looks for wholeness, for coherence of vision, for a real person infusing the work. Of course in the case of actor-managers this illusion is literally there on the stage in front of us, and accounts, I suspect, for the excitement they still arouse. But when they are not on stage they can be brought into being. Culturally competent spectators learn to recognise the individual mark, the style, of different directors. In one of the most astute analyses of this process Dennis Kennedy argues that spectators provide a discursive community around directors, with the consequence that they culturally position directors. This becomes more intensified in those circumstances where spectators are formally trained as competent readers of the stage, namely in education. He talks of the attraction to self-consciously avant-garde directors of 'small or antagonistic audiences':

> assemblies of the self-appointed demonstrating, somewhat tautologically, the advanced status of the work. Elite audiences tend to justify themselves as co-producers, effectively applauding themselves as the elect, so that their relationship to the director is likely to be more knowledgeable and perhaps more forgiving. And for their part directors continue to presume that their role in rehearsal is to be the ideal spectator, a creature who cannot exist outside the director's imagination.

> (Kennedy 2005: 45–6)

This effect on the status of directors by audiences has become reinforced over the last few decades when, as Kennedy shows, directors came to have a status similar to those authors who form the literary canon established by school and college examinations and their syllabuses (see also p. 95). The growth of theatre studies as a discipline, and the consequent publishers' lists which take advantage of and reinforce the discipline, have prompted in part a minor industry of academic writing about directors. On a very familiar model the director simply slides into the place previously occupied by the novelist or poet, and the works are considered, along the traditional lines, in terms of such things as the director's philosophy, the lineage of the works, their structure and imagery. The director as auteur is the point of origin for texts which then come to have their own discursive life and are capable of varied, and thoroughly earnest, interpretation.

We can suggest, then, that the auteur status of directors is in part constructed by the attention paid to them by academics. That attention tends to defer to the self-generated image of the director in that the mode of the 'academic' texts tends to be expository. This takes the form either of descriptions of directors' methods – the director at work – or of interviews, where the director gives their account of what their practice is and what their work intends to be. The descriptions of methods are often just that, descriptions. Where there is critique, this is fairly localised. The critique is of methods rather than of the author of those methods. The relationship between directors and the academy is therefore mutually satisfying. As Kennedy describes it:

> Directors provide commentators with a method of intellectual and historical organization, borrowed from literary examinations of authors, enabling discourse about the stylistic unity of a career, affiliation to movements, or comparative analysis with others. The approach is useful industrially as well, since celebrity directors can readily become brand names with marketing potential.
>
> (Kennedy 2005: 46)

It is ironic that soon after literary studies in the UK tore itself apart in relation to its theoretical positions, its analytic protocols, and, of course, its politics, theatre studies launched out unproblematically with its 'literary' approach to the director. And soon after film studies had started its deconstructions of stars and celebrity cultures, theatre studies set off on its romance with directors as the acceptable face of celebrity. Here were people who could be treated as auteurs insofar as they were celebrities and not as auteurs insofar as they shouldn't involve post-structuralism.

But post-structuralism has already done its ugly work. Together with its allies here, semiotics and psychoanalysis, it has broken apart the notion that the author is a unified position. As John Caughie tells us, semiotics enabled films to be treated not as completed statements but as practices where the work of 'enunciating' is ongoing. When this is evidenced in novels critics will point to the position of the narrator or the implied author and their relationship to the reader, who may sometimes even be addressed as 'dear reader'. In films this is harder to show, because there is not a similar device. So, says Caughie,

> The focus of a theory of authorship (almost of narratorship) in this context becomes to retrace the marks of the enunciating subject, the marks which constitute the film as a discourse, an ideological address rather than 'just a story', and which determine the shifting positions and relations of the spectating subject within and to the text.
>
> (Caughie 1981: 202)

Highly influential in teaching us how to read a text as an ideological address, though the texts here are prose fiction, is Pierre Macherey's *A Theory of Literary Production* which appeared in 1966, and then in an English translation in 1978. Macherey pointed out that hitherto much criticism had been a work of construction by literary critics in that they sought to demonstrate, sometimes against the odds, the basic unity of a work or alternatively they sought to elaborate on what the text was already saying. They were either taking the text on its own preferred terms or finding in it what it might be hoping to be. Macherey suggested that texts are not these complete, rounded and finalised things. They are fractured, incomplete and in a sense always in process. This is their nature because they do ideological work – taking a position within social norms – and, perhaps more importantly, they are caught up in ideological work. This is where the work of criticism comes in. For writers are always working within the ideological limits of their own time. They may be straining against these, straining to express or bring into formulation that which has not been expressed, and, crucially, is not capable at that time of being expressed, but always there is a sense of work remaining to be done – of an incompleteness figured in gaps or inconsistencies. The job of the critic is not to pretend these are not there but to attend to them: 'a true analysis does not remain within its object, paraphrasing what has already been said; analysis confronts the silences, the denials and the resistance in the object' (Macherey 1978: 150).

But, and it is a big but, as we have said, in prose fiction there are devices on which the critic can focus. So too in film there is the work of the camera as a form of scripting. But what of live theatre? How can this be done? And, more importantly, is it really necessary? Well, much academic work hitherto has sought to show how, for example, a director's productions are a sort of natural fulfilment of a process, or how they all bear the recognisable signature and achieve unity of output, or how they build on and develop completeness out of a set of influences. One of the preferred academic forms, as we've noted, is the interview – an attestation to the biological reality of the auteur there (almost) in front of us. Within a framework of literary criticism as opposed to 'theatre studies', we might, however, ask what the function of this sort of criticism is, what new knowledge it makes and what interests it serves. And we might ask whether or not there is value, for those interested in wider issues of culture and society, in reading the work on terms other than those proposed by the directors themselves.

So if we are to resist the illusion of the auteur in theatre, what do we look for? And why? An example of the need for this sort of reading is offered by Brook's *Mahabharata*. The production was praised by Richard Schechner on a familiar model: 'Of all the intentionally intercultural productions I've seen your *Mahabharata* is the finest example of something genuinely syncretic'. Here is the critic finding the real unity of the piece in a way that also, of course, performs the critic's own expertise in being able to recognise these things. But it may be that the production was not so competently intercultural and in fact did ideological work that contradicted its explicit intention. This is the critique made by Rustom Bharucha. For him the production expressed 'conceptual fuzziness' in two areas. First was a lack of 'framework of reference' providing for 'a Hindu perspective of *action* in the larger, cosmic context': Brook had indicated they were not 'presuming to present the symbolism of Hindu philosophy'. And secondly the production contained no mechanism for articulating caste distinctions 'without which the actions of the characters cannot be fully clarified'. Yet, despite the fuzziness, there were small moments when the Indian philosophical context was spoken: Bharucha specifies an 'interplay of authority and obedience in the traditional teacher-student relationship'.

Another major area of silence that Bharucha detects is the living tradition of Indian performance. This makes production of something like the *Mahabharata* rather different from doing classical Greek plays: the director of Indian material 'has both the advantage of confronting *and the responsibility* to confront traditional performances within their own aesthetic contexts'. Brook's production, by contrast, seemed to ignore how such traditional forms work and make their meaning, leading him instead to dramatise the epic 'in a predominantly linear narrative', in episodes formally linked to the 'well-made play tradition', whereas the *Mahabharata*'s own handling and concept of time are cyclical. This substitution of dramatic and conceptual form extended to the acting where it seemed that instead of finding a way to handle epic feeling, the actors were encouraged to do a sort of cod Shakespearean heroism. This was aided and abetted by a simplification, and editing, of the epic characterisations and a concomitant diffidence in attending to the text's problems around representation of gender. Bharucha said that what appeared to be a 'graceful' declaration of a refusal to impose modern concepts actually amounted to 'an evasion of responsibility'. Now although in this sort of summary it might look as if Bharucha's critique is simply a condemnation of Brook, along ideologically conservative lines, for not being true to Indian culture, what he is in fact working to demonstrate is an ideological silence which has been distorting the text: 'in his advocacy of a theatre, where the cultures of the world can be subsumed within his European structure and framework of values', says Bharucha, Brook himself is Eurocentric (Bharucha 1993: 71–81).

This critique takes us somewhere more profound, and perhaps more useful, than Schechner's praise of the 'genuinely syncretic'. In bringing us back to that, I am noting the part played by commentary in the establishment of value systems in a world of canonised directors, and, thus, the inequities which those value systems may consolidate in place. But the critical address to directors as auteurs can bring into articulation the politics not only of their productions but their processes, as the following essay by James Reynolds demonstrates. His points will then be picked up in the subsequent chapter on Organisation (Chapter 10), where not simply the process but the production company, as entities themselves authored by directors, come to be subjected to critique.

In summary, then, if directors are authors there needs to be a role for readers. These have it as their task not simply to pay witness to the production but also to state how the authoring functions, whom it authorises, and how it constitutes authority.

Chapter 9

James Reynolds: Robert Lepage and Authorial Process

Robert Lepage's theatre-making process evolved in the 1980s as a result of his encounter with Anna and Lawrence Halprin's RSVP Cycles, a method of open creativity that he learned from Jacques Lessard, the director of Théâtre Repère in Québec. The Halprins had explored architecture and dance through the RSVP Cycles, but Lessard adapted them for the theatre and changed 'RSVP' to 'Repère', a new acronym standing for Resources, Partition, Évaluation, and Representation. Lepage's creative process remains rooted in this methodology, which emphasises the mode of production over the product, and, rather than according a performance the status of a finished artwork, treats it as just one element within a continuing cycle of development. Lessard acknowledges that, although 'performance has a particular status', performances are 'not definitive' in the Repère Cycles, because 'the theatrical objective is never achieved' (Beauchamp 1994: 29). Understanding the principles of this methodology, therefore, is essential when analysing questions of authorship relating to Lepage's work. In Lessard's definition, 'Resources' constitute 'all elements from the beginning of the creation': 'Partition' is the 'exploration and organisation of the resources ... without limitations and without a precise goal'; 'Évaluation' of outcomes is evaluation conducted at the end of every cycle, and 'Representation' is 'the theatrical object presented to the public' (Beauchamp 1994: 29). The lack of a finished product raises questions around the nature of authorship in Lepage's work, but his discourse on authorship also raises interesting questions; he says that he does not apply the Cycles strictly, but rather uses them intuitively: he suggests a positive, democratic dispersal of authorship amongst his collaborators, and diminishes his own authorship by describing his role in observational terms. In what follows, therefore, I examine some of the assumptions in and around Lepage's process, in order to produce a better understanding of what kind, or kinds, of authorship might be taking place within it.

Before encountering the Repère Cycles, Lepage used an 'intuitive method' in his first company, Théâtre Hummmm ... (Charest 1997: 139). Lepage co-founded this company with Richard Fréchette in 1978, before they both joined Théâtre Repère in 1982; yet intuition-as-method remained crucial, to the extent that Lepage contextualises his break with Repère, in 1987, as a split between intuitive and methodical practitioners (dates from Charest 1997: 179, 180, 187). 'We never really respected everything', he says. 'I think that Jacques [Lessard] on his part was much closer to the Repère Cycles system. He was using it in a very methodic way. We were using a freer form and trying to adapt the rules of it to our feelings and our intuition' (McAlpine 1996: 134). Indeed, Lepage suggests that the methodology is subordinate to the content under exploration. When using the Repère Cycles, he says, we 'have to admit that the subject matter and the Resource that we've chosen and the stories that come out of that Resource are more infinite than we are' (McAlpine 1996: 141). Lessard, however, suggests that this was not a question of intuition in Lepage's work, but one of form and aesthetic. Lepage, he says, used the Cycles in accordance with his own 'creative attitude' (Beauchamp 1994: 31).

Lepage frequently relies upon the idea of intuition to emphasise or explain elements of his work. 'When I work with actors', he says, 'I tell them they have to play with emotion and intelligence. The combination of the two creates intuition', which he defines as 'the intelligence of the heart' (Charest 1997: 64). Relying on terms such as 'intuition' to explain what happens in practice creates a discourse that is inspiring and mystifying in equal measure. We might better consider how Lepage's intuition relies upon other abilities, such as making sense of his collaborators' work. Such a capacity has long been recognised as essential in devised work. As early as 1972, Theodore Shank referred to 'the conceptual ability that is requisite . . . in the making of a work without a script' (Shank 1972: 30). Furthermore, as Deirdre Heddon and Jane Milling argue in their study of devised theatre, we do not have to automatically 'accept the function of this mechanism [intuition] as an inexplicable element' of collaborative practice (Heddon and Milling 2006: 10); they cite Foucault's 'insistence' that every feeling 'has a history', as well as Bourdieu's description of intuition as 'the illusion of immediate understanding', and, in doing so, successfully illustrate the limitations of the term as an explanation of practice (Heddon and Milling 2006: 10).

In fact, in practical terms, intuition does not account for the continuities in Lepage's collaborative work. These are most evident in his montage, which consistently draws the meanings of his works together to converge in a single location, inviting the spectator to read meanings as inter-connected. Multiple meanings are brought together in Lepage's work by condensing significations into a figure or object; the thematic is thus consolidated at a symbolic level, occasionally producing remarkable emotional effects. Over and above intuition, such continuities raise the question of how directing within a devised collaboration might accord Lepage forms of authorship in practice.

Karen Fricker recognises Lepage's distinctive 'directorial signature', and his role as a 'star director' within collaboration, and suggests that Lepage draws on the cultural cachet associated with 'collective authorship' in order to brand and market his work (Fricker 2008). Furthermore, as Christie Carson asks in her analysis of *Tectonic Plates*, how can Lepage's process be intuitive, spontaneous, and 'create a truly collaborative dialogue' when 'Lepage retain[s] the role of director and therefore ultimate creative control' (Carson 1993: 46)? Carson argues that *Tectonic Plates'* 'success in creating an inter-cultural dialogue was limited both structurally and artistically by Lepage', and that these limitations created 'a demeaning and destructive process' (Carson 1993: 50). Lepage's Scottish collaborators were not able to work intuitively or spontaneously because they 'had to accept an imposed vision of Scottishness' (Carson 1993: 49):

> Because the show had already been produced in three different versions before coming to Glasgow, many of the piece's themes, characters and images had already been established. While Lepage reworked the entire show to incorporate the Scottish actors their input into the thematic dialogue was limited by the structure which had already been created. The first restriction the Scots had to deal with was the imposition of a Québecois vision of a Highland goddess... which [they] had no choice but to accept.
>
> (Carson 1993: 48–9)

Lepage's own version of events is also revealing: the Scottish actors began the process, he says, 'by drawing all the politically emphasised images, radioactivity, Greenpeace, and presenting all the troubles of the globe on which you have to have an opinion. But what do you do with it in theatrical terms?' he asks (Dundjerović 2007: 115). For the Scottish actors, Lepage's approach was prescriptive rather than intuitive, authorial rather than free; for Lepage, the work of the Scottish actors was equally limiting. What Carson's analysis allows us to recognise is that, in the Repère Cycles, the selection of the Resource which starts the process imposes conditions which collaboration must subsequently follow.

Lepage, as the director within collaboration, is privileged to determine the selection of the Resource, and thus retains possibly the most significant element of control from the outset, accomplishing a level of authorship through Resources which must be read as both formal and ideological. Before further examining the authorial dynamics which Resources might introduce into process, I here draw upon Graham Pechey's reading of Bakhtin's concept of dialogism, and particularly the notion of 'decisive privileging', in order to illustrate this (Pechey 1989: 41). Resources appear to be non-prescriptive because they are dialogic, but in actuality they must be ordered to function prescriptively, limiting collaboration to a particular dialogic 'field' of discourse and organisation of meaning. This is necessary because Resources will always push against prescription in order to accomplish further intertextuality and 'inner complexity', by connecting to other dialogic fields (Pechey 1989: 41). Every idea is a doorway to another; as Lepage puts it, the Repère Cycles reveal in practice that 'everything is larger than us', and, when working with a continually expanding field, we therefore 'have to let the story tell itself: appear by itself', because it is an 'immense force that has its own life' (McAlpine 1996: 141). Lepage's choice of initial Resource, therefore, is an authorial act of 'decisive privileging'; Resources do not only create an open, creative field for intuitive exploration, they also function as a control mechanism to focus material, and prevent it from spilling over into the chaos of excessive intertextuality (Pechey 1989: 41).

The dialogism of Resources plays a key role in producing the intertextual connectivity that characterises Lepage's work. But this understanding also leads us to recognise a key critical difficulty. The collaborator works as a referent for the Resource, engaging in a renegotiation of subjectivity between the Resource that they are working on and the Resource that they are. For the collaborator is also a Resource within Lepage's process, a condition both agreed to and imposed upon them. The capacity of the Resource to reposition subjectivity may be welcome, but it could equally be alienating. Firstly, engagement with a Resource produces an increasing level of intertextuality between it and the collaborator. This is probably why Lepage feels his process sometimes has a 'life' of its own. The Resource becomes uncanny, animated by the significances accorded to it through the process, and it continuously produces new connections in a seemingly autonomous way. Secondly, when the intertextual connections of the Resource are recognised, they are experienced as discoveries. Because Lepage's emphasis on intuition frames the Resource as open to inscription, rather than already inscribed, these discoveries appear powerfully random (rather than predictable) and gain the authority of an intuitive breakthrough. Thirdly, the Resource can alienate the collaborator by coming to possess an authorship which seems to exceed their own, even though it is the collaborator's subjectivity which is used as an intertext in order to animate the Resource. The 'Resource that we've chosen and the stories that come out of that Resource are more infinite than we are', Lepage says (McAlpine 1996: 141). Like his theatricality, Lepage's process itself is uncanny, because Resources appear as if animated, and, as a result, are accorded an unusual authorship.

The implications of this can be illustrated with reference to productions ranging from *The Seven Streams of the River Ota* (1994) to *Lipsynch* (2007). *Ota* emerged from Lepage's own preoccupation with, and visit to, Hiroshima. Takahagi Hiroshi, programme manager at the Tokyo Globe, describes *Ota's* inception. Lepage directed *The Tempest* in Tokyo in 1994, and Hiroshi put him in touch with a Shakespearean scholar based in Hiroshima. This professor, Hiroshi says,

> had no idea who Lepage was, but he did his best to give this talented young director a good account of Hiroshima's history, as well as of his own experiences of the bomb. Some two weeks later, Lepage went home; we couldn't have imagined at that time that his visit would become the germ of his Hiroshima project, begun in 1994.
>
> (Hiroshi 1995: 39)

The professor had, in Lepage's words, given him 'a fantastic two days of these little stories', including one about a 'woman who had been disfigured' in the bombing reacting to the sight of her own face in a mirror, and another about a plan to give the city back its 'sexual organs' through bridge building (McAlpine 1996: 137, 136). The professor's narratives appeared both as specific elements – the character Nozomi indeed studies her ruined face in a mirror – and as the Eros-Thanatos thematic that haunts the piece. Hiroshi also became one of Lepage's collaborators, somewhat unwittingly, being 'surprised to discover that, at its opening in Edinburgh, Lepage used throughout his production a sound-over of Hiroshima station noises I had recorded for him that summer' (Hiroshi 1995: 39). Obviously these small contributions are the kind of things artists simply pick up along the way. But in *Ota*, Lepage's Resource dominated the through-line, in that Nozomi and her family connections provided its core narrative triad, and the Eros-Thanatos motif provided its thematic force. And this shows not only that the Resource can be an already ideologically informed selection, but also that the Resource can be already mediated, and this complicates claims that non-intellectual Resources have immediacy.

Lipsynch (2007) also began with a Resource introduced by Lepage. The Resource was a rough sketch of an aeroplane interior; a screaming baby sits at the back of the plane, while an adult with a cultured voice sits at the front in club class. Lepage asked his collaborators what happens between the two to connect them (Blankenship 2006). In keeping with Lepage's established 'creative attitude', *Lipsynch's* explorations began with an image. This in itself is hardly significant, as Lepage is both collaborator and director. However, while each of *Lipsynch*'s nine sections was devised from collaborators' individual Resources, the dominant narrative derives from Lepage's picture; indeed, this Resource was translated directly, as if pre-inscribed, into the opening, where Ada, an opera singer, sits at the front of the plane, returning from a performance; Jeremy is the screaming baby at the rear of the plane, unaware that his mother, Lupe, has died. These events contribute the narrative spine of *Lipsynch*, and provide it with three of its sections. Furthermore, this triad of characters is reunited to form the grand metaphor of *Lipsynch*'s ending, where Jeremy is symbolically re-united with Lupe in an inverted image of the opening; it is now the son who holds the mother. The cyclical journey of discovery is completed in a gesture that gives closure to the audience, but which also reduces the dialogic field to one prescribed by Lepage's editing, and originated in his Resource, namely, the parent–child relationship.

By returning to the already established image, Lepage imposes organisation and interpretation upon the work. He does not do this by imposing a specifically authored 'meaning', but it is, nevertheless, a moment of closure, and a movement away from the open dialogism of the Repère Cycles. The selection of Resources provides Lepage with the decisive privileging Pechey describes, and, consequently, with a form of authorship that is not shared with other collaborators. Lepage's discourse on intuition and creative freedom does not sufficiently explain his practice, and he clearly does more to determine the meaning of his work than just facilitating 'the final composition of the piece' (Dundjerović 2007: 33). Lepage may not be a traditional 'director'; nevertheless, the decisive privileging that the selection of Resources, theatrical forms and sequence accords to him needs to be recognised as a form of authorship.

This form of authorship can be characterised by recognising the movement within Lepage's process away from the playful dialogism of Resources, and towards a more monologic and authored condition. In 2007, Yves Jacques replaced Lepage in *The Andersen Project*, as he did when Lepage finished performing in *The Far Side of the Moon*; and, as Fricker notes, this 'unofficially mark[s] the end of the production's creative development, in that Jacques will perform a set script and does not have licence to change the production' (Fricker 2007: 140). To recognise this as a movement from a dialogic to a monologic condition allows us to understand the emergence of Lepage's authorship over the duration of the creative process. Despite the apparently open authorship of the Repère Cycles, the choice of initial Resource sets the dialogic field in a significant way from the outset. An act of authorship is, therefore, present from the beginning, and both the control over, and packaging of, these works as Lepage's ensures it is also present at the end. Lepage's methods produce not only the work itself, but ultimately ensure that he is identified with the work. In this sense, the method produces both work and author, and, to reflect this, we might therefore describe Lepage's application of the Repère Cycles as constituting an authorial process.

This does not mean that Lepage performances are, to use Barthes' terms, 'works which follow the law of solidarity which governs the readerly', where 'everything must hold together as well as possible' (Barthes 1992: 181). Lepage performances are not completely 'readerly', because the interpretive activity they demand in reception does not position the spectator as a 'consumer' but as 'a producer of the text' (Barthes 1992: 4). But the movement from a dialogic to a monologic condition shows that Lepage performances are not completely 'writerly' either. Seán Burke suggests that the writerly and the readerly can be reconciled: 'authorial return', he says, need not 'impinge upon the birth of the reader' (Burke 1998: 30). Rather, the 'univocal conception of the text' and its authoritarian hierarchy, in which 'the authorial voice' dominates 'other textual voices', can be replaced by Bakhtin's idea of the 'carnivalesque author' (Burke 1998: 48). This demonstrates that 'the concept of the author can be renewed' without sacrificing the values of the writerly text (Burke 1998: 49). The issue of authorship here, then, is to do with the control Lepage has over process, and therefore over the authorial voice of his collaborators. Is Lepage a 'dead' author, the writer whose 'only power is to mix writings' (Barthes 1993: 146)? While Lepage undoubtedly combines the writing of his collaborators in a way that gives his method the appearance of carnivalesque authorship, I contend that it is a combination that constructs his own authorship.

It is not my argument that the recurrence of dramaturgical forms or narrative patterns in Lepage performances is evidence of a 'design or plan in [Lepage's] mind'; or that they represent a 'design or intention', which might be 'a standard for judging the success of [his] work' (Wimsatt and Beardsley 1995: 90). But continuities of practice suggest that the '*Lepagean*' in Lepage performances cannot be ignored. Through editing, Lepage becomes the author he already was – a position accorded to him through the selection of Resources – the 'big' author in the process. This power is also in evidence where Lepage introduces his personal obsessions into collective work. Lepage uses *Hamlet* so frequently that Ric Knowles wonders what 'makes Lepage return to it so obsessively?' (Knowles 1998: 200). Marianne Ackerman, Lepage's co-writer on 1992's *Alanienouidet*, describes the effect of Lepage's late-in-the-day introduction of material from *Hamlet* into their creative process. Lepage, she says, came

> upon the idea that *Hamlet's* gravedigger's scene should be performed on or near the climax of the play. This seemed like a great idea, and (but? how?) I felt the entire play would now have to be pointed in that direction. I decided not to panic.
>
> (Ackerman 1992: 34)

But it is not only text which can be introduced as a Resource in this prescriptive way. Ackerman describes the beginning of their process, in which she agreed to 'summarise [her] research notes', which they would then workshop; then, if Lepage 'came up with a set', she would 'start writing the play'; but, she says,

> As it turned out, he had already started, and described a set which would be a life-sized longhouse on stage, with large windows, and a playing space on the roof...he sketched out a rough plan for the longhouse...and continued to refine and discover the possibilities of this concept throughout the building of the play.
>
> (Ackerman 1992: 32)

Although it is far from Ackerman's intention to criticise the process of working with Lepage, it is fairly clear that this collaboration cannot be idealised on the terms of intuition or creative freedom. These Resources pre-inscribe Lepage's creative vision into the process. Furthermore, while introducing a new direction through a Resource might be presented as following one's intuition, it hardly seems like a collaborative act of authorship when it reflects a personal obsession, especially when it reorders the 'entire play'. Lepage does not occupy a position which could be described as that of sole author. And yet, as Jen Harvie says, while it is 'possible to see Lepage as insistent on a democratic dispersal of authorial power in his productions, it is nevertheless also possible to see him as monopolising much of the authority – and certainly much of the credit – for the productions' (Harvie 2002: 229).

When a practice is described as intuitive and collaborative, but actually produces works with a distinctive authorial signature, criticism also needs to consider the ethical questions that arise regarding undeclared uses of subjective material. On the terms of the Repère Cycle, the collaborator is a Resource. As Dundjerović suggests, therefore, Lepage's collaborators must 'work with and accept transformation', as they bring subjective material to the process which is then investigated creatively by the ensemble. Lepage's process 'starts as individual research and solo improvisations but there is no ownership over the material'. Indeed, once this 'very subjective inner work' is 'externalised', it becomes the property of the group. Subjective material, therefore, has to be 'open for collective playing' (Dundjerović 2009: 91–4). As a consequence, Lepage's collaborators must 'allow themselves to explore new ways of seeing their own identity' (Dundjerović 2007: 116). Personal transformation may be what collaborators desire in Lepage's work – it may be exactly its appeal. Indeed, Patrice Pavis remarks that actors 'are marked, almost stigmatized' even by the performance techniques they learn (Pavis 1998: 83). Transformation can be *ordinary*. But it may nevertheless be that performance practices which do not fully declare the nature of their authorial control over subjective materials are unethical, and might mark the performer in ways that risk producing an alienation of self.

Lepage acknowledges that his application of the Repère Cycles can be highly problematic, but he weighs this against its transformational power, saying that 'There are people that this murders, this way of working, but there are also people it awakens . . . . I can't tell when I select people. I can't say: "Oh yes, with him it'll work, with her, it won't" ' (Bureau 2008: 30).[1] Lepage's demands on collaborators are not grounded in an ethical basis: this is a risk-based practice. And this is problematic, I suggest, because where subjectivity is open to alienation or transformation, the terms of such work should be properly declared. Lepage's process may have the effect of 'signing' and producing his collaborators. Thus there is an ethical need for him to declare his authorship within the collaborative process. Without precise acknowledgement, his process risks the appropriation of subjectivity. Thus adaptive, rather than intuitive, collaboration seems a better way of describing his process.

Lepage would almost certainly reject any call to acknowledge such authorship as ideological; after all, he sees his work as self-producing: 'let the story tell itself: appear by itself', he urges (McAlpine 1996: 141). Yet this abdication of authorship, and proposal of the work's production of itself would be, if it were accurate, what Burke calls a 'true Platonic nightmare' – creating an 'anonymous discourse, a discourse genuinely orphaned, irresponsible and without any ethical trackback whatsoever' (Burke 1995: 290). Burke argues that 'The act of signing a text . . . carries with it an intricate substructural set of ethical assumptions', creating a 'channel of enquiry' between text and reader which is activated if or when 'an ethical demand or interrogation is made of the text' (Burke 1995: 289). It is precisely this signature that is lacking in Lepage performances. Yet Lepage is engaged in forms of authorship, and his work is engaged in ideological expression, whether this is acknowledged by him or not. It may be that a greater acknowledgement of authorship would release Lepage's practice from the introversion of its formalism – the 'self-satisfied and self-interested play' which Harvie suggests has led at times to 'a chronic failure of political critique' in his work – by creating engagement with the contexts it operates in (Harvie 2002: 229). Signature, furthermore, would announce the risks of Lepage's process to potential collaborators, and thereby counter the alienation of subjectivity possible in undeclared working conditions. Lepage says that he and his company 'want to be connected with what goes on in the world' (McAlpine 1996: 154). Signature would provide an ethical counterbalance to the formalism of Lepage's theatre. And it may then create the actual connection Lepage wants between his performances and the world that they travel.

NOTE

1. My translation: 'Il y a des gens que ça assassine, cette façon de travailler, mais il y a aussi des gens que ça éveille . . . . Et ça, je peux pas distinguer ça quand je sélectionne les gens. Je peux pas dire: "Ah oui, avec lui, ça va marcher, avec elle, ça marchera pas" '.

James Reynolds lectures in drama at Kingston University.

An Interview with Michael Grandage

Trained at Central School of Speech & Drama, Michael Grandage worked for 12 years as a professional actor before directing his first production in 1995. Between 1999 and 2005 he was Artistic Director of Sheffield Theatres. During this period, in 2002 he also became Artistic Director of the Donmar Warehouse. At the Donmar he expanded the repertoire to include European work, an education programme and touring work. His own productions have toured internationally, including transfers to Broadway. In recent years he has developed his work in opera. He is now Artistic Director of the Michael Grandage Company.

Shepherd: Let's begin at the beginning. What do you think is the most important skill of a director? And what's the most important task that a director does, if it's possible to single that out?

Grandage: Well the first thing to say about any of these questions is that I'm answering from a personal viewpoint and anything I say does not necessarily relate to how directing should be done. One of the interesting things about directing anyway is that there are as many ways to direct a play as there are directors to do it. The only thing that we probably share in common is that we all sign a piece of paper at some point to agree to deliver something on a certain date. How you get there from the beginning of that process to the delivery date is different for everyone. I know that because one of the few interesting things in twelve years as an actor working in different rehearsal rooms and with different directors is that every single one was different. The only thing they all shared in common was that on a particular date they'd open to the public.

My view is that one of the most important things to provide as a director is leadership and a vision of some kind. A team has to be formed and it's you that has to do that. So you draw together a collaborative team of designer, lighting designer, costume and scenic designer (if they're separate), a composer, a choreographer, a fight director, each where appropriate . . . a whole team before the actors are even on board. With them you come up with a vision for the piece you are presenting. Assuming you're working on a piece of text-based theatre, which I do, it's about getting into a room months before a single actor is employed and talking about why I would like to do this piece. In doing that I hope to excite and motivate the team, and particularly the designer in the first instance, to start coming up with something which informs that vision and then goes into a collaborative place that takes it on and develops it in other areas that you weren't expecting. So leading that first off is the important thing.

The next thing is that you hire the actors. Then when the rehearsals begin it's the director's job to lead the company of actors with the vision that you have.

Whatever you started with when you first sat down with your key collaborators may well be different, but hopefully when you start with your actors it will be a complete vision for the way to do a piece. The only thing that's left open after that moment is what the actors bring – which is considerable. They can alter your perspective and take you in different directions, but the actual nature of the physical presentation will follow the parameters already set down, which is the way we work in England – five weeks rehearsal, delivery date fixed.

Another key thing for me – again not for a lot of directors who don't work on written text – is that it's quite important to get up every morning and say 'I am an interpretive artist, not a creative artist.' Of course I believe myself to be an interpretive artist with a huge creative brief, but I am the interpretive artist in the mix while the creative artist is the writer. They are the source material: that's what we are all gathered in a room to interpret. I say it's important because for me, in the past, working with directors who believed themselves to be more important than the writer immediately made for a tricky dynamic. You've got to decide you want to do the play and then interpret it; what you shouldn't do is decide you want to do the play and then completely rethink it. That's not our job. If we want to do that, then go to someone else and commission a new version of something. Once you've decided to take the piece, interpret it.

Shepherd: I've encountered that before around doing classics, where the author's dead and the director's become the guardian of the text.

Grandage: But *Twelfth Night* was a new play once, and it got its first performance in front of a group of people who had never seen it before. Why he wrote what he wrote for the day that it was going to be performed is of crucial importance to a good interpretive artist because getting back into the dead writer's head to try and understand why he wanted to say this in one scene and that in another will open up the play to you. Then you as an interpretive artist will be able to present that clear narrative to an audience which will allow them access to the deep path of the play. If, however, you decide to ignore whatever the writer was trying to do, even if they've been dead for four hundred years, and what you do is entirely something that you've come up with separate from the process of its being written, then something will be missing.

Shepherd: Do you work with living authors and, if so, how does that work best?

Grandage: When I've worked with living authors it is quite often not on new plays. The way we've done it here at the Donmar, the way we've made this a writers' theatre – if we have – is by asking living writers to work on old texts. So we've taken plays from the European repertoire by dead writers and invited living writers to do new versions of them. What's absolutely fascinating to me, and most of these writers have it in common, is that they say there is always a point in the process they'd love to have picked up the phone to the dead writer and asked what's going on in a particular scene. I think in the room we have a similar feeling, whether the writer's alive or dead. If the writer's alive and they're in the room with you, you do turn to them and say 'help us' – and quite often, interestingly, they can't. When the writer's dead and you've got nobody to turn to, that's part of the wonderful unlocking of the play process, which I think is integral to what we do. You've got to try and get back into the writer's head at the point of writing. If you're ever needing to unlock a moment, the best way to do it, for me, is to try and understand. And it doesn't necessarily need to come about by trying to understand the life of the writer.

Shepherd: Because the writer won't often understand that herself.

Grandage: Correct. It's about what the writer was trying to do in that moment when writing that line – and trying to unlock it. Sometimes that is literally like a mathematical equation.

Shepherd: When you said right at the start all this can only be your personal take because no two directors will work alike, no two processes will be the same, presumably there's not much point in trying to train a director, because, if nothing's held in common, what can be taught?

Grandage: It's a good point, but there are basic skills that may be shared even though they don't manifest in the same way. The most obvious is communication skills. All directors should be able to communicate easily with an actor as to what they would like to do, how they would like to do it and what they want to achieve from the process. Maybe training can help people that have rather extraordinary minds but an inability to communicate what's in those minds. It's easy to say that people either have it from birth or not, but actually things like that can be trained up. There are also some basic skills in understanding how a production is physically put together. Directors can be taught the language they need to talk to a designer, they can be taught how a technical period works. None of that's instinctive. In a technical period you go into a theatre for the first time and you need to allow this much for lights and you need to do this with costumes, and this is how the composer works – all those things can be taught. A training for the nuts and bolts of the process, even though the process might be different each time, that can be taught.

Shepherd: Some people say that directors need to have been actors first.

Grandage: Yes. I disagree with that quite profoundly. All the best directors I worked with as an actor had not been actors. The one thing I have that I use frequently, as an ex-actor turned director, is an understanding of the internal fear that actors sometimes have. If you haven't been through it maybe it's difficult to understand. That's about the only thing I've got over a director who hasn't been an actor.

Shepherd: In this current phase of your life, you're known for your work in this particular theatre. How important do you think it is for a director to manage and be associated with a building?

Grandage: I don't think it's important for a director to do it at all, but it's important for me to do it. The role you've just described is the role of a producer, so there's a sort of duality I enjoy because one feeds the other. Being a director of plays is very different from the part of me that is required to run a building, producing work which I don't direct. They're two completely different roles but they support each other emotionally and intellectually. I like the idea of building a body of work under one roof. It's like creating a house style, where audiences are invited to come and interact in one space to get variations on a theme. If you're a freelance director you go out there and you work wherever and people come to see it and quite frequently don't know who's directing it.

Shepherd: You could say that as director you're making individual productions but as producer you are making the house style through a set of productions. That is also a quite creative job of work.

Grandage: It is creative, there's no doubt about that. Producing the body of work which gives a house style into which you put yourself and your individual productions as a director is all connected. It's enjoyable because each decision feeds another decision in a positive way.

Shepherd: You can come across people who say 'It's rubbish being a director because you've got to satisfy them upstairs in the big offices.' That suggests a sense of alienation – where running the building and doing that stuff feels deadly, while the 'artistry' is doing a show.

Grandage: It doesn't need to be though. Last week I was in New York auditioning *Evita*, which is going to be on Broadway as a freelance production. In the room were the two producers for the auditions with views about who was singing well and who badly, and who looked right and who didn't. It was the very first time in fifteen years that as a director I haven't been my own producer in the room making those decisions. It was weirdly liberating, but it was also slightly out-of-body. It brought home to me that for fifteen years I've been both producer and director of my own work.

Shepherd: That ties in with something that you've talked about in terms of the formation of the basic core of the company. What do you look for when you're assembling the team? Do you have particular guidelines for assembling the company?

Grandage: Yes, but before I answer that it's worth saying that it's the bit that nobody tells you about when you say you want to be a director. I think people imagine that it's about just putting on plays, developing a vision and creating work. The bit that nobody ever really talks about, and for me is the single most exciting part of being a director, is the huge and quite profound collaboration that happens between a very small group of people in terms of creating an aesthetic together. I use about four or five designers, only about two lighting designers and two composers – and that's over fifteen years. You start to develop a language with these individuals that comes out of a deep understanding with each other. If each time you start a fresh relationship, you're spending quite a lot of time just getting to know each other. If you start a project with people who all know each other's tastes, the new bit is the play. And then you pool all your collective knowledge in the interpretation. That is a thrilling part of the process because it's about a life journey. It's like a friendship, something you develop all your life, and it gets richer as you get older. And in our case in the theatre it's about growing old together. You then get to a point when you think some seam of it has been exhausted and the friendship can continue but you need new blood in your veins. That's when I turn to somebody much younger and start the relationship all over again. So, for instance, for my final production at the Donmar, I've decided to work with a designer I've never worked with before. I see that as a new point for me, this final production, but I've done it at many key moments in my career so far. It's quite good to keep yourself on the edge of your comfort zone and start new relationships that might develop into the future with you.

Shepherd: The director produces and manages and works with and grows old with a group of people who do aesthetic work which is bigger than each individual production – so the director is actually creating at different levels things which are much bigger than particular productions?

Grandage: That's right. And you've just used an interesting word that I think sometimes we should talk about. 'Manages' you said: words like 'managing' are ones that directors are not always happy to talk about. They're so obsessed with creating the poetic – which I think is a given – that they actually forget to talk about the practical, and it's the practical which will ultimately deliver. The poetic is something you can't teach on one of those courses. When you ask 'what's the point of training?', it's the practical, it's the managing of people, it's the bring-ing together of groups, it's the need to inspire and the leadership qualities that you can actually develop and learn. And it's the bit that never gets talked about, because it's regarded as somehow bringing a job that a lot of people want to believe is 'up there', beyond most people, down to a basic level. But it's a com-bination of the two that makes a good director. Most interviews are all about the emotional, intellectual and poetic journey of the artist and very rarely about the nuts and bolts because somehow talking about it makes them feel that they're ordinary. But directing a play is ordinary on one level. You've just got to trust yourself, let it develop with the artists you work with, keep your instinct sharp, and all of those things – but make sure that this bit, this bit at the bottom, this grounded bit is also working at full stretch.

Shepherd: I have become very interested in the organisational role of directors.

Grandage: You will be very hard pushed to find a director talk literally about how their rehearsal room is organised. It becomes some weird secret pact where we can't talk about the so-called alchemy that happens in the room. Mine is very straight-forward. I ask all my actors to learn their lines before the first day of rehearsal. On the first day of rehearsal, I don't do a read-through. I talk a little bit about the vision for the piece and show them a set and then we get up within one hour of coming through the door and start rehearsing the play. And we usually go through the whole of the play in the first week and in the second week we're already standing in the room without a book in our hand discussing every single part of what that scene needs. The next two or three weeks are the dissecting of the piece. Quite a lot of time that happens round a table, and often in the context of a read-through. But a read-through for me is not a level playing-field. I've seen people completely destroyed by read-throughs, because some actors show off what they've been doing for the last six weeks while other actors don't quite know who they are at the read-through, so they watch the flamboyant, brilliant actor at the other end of table...and in one case nearly had a nervous breakdown because they can't compete. You don't need to do that. Better to create a level playing-field: have them all start together in the room and let the discussion come out of that. The discussion that we have in week one is more about creating some kind of spatial awareness as to how the piece can play out. The great joy is that it all starts from a place of standing up, without a script. What we will be doing in week two is the Stanislavskian approach – who are you, where are you, why are you there, where are you going, what is your motivation? There is a development of skills during the process. That has been a technique I've adopted for most of the productions I've done – but I've hardly ever heard any other director talk about their technique in the rehearsal room.

Shepherd: You talk about directors and closed doors and the magical arcane mys-teries of the rehearsal room...let me ask where you place yourself physically in the room and does it change through the process?

Grandage: I am in a chair without a table but with a music stand in front of me with a script on it. That's where I am for about three weeks, and then in weeks four and five I sit all around. I get up from the chair, direct and then stand around the room to watch it happen. When we run a scene I sit back down in a seat with just the music stand in front of me.

Shepherd: Is that a deliberate choice?

Grandage: Yes, because it says: 'I am here and you, the actors, are over there. And I want nothing to be between us.' The other thing that never gets said enough is that we're a recent invention, the director. The producer is far older, you know. It was the producer and the actor that made theatre happen at the beginning and directors didn't exist. In that respect we've invented our role and we've invented our place in the room.

Shepherd: Carrying on from what we were just saying about organisation, would it ever be possible to say that the way the process is organised itself has bearing on the aesthetic effect, so that the way in which the director organises the production shows in its aesthetic qualities?

Grandage: The one thing that is in the finished product is the director's sense of spatial awareness, and the spatial awareness is the aesthetic for me. That is what creates the piece, and constructing a picture can only be done by organising it in some way. One director I've worked with, Peter Gill, has a belief that the less articulate you are, the more you'll get. (And how do you teach *that* on a course?) There was a famous incident of him saying to an actor: 'you know that bit where you do – you know – you know . . .', and the actor said 'yes', and he said: 'well, I think you should do a little bit more – you know', and the actor went 'OK, let me try.' And out of that little conversation came what the director wanted and what the actor needed. Something was unlocked. His point is that: 'If I'd been more articulate I'd have buggered the actor up, but by being inarticulate I got the actor to understand he or she needed to do a bit more *uh* and the *uh* happened with the actor taking the authority to do it.' Now that is organising. It doesn't sound very articulate organising, but somewhere in that brief and inarticulate dialogue, the director organised the actor to be released and the picture to be created. So the aesthetic was born out of organisation in that scenario.

Shepherd: You were an actor but you've been a director for many more years than you've been an actor. Sometimes when I'm reading directors' accounts of their work it seems that somehow the director is still imagining him or herself in the piece as well, is somehow physically modelling the thing on how they would do it themselves. Do you think there is always that sort of urge somewhere deep inside a director that wants physically to represent themselves on stage?

Grandage: There isn't in me. One of the reasons I gave up acting was because I couldn't do it anymore, so I don't want to go back there. But in mentioning those sorts of directors you've picked up on something we should touch on, which again is something that's unspoken. You can't be a director if you're not a control freak – let's just say it. Why would you choose this profession if you're not interested in control? Somehow you've got to understand that wanting to control a scenario needs to be an expressive, joyous, creative, positive thing – because in our society 'control freak' comes with a whole load of negatives attached to it. I think wanting to help control a piece, wanting to help control the look of a piece and wanting to help control the outcome of a piece for an audience are integral parts of what a director needs to be able to do. It is unfortunate that, in talking about control, people immediately assume personality traits and things which dictators do. But there's control and there's control. Actors want to know that there is a controlled environment that can be free but that somebody is in charge of the environment and decisions can be made, an umpire. Equally actors and collaborators need to know that somebody somewhere is leading the process on a purely practical level within a building. The buck needs to stop somewhere.

One of the reasons a director might get paid more than his other collaborators is because he has to take the overall responsibility for it, the buck stops with him. And in the critical analysis of the piece, whether it's the audience watching it or a newspaper critic, it is the director who, particularly in a revival, is taken to task for the vision, positively or negatively. So you can't start having your cake and eating it and arguing 'we're all just one big co-op and we're all in it together' because actually that isn't the way it works.

Shepherd: Mnouchkine describes herself as a sort of midwife and mother.

Grandage: Well, we are. We're therapists, we're mothers, fathers, all of those things. And it works two ways because of what I get from the process. In the hands of a wonderful actor they can unlock something without the aid of the director coming within a hundred feet. But, when they do it, the director in the room gets the great privilege of watching somebody touch something deep in themselves that in turn can help a director as a human being understand more about themselves. I've always used my work as therapy because what can happen in a rehearsal room can go so, so deep and unlock so many things that help me understand who I am, so that I feel very privileged not to have to fork out a lot of money to somebody I don't know to help me do that.

Shepherd: When the rehearsal process comes to an end, and the show opens, where are you?

Grandage: That's an interesting one. I can experience a loss of the control I talked about earlier and feel slightly surplus to requirements once the show is on. But at the same time I realise there is something needed of me by the actors to know that they are still on track or developing into a better place. I lose interest a little bit, once the process has been completed in terms of presentation. The show continues to develop, and how we get there is exciting. But by definition you have to give the control over to them.

Part

V Directors as Organisers

Chapter

10 The Art of Organisation

The role of the director is customarily described with a whole cluster of nouns. Stanislavski is typical: 'The role of the producer ... comprises an aesthete, a poet, a psychologist, a teacher and theorist, a critic, an administrator, a man with creative initiative, and so on' (in Magarshack 1950: 284). Quite a long way down the list is the word 'administrator'. There is usually a word of this sort, but it fades in and out of prominence depending on the speaker. It has always been there though: in 1922 MacGowan notes 'The director must be an executive, and this implies a cold ability to dominate other human beings, which the artist does not ordinarily have' (MacGowan and Jones 1964: 128). For MacGowan, writing at the height of Modernism, the entry of this new executive figure into the world of art had about it a glamour and heroism. This was literally enacted when Reinhardt took his place on a podium high above the ground at Olympia in 1911 in order to oversee and organise the hundreds of performers and technicians below. In a sense the new movement in theatre could be said to break with the past precisely because it was a creative activity now shaped by explicit organisational drive. Brecht tells how, among other experiments, they 'organized small collectives of specialists in various fields to "make" the plays' (Brecht 1964: 78). Modernist direction was both new and valuable because it was art as management.

In the decades after Modernism the role of director as heroic manager lost its cultural currency; the concept began to fade from view. But it remained the case that, with or without glamour, the person who did the directing was also the person who, in all sorts of mundane ways, organised the show. And among directors, it seems, that work of organisation is regarded as a very substantial part of the creative activity: 'Peter Brook and Peter Stein are very fine directors,' says Max Stafford-Clark, 'but what I envy is not their talent but their ability to organize lengthy rehearsal periods' (Stafford-Clark 2004: xiii). The organisation that directors do might appear to be something separable from the fine art that they make. This chapter, however, takes the relationship between organisation and art as its subject, to argue that this relationship may well be a defining feature of what directors create.

THE GUARDIANS OF PURPOSE

In their ability to organise lengthy rehearsal periods Brook and Stein display their high status as directors. Lengthy rehearsal periods are very expensive. Somewhat lesser directors might find themselves taken up with accommodation and schedules. In a company which apparently is totally collective, with no director role, the director is the person who organises the process that makes the show happen. When Freehold Theatre Company tried to work without a director in the early 1970s, in rehearsals, as Nancy Meckler puts it, 'what it really amounted to was that one person had an idea and was able to impose it. You couldn't say in the end that it hadn't been directed' (in Schneider and Cody 2002: 229).

Where there is a clear role of director, that person must be prepared to undertake tasks which are often more managerial than simply administrative. Katie Mitchell advises that there is an HR role for directors: 'Be even-handed and make sure you note all the actors involved in the scene or called to the note session' (Mitchell 2009: 129). And it falls to the director to ensure that the collection of individuals becomes a group: 'I always look for some kind of a physical theatre language that links everybody so that they are, in some way, in the same world' (Lecompte in Shevtsova and Innes 2009: 104). For Lepage, who has often engaged in large-scale collaborations, the director is the primary budget manager: of his work with Peter Gabriel he remarks: 'It's a dialogue, which begins with Peter's unrealistic visions, because Peter comes out, forgets the cost, the practicality of the thing' (in Shevtsova and Innes 2009: 139). But it's not quantities of money as such that directors tend to talk much about. It is, instead, time, as evidenced in rehearsal periods that are as long as they think they need. This aspiration to have adequate time at one's disposal is a symptom of a job that spends much of its creative and emotional energy wrestling with basic resources.

But that is a rather reactive way of putting it, implying that directors have to be organisers because of the conditions in which they find themselves. While that is indeed true, it is also the case that, as the role of the director emerges historically, it comes with organisational activity as a primary component, even an ideal. As we learnt in the case of Goethe (see Chapter 1), he was a civil servant amongst whose lighter duties was the organisation of entertainments for the court. When directors began to appear in different settings, at the turn of the twentieth century, their mission was often articulated as a plan to change the organisation of the contemporary theatre. Antoine wanted to abolish the star system; numerous directors acquired their own theatres to put themselves outside the commercial framework controlled by actor-managers. Reinhardt adopted the repertory system for the Kammerspiele and Deutsches Theater, which influenced Granville Barker, who visited in 1910. Granville Barker had already, however, modelled an application of the repertory system, based on Annie Horniman's company at the Abbey, Dublin, in the proposal which he and

William Archer published in 1904 for establishing a National Theatre in England. Perhaps, then, the most significant aim and impact of the newly emerged role of director were that it assumed to itself the duty of organising theatrical activity. Although this duty expressed itself in heroic fashion in the Modernist directors' challenge to the way that theatre was organised, it remained a consistent feature of directors' attitude to their art and role that they should be naturally, as it were, the ones who organise.

That organisational mission applies itself to a range of activities. Directors, from the beginning, have done some or all of the following: they run a process that makes a show, or a series of shows; they create the structure and mode of working of a theatre company; they buy and/or run a theatre building; they establish themselves as a corporate enterprise, sometimes of global reach; and, we ought not forget, they engineer their own artistic profile and manage its impression.

This list can be broken down further. When directors create the structure and mode of operation of a theatre company they are in effect organising the relationships within that company. For example, one effect of the repertory system is that it can ensure that nobody is a star. Those who take lead roles in one production take lesser roles in the next. This is partly what made repertory attractive to those who were opposed to the star system of commercial theatre. Even without a repertory system, however, a director can establish a company that feels itself to be largely unhierarchical. Stanislavski insisted on the actors all going through the same shared process; Brecht apparently encouraged critique from everyone including technical crew. The methods of creating the art can themselves establish or embed the organisation.

A different way of approaching it is to invent the organisational principles and then discover what art emerges. From the 1970s onwards there was considerable experiment with models of companies run as collectives or cooperatives. We shall look at this in more detail in the next section but for now it should be noted that a considerable part of the energy of such companies is spent on the active maintenance of the mechanisms and operation of collectivism. The British Marxist company Red Ladder 'had weekly meetings, a whole afternoon to discuss the group, to ensure that everybody had an equal role, that all work was rotated, including the Chairman of the Day' (Itzin 1980: 47). Now that rotation of duties is not necessarily very far removed from the effect of a shared system of regular training. Each gives to the company members a sense of purposeful work. What then becomes interesting is the role of the director in relation to that purpose.

Where directors train actors for their own artistic ends they as it were mould their raw material. The director's role is qualitatively different from that of the actors: the director is the one designing the exercises, not taking part in them. The distinction must have been clearly marked for Stanislavski's company at those moments when he took a group of performers to work with them in his home (see Houghton 1938: 79). They are watched by him in his space as they attempt to produce the effects which he requires. In these sorts of circumstances the director controls not only how the company interrelates but also how the performers define themselves and their job: 'Since there is no existing discipline to use, an acting company must invent its use. The discipline comes about through creating exercises which bring up a common ground to those who study together.' This is the founder of the cooperative company The Open Theater, Joseph Chaikin (1935–2003), reflecting on the social effects of the 'discipline' of training, and he goes on to suggest how that discipline produces a sense of personal identity: 'where we are fully focused, the process of work suggests itself through the involvement, and the actors become "theater workers"' (Chaikin 1972: 15, 28).

As the source of that discipline, the director comes to be not simply the guardian of the values and purpose of the company, but also a personal embodiment of it. According to Kazan, Strasberg's temperamental behaviour had specific function and effect: 'Lee ... had a gift for anger and a taste for the power it brought him ... His explosions of temper maintained the discipline of this camp of high-strung people. I came to believe that without their fear of this man, the Group would fly apart' (in Cohen 2011: 58). It is not here simply the discipline invented by the director but the very nature of the director, the personality, which becomes the guarantee of the whole structure.

And in this respect the director begins to resemble the chief executive officer of a company. For much of its history to date, as we have seen (pp. 31–5), there has been uncertainty as to what is the craft or art which pertains specifically to directing. Similarly there is not really any training, or indeed craft, that pertains to a CEO. What we can now suggest, however, given the narrative so far, is that a primary function, and even maybe the craft, of the director has to do with organisation of others. Thus when Goethe wrote his Rules for Actors in 1803 he was also describing the directed theatre's potential as a disciplinary machine. For his Rules do not simply specify behaviour on stage but also behaviour off it: 'it is an important actor's rule to strive to adjust his body, his behaviour, indeed his whole external appearance in everyday life just as if he were involved in a continuous exercise' (in Carlson 1978: 317). When it instructs as to actors' private lives, the theatre is not just making art. As we noted above, Chaikin saw the job of an acting company as inventing discipline. What a director may be said to create therefore is, in short, the organisation of people. And what gives purpose to the director is that the director is the guardian, if not the actual embodiment, of purpose.

WHAT THE STRUCTURE SAYS

Ruminating on his role, Robert Lepage reminds us that 'The thing is, you don't just invent gadgets. You invent ways of working. It becomes the philosophy of what you do' (in Shevtsova and Innes 2009: 140). While for many audiences the gadgets might be the most noticeable thing, for the director it is in the way of working that the philosophy lies. And, although the philosophy is mainly noticed in ways of working with actors, it is present too in something rather larger, in the way that the company works, in its structure and organisation. We have seen in other chapters something of the nature of the work undertaken by the company. This section will look at the work done by the structure and organisation of the company, at the way these express the philosophy, and to whom they express it.

To illustrate how the philosophy is expressed by the structure we can turn to those theatre groups that formed explicitly to make political theatre in the years after 1968. We noted one such above, the Marxist group Red Ladder. Similarly there was the socialist group 7:84: its principal director John McGrath used to argue that their first impact on the audience was the moment they arrived in the community and began to unload the van, working together as a company. But a much more deliberate example of expressive structure, or lack of it, was the feminist company Common Ground.

In the mid-1980s the United States military base at Greenham Common, near Newbury in Berkshire, was the focus of sustained political opposition by women peace activists. Among the many and varied means by which they pursued their struggle was theatre. Seven activists formed themselves into a company, Common Ground, for the purpose of doing one play, which had two performances in 1984. In a context within which the enemy was, in part, militarism itself, with its discipline based on obedience and hierarchy, the women of Common Ground structured their company in such a way that it did not reflect the dominant models of theatre production. It not only sought to be non-hierarchical but also it built reflectiveness, the capacity for philosophising as it were, into the roles. These included: 'OUTSIDE EYE (the director)', 'THE SEEKER OF TRUTH (the challenger)', 'REALITY CHECKPOINT (to keep communication with audience in view)'. In a sense, all the roles are aspects of the directing role: they list, separately, director, motivator, focus keeper, facilitator, morale booster, and being concerned with effect on audience (Common Ground 1985: 128).

In renaming the organisational roles, and perhaps especially in having a group version of the individual role of director, Common Ground was speaking both to itself as a company and to the outside world. It said that this was feminist theatre that stood apart from largely male-dominated hierarchies. Quite apart from the show it made, the manner of organisation could be said to be one of the messages communicated by the company.

A rather more complex example of a similar sort, albeit with the director in place, and a male one to boot, is that of the Schaubüne am Halleschen Ufer in Berlin when Peter Stein was invited to take over in 1970. It was a subsidised theatre with a full staff of technicians, administrators and actors. Stein's plan arranged them into a structure that allowed for democratic representation, with a monthly general meeting which could block 'management' proposals. Wages were set at levels to inhibit the development of a star system. Regular seminars were held on the theories of Marx and Lenin. The theatre opened with Brecht's play of revolution, *The Mother*, but the organisation around it, as a whole entity, spoke of socialist politics. The two were interlocked: as Stein said, 'I cannot separate my work from the institution ... I find it necessary to consider how the organization of this institution can be changed' (in Patterson 2010: 40). The 'work' is, in a sense, the organisation. And the organisation, in the case of Stein, or indeed Common Ground, was a major part of what the theatre communicated.

But it seems that the organisation, come what may, always says something, irrespective of whether the company members aim so to do. Ariane Mnouchkine discovered this to her surprise. She tells a story of going to seek funding from the Ministry for Cultural Affairs. She eventually gets the money but the Ministry indicates it feels that Soleil are 'intransigent': 'Then suddenly I understood. I can stage a production that seems totally opposed to them, they couldn't care less. But the way in which the company functions and produces its shows, the simple fact that we don't fit ourselves into a pre-existing framework – this throws them and worries them' (in Williams 1999: 22). The organisation, as much as an individual show, is a vehicle for communicating the philosophy. This is how the Japanese director Tadashi Suzuki (born 1939) sees it: 'the most important work of a theatre troupe does not involve any simple spreading about of its message, whatever that may be. The group must instead take charge of expressing a felt responsibility for finding a means to pass along the unique experiences that the group has undergone' (Suzuki 1986: 60).

Suzuki's comment nudges us into a different place. We have so far looked at what the organisation of the company says about it to those outside of it. Suzuki invites us to turn towards those inside, who have to regard their experiences in the company as something to be disseminated. This point of view assumes not only that the company organisation has its effect on its members, but that this is inherently valuable. But before we follow through this impact of organisation on those who are part of it we need to see where, in Suzuki's opinion, the director in particular fits in.

'In many ways,' he says, 'the life of a theatre director actually does resemble the life of someone like the mayor of Toga-mura.' This analogy aims to make clear not only that directors are responsible for the management and survival of their group but also that they are themselves shaped by the process:

> the problem the director faces is how to bring about the necessary development of his troupe and, just as important, how to maintain the means to do so ... He must bring about the communal work with the actors that allows them to change and develop, while growing himself as an individual. The work of the director requires that he build, on the basis of those changes ... a larger, future vision. Not only does the object of his concerns change over time; the director himself alters as well.

In the case of Suzuki the inventing of the gadgets, the making of the art, has limits put upon it by these primary duties:

> Even though I am an artistic director, I am responsible in addition for the economic welfare of my troupe, I cannot simply decide what to do based on some personal emotional enthusiasm. I must observe changes in our audiences, even in society itself, and my plans must be based on what I perceive. There is no possibility of my simply amusing myself with my work in some narcissistic fashion.

It is for these reasons that Suzuki says that, unlike other creative artists, 'The work of a stage director has no independent life' (Suzuki 1986: 108).

In Suzuki's model, the role of the director, although it has no independent life, is still clearly defined. He sets himself against those groups whose unity 'is based not on economics but on the purity of a common response to a set of theories', which he calls 'communal absolutism' (Suzuki 1986: 58, 59). His analogy is with the Japanese Red Army. But he could also perhaps have pointed to those theatre groups formed in the wake of the revolutionary moment of 1968. We have already noted Red Ladder's rotation of duties and arrangements for Chairman for the Day. Similarly in the running of Ariane Mnouchkine's Théâtre du Soleil, as one of its actors, Jean-Claude Penchenat, describes, 'The company is constituted as a workers' cooperative, directed by an elected committee. Members of the cooperative have more duties than rights' (Williams 1999: 31).

A structure that makes its constituents understand that they have duties in relation to rights is one which not only establishes the mode of relationships within the group but also creates a sense of personal identity for each individual. It does this by means of the controlling set of ideas and values of the group, its belief-system or, perhaps, ideology. It could be said then that the 'philosophy' is a way not only of organising the company but of shaping its members. And it often does so not by disseminating anything as explicit as philosophy but by more implicit, organic, means. So, while Suzuki repudiates the 'communal absolutism' of the political groups, his admiration for classical Japanese theatre leads him into similar territory: 'the fundamental structure of a traditional arts ensemble is not based on individuals; rather, its assets accrue from the wisdom passed on by the group, the vision created from the communal experience of a whole family of actors'. And, while this 'family' is no longer based on ties of blood but on 'the economic necessities of performance' (Suzuki 1986: 53), it's clear that the belief-system, the 'vision', is still being disseminated organically, in 'communal experience'. Thus here as elsewhere the company member comes to inhabit a subject position that is shaped by the belief-system, through the process of being, for example, addressed continually as an equal member of a collective or family.

Or as a member of genteel society: when David Belasco's actors first arrived at the theatre – *his* theatre –

> I always make it a practice to be on hand to receive them ... I introduce them to one another and treat them as guests in my drawing-room, rather than as employees on my stage. After a few moments spent in general conversation I then invite them to accompany me to the reading-room, where they find a long, well-lighted table surrounded by comfortable chairs.
>
> When we are all seated – I at the head of the table with the scene models beside me – I invariably give a few preliminary instructions. First of all I caution the members of the company not to discuss the play outside my theatre.

He talks to them of the 'spirit of co-operation' as the key to their success, and then he reads the play to them, without interruption. Lunch is then served. After lunch the actors read their own parts, pausing as necessary for discussion. Belasco notes the 'stage fright' exhibited by actors reading in a situation where he is the only audience (Belasco 1919: 65–6).

Note the elements of the process: the actors are treated as guests to whom lunch is served; Belasco at the head of the table instructs, beginning with a caution as to secrecy; they are told about co-operation; they show fear. It is clear where the power lies but that power does some of its work through management of discourses and behaviour. Treated as guests the actors know they are both special and yet vulnerable employees. Whether it is in the circumstances of being regarded as a member of a collective or a guest at a lunch party, the mode of address is doing crucial managerial work in communicating ideological positioning.

The term given to this mechanism is 'interpellation'. This is a term developed by the post-structuralist Marxist Louis Althusser to explain the operation on us of ideology. He argues that we 'constantly practice the rituals of ideological recognition' – you shake hands, you are called by your name, somebody recognises that you have a name: these rituals 'guarantee for us that we are indeed concrete, individual, distinguishable and (naturally) irreplaceable subjects'. Thus we can say

> Ideology 'acts' or 'functions' in such a way that it 'recruits' subjects among the individuals (it recruits them all), or 'transforms' the individuals into subjects (it transforms them all) by that very precise operation which I have called *interpellation* or hailing, and which can be imagined along the lines of the most commonplace everyday police (or other) hailing: 'Hey, you there!'
>
> (Althusser 1971: 172–4)

We could liken this to the operation of classical Japanese theatre as Suzuki sees it:

> as an actor grows older, his personal experience, gained in the context of a set of restrictions, comes into play. The actor undergoes various experiences so that

eventually he achieves a kind of communal self-consciousness (another term, if you like, for artistic freedom).

(Suzuki 1986: 51)

So 'freedom' amounts to a sense of self, of being a subject, which is 'communal', where the communal is in effect the absorption of a set of 'restrictions'. This is a fairly classic exemplification of what Althusser understands as the illusion of ideology.

But let's now follow Althusser's argument one step further. He takes as illustration Christian religious ideology, in which he observes that the establishment of 'Christian religious subjects is dominated by a strange phenomenon: the fact that there can only be such a multitude of possible religious subjects on the absolute condition that there is a Unique, Absolute, *Other Subject*, i.e. God'. This leads him to add to his model of interpellation: 'the interpellation of individuals as subjects presupposes the "existence" of a Unique and central Other Subject, in whose Name the religious ideology interpellates all individuals as subjects' (Althusser 1971: 178–9). The Absolute Subject is only God in the case of religious ideology. It might be that policeman. Or indeed it might be a visionary leader of a theatre company.

If we are using the model of interpellation to try and account for the effect on a company of the visionary director who is guardian of its purpose, we might see this as more than coming to inhabit a belief system, in that the belief system seems to reside in, to be embodied by, a particular person. That person may well make no pronouncements about organisation as such but they nevertheless operate as, through their own person, the organisational principle which structures the work, and perhaps above all the thinking, of company members – or as Komisarjevsky put it, a successful director 'forms an interpretative unity of the individualities of all the performers' only when such a director is 'a spiritual leader, a kind of magician, psychologist and technical master' (Komisarjevsky 1935: 18–19). Let's take two possible instances of such interpellation.

Eugenio Barba insists on the difference 'between a theatre company and a group. In established theatre companies the director is at the top of the hierarchy. In a group, there is no hierarchy; there is competence – what each individual member knows.' His actors, he says, stay with him not because they have signed a contract but because 'they feel that I'm still able to give them something'. How he does this is to remain 'alive' as a director and 'make my group react to the manifestations of this "life"'. He then defines what 'life' is: it 'consists in being unpredictable, astonishing, challenging, heading towards a bizarre or even dull aim, changing the demands, assigning new and unprecedented tasks'. In his book on directing he explains how he deliberately creates obstacles for the actors. He concedes it is an 'agonising process' for everybody. The cast will work to develop up to 90 minutes of material and 'I might select only five minutes of it. Perhaps I'll take a few minutes of what they had been preparing for one year, even two years.' He remarks that it's a 'privilege' to have actors who 'accept these sorts of demands', but adds: 'You have to educate them to think and act like this' (in Shevtsova and Innes 2009: 12–13). Or as he put it later: 'there are actors who love their director and are ready to sacrifice themselves for this person who stimulates and represses them. But I don't believe that love, in theatre, is spontaneous. It grows little by little, as in arranged marriages' (Barba 2010: 152).

So although the group does not, by definition here, have hierarchy, it would seem to be hierarchy by other means, where the director is able to get away with being extremely demanding and selective in relation to other people's work because of his invented personality, his having 'life'. That 'life' doesn't, however, operate on its own: the actors are educated to accept its consequences. So the director's personality becomes an organisational tool for delivering hierarchical labour that is not called hierarchy. 'As the director, I was not only *the first spectator* for the actor: a competent external look, a nervous system and a memory which reacted. I also represented a principle of justice. The true tragedy, for an actor, is not being able to find in his director an individual to whom he can offer his total trust' (Barba 2010: 205). The actor offers, and the director judges – his look, literally, oversees.

As artistic director of the Maly Drama Theatre Lev Dodin has a policy of incorporating into the company students he has trained at the St Petersburg Academy of Theatre Arts, having the younger actors work alongside the more experienced ones. The language in which Dodin describes it explicitly evokes the family:

> To a certain degree, yes, I suppose I have to be a father figure. There is perhaps some close feeling at any rate, I love them because, to a certain extent, they are my creations, and also I am their creation. When something happens I am really upset and sad, and I get nervous and the actors know this. When I have to scold someone – and it happens – when I sometimes have to use very harsh language, the next day we may kiss and embrace and be quite tender to each other, because I think that with very, very few exceptions they understand that I do it because I want things to get better.
>
> (in Delgado and Heritage 1996: 73)

Where the company is seen as a family it is suggesting about itself that it puts high value on personal relations that are close, not because they share political mission, but because they are bonds of blood. The closeness thus appears to be not so much worked for as natural. What the organisation communicates is that the company is a heightened instance of a thoroughly productive family, where relations based in nature provide a context for the individual artworks. It is perhaps an impossibly utopian model. The organisation thus could be said to be as much of a production, as heavy with message, as any individual show. 'In the theatre, today and tomorrow influence the past. This is a law of theatre-making in that the most important work is not the creation of individual productions, but of theatre as such' (in Shevtsova and Innes 2009: 49).

The shows might then be said to be mechanisms for staging not just 'theatre as such' – whatever that is – but also that more tangible larger production, the company organisation. And as such a key part of what is staged might in some sense be the director.

THE DESIRE TO DIRECT

We have seen, in a fairly abstract way, that the director functions as part of that which organisation communicates, is part of the mechanism of interpellation. We have also seen, in the case of Authors (Chapter 8), that the role of the director can itself become a performance, as it were a self-authorisation. But we should not forget that the director is in the most straightforward way a person, a physical entity that makes a noise and takes up space, and who, in doing these things, has an impact on the other people in the room and possibly on the show that emerges from it. How does the director's body, the physical presence of the director, inhabit the process? Where, we should ask, is the director in the work?

In the chapter on Methods (Chapter 3) we noted some examples of where directors place themselves in the rehearsal room. Let us return to these sorts of examples, but this time considering them in a new frame. That frame comes from the assumption which governs exercises and games for actors, namely that actors' bodies, and the relationships between actors, can be altered, freed up, creatively released as a result of physical interactions. These are mainly thought of as interactions between actors, but Mitchell and Bogart both suggest that the director can be a part of these interactions. So it follows that where directors place themselves and how they conduct themselves physically may well have an effect on the bodies, and thus perhaps too the subjectivities, of the actors – and indeed the rest of the company. Mitchell notes explicitly that directors' 'sitting positions and physical activities affect how the actors work' (Mitchell 2009: 131).

Anne Bogart is refreshingly frank about the fears and uncertainties faced by directors, and she tells a story about what she does when she is stuck in rehearsal:

> Right there, in that moment, in that rehearsal, I have to say, 'I know!' and start walking towards the stage. During the crisis of the walk, something *must* happen; some insight, some idea. The sensation of this walk to the stage, to the actors, feels like falling into a treacherous abyss. The walk creates a crisis in which innovation must happen, invention must transpire. I create the crisis in rehearsal to get out of my own way.
>
> (Bogart 2003: 86)

This presumably has a different effect than when the director who was also the theatre owner met difficulty. We hear of David Belasco that 'sometimes when he met difficulty he would suddenly stop the rehearsal and walk up and down the stage for as long as half an hour in absolute silence ... He had really no idea of time' (in Marker 1975: 107). Belasco's actors were very much his employees and knew it, and presumably while he had no idea of time those others waiting in silence did. His crisis walk could be seen to perform the power differential between them.

But Bogart's walk isn't in all respects different. She has the power to create the crisis which she needs, and in taking action she moves towards the actors' space, the stage. Belasco, we note, walked up and down on the stage. The ownership or otherwise of particular spaces in the rehearsal or indeed the theatre is used, consciously or not, by directors. For example, we hear of Antoine at the Odéon: while watching a rehearsal from a darkened auditorium, he 'would suddenly appear on the stage, his voice "sharp, mordant, authoritative: the voice of a master", to demonstrate his idea or to replay a sequence' (Chothia 1991: 118). The director suddenly penetrates the actors' space. Less suddenly, but perhaps as invasively, Joan Littlewood left notes for the actors in their dressing room after a show. Clive Barker reports feeling trapped by the negativity of these notes, and their inevitability.

Houghton, observing work at the Moscow Art Theatre, notes a moment at which the rehearsal process changes gear. This is done through management of spaces, and, consequently, atmosphere: 'with the final stage in the rehearsal period, the producer leaves the stage, drops his whisper, goes out into the house, and becomes at the same time audience and full-voiced master. He must now give the performance unity and form' (Houghton 1938: 94). The physical conduct of the director operates as a signal. Only the director has the power to move through spaces and change conduct in this way. Often the change is orderly in that it coincides with, or produces, a phase in the process. But at the same time it may be disorderly. Antoine appeared in a way designed to surprise. Other directors adopt a manner which is hard to read, as Selbourne reports of Brook. As the source of order, a director who sends inscrutable signals – or is liable to surprises – can have an unsettling effect.

The issue here is not simply about the readability of the director's actions. It is also about interpersonal transactions, the effect of the physical presence of the director in relation to everyone else in the room. That physical presence is underlined by the regular piece of furniture, a director's table. It is not any old table, not the table in the pub next door around which you might have discussions. Historically the director's table literally belonged to the director:

Rehearsals normally began in Goethe's own accommodation with a read-through .... Goethe would sit at the head of the table and begin proceedings by rapping with his key. At this stage no roles were allocated, and the whole play was read aloud by the actors in turn, with Goethe controlling the change of reader and pace of delivery with the tapping of his key.

(Patterson 1990: 75)

No actors had a role at this stage; only Goethe had a consistent role, rapping his key. The actors, sat around Goethe's table, were literally in his space, organised by his furniture. A similar effect might have been created when Stanislavski rehearsed in his own accommodation.

Certainly Stanislavski had mastered the use of the director's table as a disciplinary mechanism. He learnt it from the Regisseur of the Meiningen company, Chronegk: 'He, too, like Kronegk, sat at the producer's table with a watch in his hand, waiting for the appointed time of the rehearsal, and when the time came he struck his bell and the rehearsal began' (Magarshack 1950: 74). The table furnishes the director with a physical extension of his presence, literally making him the largest entity in the room and giving him the material means spatially to structure others. It also allows emotional expression, as Komisarjevsky tells us when he relates an 'exhibition of youthful temper': 'After keeping my patience with great effort for an hour, I could stand it no longer, and blowing out the candle on the producer's desk, said something rude and left the Theatre without hat or coat' (Komisarjevsky 1929: 55).

If the table can establish formal physical relations between director and actors, it can also be ignored. The director can penetrate actors' space. This penetration might be supportive and caring, as Houghton implies about Stanislavski: 'He walks about with them on the stage; whispers suggestions to stir their imaginations. If the actor wishes to make movements of which the producer does not approve, he is allowed to try his way' (Houghton 1938: 92). A similar activity was recommended by Barrault: a good director

> works on the stage at the side of the actors...He stands in front of them, nose to nose, in order to hypnotize them. He takes them by the arm, as if he were suddenly leading a blind man. He hides behind them, his mouth against their ear.
> (in Leiter 1991: 206)

Barrault makes it sound very close. Slowiak and Cuesta likewise report Grotowski during an improvisation: 'he would enter the action without interrupting and physically move the actors in the space'. Apparently the actors simply carried on, unconfused and unquestioning. A perhaps more invasive effect might have been felt at some level by Grotowski's leading actor Cieślak who worked alone with him for several months preparing *The Constant Prince*, the text of which Cieślak had to know by heart: Grotowski would appear at his actor's bedside 'in the middle of the night, wake him up, and make him recite the text word for word' (Slowiak and Cuesta 2007: 88, 97).

Describing his relationship with Cieślak Grotowski said: 'His growth is attended by observation, astonishment, and desire to help; my growth is projected onto him, or, rather, is *found in him* – and our common growth becomes revelation' (Slowiak and Cuesta 2007: 97). Houghton says something similar about Meyerhold's approach. Meyerhold, we may recall from Chapter 3, was encouraging the actor's reading of a line to be 'as close as possible to the way *he* would read the line'. The reason, suggests Houghton, is that Meyerhold 'must project himself into the performance and this he has to do through the medium of each actor' (Houghton 1938: 127, 141). The suggestion that the actors are a surrogate for the director's own presence in the show takes us into ambiguous and difficult territory. At stake is the operation of desire between director and actors, and the uncertainty is whether a director wants to have the actor or be the actor: 'my growth' is 'found in him', Grotowski says.

Of this desire some directors are very conscious. Mitchell warns against any form of unguarded closeness: 'If you mix with actors socially, keep the boundaries clear' (Mitchell 2009: 123). But Kazan bluntly suggests the reverse: 'It is not essential that you should want to fuck the leading lady, but it is essential that you should feel emotions well past those of ordinary friendship and respect' (Kazan 2009: 276). Bogart too suggests that 'Erotic tension between a director and an actor can be an indispensable contribution to a good rehearsal process', and, while she does not encourage 'physical consummation' of this, 'A rehearsal should feel like a date . . . The best productions I have directed issue from a rehearsal process charged with erotic interest' (Bogart 2003: 67). The argument gets more interesting when its rationale is developed. Kazan suggests that the reason for the necessary intimacy is that the director works with the life experience of performers, and this is deeper inside them than their learnt techniques. But, and here's the interesting turn, not only does the director participate in the life experience of the actors, they should also 'stir you . . . as you hope the characters in the script will stir the audience' (Kazan 2009: 276). Now the audience is frequently stirred not just by watching but by empathy, feeling with the characters. That analogy between the director's and the audience's engagement potentially has the director both watching erotically and at the same time feeling with: both desiring and being the actors.

But the mechanism might not be eroticism. It might also be violence. . . . Albert Hunt tells a story of Patrick Magee in Peter Brook's production of *The Marat/Sade*: Brook 'set up working situations in which the performers would have to confront the violence inside themselves'. Magee played Sade, whose name is not only associated with a form of sexual play involving cruelty but who, in the drama, is also a theatre director. 'Sade's relationship to the inmates is a mirror image of Brook's relationship to an acting group. And Brook had pushed his group, not to "act" as inmates, but to "be" inmates.' In the filmed version, notes Hunt, as Sade watches the actors destroy the set Magee seems to quote the 'enigmatic smile' with which Brook watched his own actors destroy the rehearsal set of *Lear*. It was when Brook talked to Hunt about 'the need to be aware of the violence inside oneself' that Hunt realised that 'Magee wasn't simply playing Sade – he was playing Brook as well' (in Hunt and Reeves 1995: 92–3).

By way of summary of our reflections on the body of the director in the process, let's recall the instances above of directors' control of space and sound and bodies – and timekeeping – as we read Bogart's account of Robert Wilson in rehearsal.

> The production was Heiner Müller's *Hamletmachine* performed by undergraduate acting students at New York University. The rehearsal was scheduled to begin at 7 p.m. I arrived early to find a buoyant atmosphere. In the back row of the theatre, PhD students and scholars waited expectantly, pens poised, for Wilson's entrance. On the stage young actors warmed up. A stage management team sat behind a battalion of long tables at the edge of the stage. Wilson arrived at 7.15. He sat down in the middle of the audience risers amidst the bustle and noise and proceeded to gaze intently at the stage. Gradually everyone in the theatre quietened down until the silence was penetrating. After about five excruciating minutes of utter stillness, Wilson stood up, walked towards a chair on the stage and stared at it. After what felt to me an eternity, he reached down, touched the chair and moved it less than an inch. As he stepped back to look at the chair again, I noticed that I was having trouble breathing. The tension in the room was palpable, almost unbearable. Next, Wilson motioned an actress towards him in order to show her what he wanted her to do. He demonstrated by sitting on the chair, tilting forward, and moving his fingers slightly. Then she took his place and precisely copied his tilt and hand gestures. I realized that I was leaning forward on my own chair, deeply distressed. Never having experienced another director at work, I felt like I was watching other people in a private, intimate act. And I recognized that night the necessary cruelty of decision.
>
> (Bogart 2003: 44)

The set of devices used by Wilson here demonstrate his mastery – in every sense of the word – in a way that feels very similar to the self-production of charismatic individuality by the actor-manager. But it also forcibly reminds us that while the director's being might be said to inhabit the whole process as a dispersed organising entity, that entity is at the same time a very real, and often very demanding, body.

ORGANISATION AND AESTHETICS

It may be that the cruelty of decision – or at least the romance of cruelty of decision – is deep at the heart of directed theatre.

What seems to have impressed many watchers of performances by the Meiningen troupe were its efficiency and discipline. Most of the acting was not very good but the actors obviously worked together, didn't upstage each other and knew what they were doing. Komisarjevsky says 'the bad actors of the Meininger troupe looked very much as if animated figures were moving about in Madame Tussaud's "natural" surroundings'; but he also notes that 'instead of playing for themselves, as was customary under the "star" system' the actors 'became dependent one upon the other, thus creating an "ensemble" ' (Komisarjevsky 1929: 58). For Stanislavski what shone through clearly was the power of the person who had produced this discipline, the Regisseur Chronegk: 'I liked Chronegk's control and sangfroid. I imitated him and with time became a dictator-director, and other Russian directors began to imitate me just as I had imitated him' (Stanislavski 2008: 115). So like Chronegk he sat at a table and marked the start of the rehearsal with a bell. But he then went further by reducing leading parts to walk-on from one day to another, in order to promote interdependence.

The Meiningen company produced, by strong company discipline, the effect of ensemble playing. In a similar way when the Compagnie des Quinze took London by storm in the mid-1930s, they were celebrated for their ensemble work. This ensemble work was in fact an ensemble effect, and the effect was created by their director, Michel Saint-Denis, who meticulously positioned actors according to his pre-written notes. The actual organisation of the work was that of a hierarchical system where the director had the ideas and fitted the actors into them. Its aesthetic effect, however, was of ensemble playing. The same is true of the man who apparently brought ensemble playing to England, Komisarjevsky. He is very clear that success in the theatre comes from being led by a single man with a vision. The same, he says, holds true of life, a matter on which he cites approvingly the Italian fascist Mussolini. 'Stage work', he observes, 'involves many people, but it does not therefore follow that it is necessarily a communal work' (Komisarjevsky 1935: 18). This might prompt us to suggest that the enjoyment of ensemble playing has to do not with the reality of democratic company organisation but simply with an image in front of us that feels thoroughly worked-out, disciplined, organised.

That suggestion raises the question of the extent to which organisation can be imaged in performance. Certainly military displays, especially of marching, exhibit – are designed to exhibit – discipline. That discipline implies respect for an organisational approach in which obedience and hierarchy are valued. In a similar way – and indeed with a similar sort of discipline – the performances by early twentieth-century chorus girls were seen as an image not only of automated labour but of its values. As Siegfried Kracauer said in 1931, 'when they stepped to a rapid beat, it sounded like "business, business"; when they raised their legs with mathematical precision above their heads, they joyfully affirmed the progress of rationalization'. The image they embody, for Kracauer, was 'The functioning of a flourishing economy' (Kracauer 1994: 565). But while Kracauer was sardonically identifying the chorus line as a sort of industrial product in keeping with the new values of automated labour, in the new Soviet Union Meyerhold's development of biomechanics (1922) attempted to create performances that drew from, and celebrated, the artistry of productive labour: 'The work of the actor in an industrial society will be regarded as a means of production vital to the proper organization of the labour of every citizen of that society.' To that end he recommends that the performer 'discover those movements in work which facilitate the maximum use of work time', for this will have aesthetic effect: 'a skilled worker at work invariably reminds one of a dancer' (Meyerhold 1969: 197–8).

In these early twentieth-century examples the performances may be said to be mimetic images of a felt world of new industrial organisation. In that sense they are doing the customary job of performance in making imitation. But it may be a different matter to ask whether a performance might as it were express the actual organisation of the people that make it. The choreographer and dance historian Mark Franko suggests this might be the case. In his exploration of dance in the 1930s he traces how 'choreographic rationales influenced the goals of structures administering the organization of the mass'. The term 'organization' here entails 'both the aesthetics of social engineering and the politics of artistic genre'. As he sees it choreography can contribute to the organisation of the mass by working at a very deep level in the individual on their emotions and musculature: 'The vibrant qualities of readiness and expectancy in the proletarian body were central to the politically radical meanings of *organization*. When ignited by the prospect of emancipation, the masses were "organized" emotionally.' Thus, for example, in the mass dance movement dancers as individuals were given a sense of personal freedom in exploring choreographic possibilities but at the same time they worked in groups to develop a sense of shared focus. This operated to organise them insofar as it produced 'the emotional and physical coalescence of their energetic resources'. They did exercises to enhance their understanding of 'what it means to move together as a group'. So, says Franko, 'The amassing of physical and emotional energy within the group is the result of choreographic directives, which became an effective means of emboldening political consciousness.' By contrast the chorus line was strictly disciplined in a way which gave no opportunity for 'creative adjustment to others' impulses'. If mass dance created a freed individual working as part of a group, the chorus line presented an image of unskilled labour in a machinic discipline. And this, argues Franko, was no mere image. The arrangement of the choreographic work was such that subgroups had particular specialisms and any one dancer therefore had a narrow range of movement options. At this point the actual organisation of the dancing coincides with its aesthetic effect: 'Such organization limited the dancing body to specialized tasks on the model of scientific management' (Franko 2002: 21–32). Hence the mathematically precise high kicks noted by Kracauer affirming, albeit not joyfully perhaps, the progress of rationalisation.

Now while dance would seem to give a fairly clear example there are examples of other stage forms from the Modernist period that show a similar connection between the organisation of the work and the staged effect. When Charlie Mann advised amateur players how to perform his agitational sketch *Meerut* (1933), he was clear that what they did in performance should – and would – express their political discipline: 'a strong feminine voice vibrating with the conviction of the message can be just as effective as a masculine one' (Mann 1985: 106). Two decades before, the voice trainer Elsie Fogerty had developed techniques of choral speaking. A moment of breakthrough came when her chorus was able to speak together with such unified precision that they could dance to the rhythm of the words they were speaking. This is a staging of the organisation of the chorus as a group entity, where the discipline enables a greater expressivity of the body in that it now dances to its own words.

That sense of greater expressivity is important because it implies an emotional element which correlates with the physical just like the physical and emotional coalescence that Franko sees in mass dance. The staged image of organisation can position the individual subject – or at least an image of the individual subject – in relation to it. The chorus line all apparently take delight in what they are doing by all showing the same identical smile. More interesting in this context perhaps are those responses to the Meiningen troupe where what was seen was actor discipline in conjunction with, it seems, not very good acting. The focus of the actors was on their learnt rules perhaps rather than being able to inhabit their own bodies. The failings observed by Antoine appear to belong with a mindset that meticulously prepares each element without having much sense of what it is being used for (a rain cue that stops abruptly on the appropriate cue-line). He set about creating a crowd utterance which had more diversity by dividing his crowd into subgroups with different responsibilities for the sound. Granville Barker was a step more detailed when he wrote lines for members of an onstage crowd attending a political rally. Both he and Antoine were intending to make the crowd feel more real by giving parts of the crowd, even individuals within it, specific things to do. In the radical arts theatres that pioneered realism the organisation of a crowd felt more like reality when it expressed individual presences.

What the crowd offered to the director was the opportunity to work like a conductor, organising the elements in relation to one another without losing their individual character. Performances of very large crowds or mass rallies required, and brought into being, new organisational methods. And it is therefore significant that in various different forms the interest in group movement, in chorus and in crowd persisted through the years during which the role of director emerged. For although there are different emphases here, and different values at work in the image of organisation, from its earliest days directing seemed to be associated with the ability to stage groups of people. The successful staging of groups required organisation and then could turn that organisation into aesthetic object. This relationship between organisation and aesthetics was formulated early on by one of the great directors of the twentieth century, Erwin Piscator (1893–1966).

STAGING ORGANISATION

Piscator's politics insisted that the theatre organisation should be collective and should then turn its audience into politically aware opponents of

Capitalism. He laid down these two 'fundamental principles' when he founded the Proletarisches Theater in 1920:

> as an organization it must break with capitalist traditions and create a footing of equality, a common interest and a collective will to work, uniting directors, actors, designers and technical administrative personnel, and then uniting these people with the consumers (that is, the audience) . . .
>
> The second task facing the Proletarisches Theater is to make an educative, propagandistic impact on those members of the masses who are as yet politically undecided or indifferent, or who have not yet understood that a proletarian state cannot adopt bourgeois art and the bourgeois mode of 'enjoying' art.
>
> (Piscator 1980: 46)

Aesthetically the challenge was to bring audience and stage together in a way that felt like a public meeting.

Such a meeting required the tight organisation of its material elements. But it also required formal innovations. When Piscator did *Flags* in 1924, he handled the 19 scenes so that they moved in quick succession, forcing sharp contrasts and ironic elision. This was done by means of a revolve, together with projections of linking texts, an initiative which may well have been innovatory (and all requiring a great deal of last-minute rehearsal). This mechanisation of the theatre combined with the attitude of public meeting led to the invention of one of the great new forms of the twentieth century, epic theatre. As Piscator saw it,

> it was about the extension of the action and the clarification of the background of the action, that is to say it involved a continuation of the play beyond the dramatic framework . . . This automatically led to the use of stage techniques from areas which had never been seen in the theatre before.
>
> (Piscator 1980: 75)

This work of 'clarification' involved going beyond the individuality of characters in order to show the relationship between events on stage and, at the same time, their relationship to abstract historical forces in the world beyond the theatre. It amounted in effect to finding a way of staging an argument, where two levels of organisation become necessary. First there is the organisation of materials – getting the groups of people and the machinery into the right relationships and rhythms. Second there is the organisation of ideas so that an audience appreciates the connectedness of things:

> the way to do this is to show the link between events on the stage and the great forces active in history. It is not by chance that the factual substance becomes the main thing in each play. It is only from the facts themselves that the constraints and the constant mechanisms of life emerge, giving a deeper meaning to our private fates. For this I need some means of showing how human-superhuman factors interact with classes or individuals. One of the means was film.

This interconnectedness was made materially manifest in the staging arrangements:

> For the basic stage I had a so-called 'Praktikabel' built, a terraced structure of irregular shape with a raked platform on one side and steps and levels on the other. This structure stood on a revolving stage. I built the various acting areas into terraces, niches and corridors. In this way the overall structure of the scenes was unified and the play could flow uninterrupted, like a single current sweeping everything along with it. The abandonment of the decorative set was taken a stage further than in *Flags*. The predominant principle was that of a purely practical acting structure to support, clarify and express the action. Freestanding structures, a self-contained world on the revolving stage, put an end to the peep-show world of the bourgeois theater. They can also be set up in the open. The squared stage area is merely an irritating limitation.

In this project Piscator argues that he is going beyond Reinhardt in that he was not merely putting the social mass on display but actually involving it, and, as he would have hoped, developing its class consciousness. The theatre production becomes 'one big assembly'.

This was done not simply by aesthetic staging means, but by audience organisation:

> In our case arena and stage were fused into one. In this there was one decisive factor: Beye had organized block bookings for the trade unions that summer. Class-conscious workers were sitting out front, and the storm broke. I had always been aware that we were not filling the house, and had wondered how we could actually reach this mass audience. Now I had them in my hand – and even today I still see that as the only real possibility for mass theater in Berlin.

What Piscator is describing is an ideal of socialist theatre, where firm organisation – as it were a version of the vanguard political party perhaps – brings about mass mobilisation. His description of opening night is thus infused with the energy and sentiment of revolutionary aspiration:

> On opening night there were thousands in the Grosses Schauspielhaus. Every seat was taken, steps, aisles, entrances were full to bursting. The living masses were filled from the outset with wild excitement at being there to watch, and you could feel an incredible, willing receptivity out in the audience that you get only with the proletariat.
>
> But this inner willingness quickly turned into active participation: the masses took over the direction. The people who filled the house had for the most part been actively involved in the period, and what we were showing them was in a true sense their own fate, their own tragedy being acted out before their eyes. Theater had become reality, and soon it was not a case of the stage confronting the audience, but one big assembly, one big battlefield, one massive demonstration. It was this unity that proved that evening that political theater could be effective agitation.

(Piscator 1980: 92–7)

Clearly Piscator's account is inflected by his own political ideals, and quite right too, some may say. But the account does also offer an insight into how the effort to make theatre into 'one big assembly' produces new ways of organising the stage, the material, the company and, indeed, the audience. This was not a pictorial image of bodily discipline or group organisation. Instead it was in effect an aesthetic expression of the company values and mode of work, creating both an assembly and an assemblage.

PROCESS AND AESTHETICS

It could be observed that of course for Piscator as with his contemporaries and immediate predecessors an interest in organisation as such was part of a Modernist ethos, so that in various ways groups were reflecting on their own organisation and in many cases deliberately trying to stage an image of it, or, to be more precise, an image of what they thought it was. But how far is it viable to move beyond Modernist directorial practices to ask whether the form of organisation of a company's structure and process make themselves manifest in performance?

Some would argue that this always happens in some way. A member of the Théâtre du Soleil collective, Louis Samier, said: 'I can no longer imagine working in "the profession" as it's usually understood. Here an actor is required to be a creator *in the production*. What comes through in the performance stems from what's outside the performance and it's intimately connected to the group's life and work' (in Williams 1999: 30). What's outside the performance is often the material environment of its making. Max Stafford-Clark describes his style: 'I suppose it's based on simplicity. What I've had to do is make a virtue out of poverty ... all aesthetics come from economics' (in Shevtsova and Innes 2009: 256–7). Similarly Deborah Warner noted that the extremely limited means of her company Kick figured aesthetically: 'It was not only a way of working in rehearsal, it was a production style' (in Cook 1989: 101). Although Warner's comment doesn't spell it out, one mechanism by which the organisational arrangements show themselves in performance is that the director and company choose to embrace their given circumstances and articulate them aesthetically. That sort of choice is particularly apparent where the director has an intellectual or political commitment to a particular mode of working.

By way of a very obvious, and fairly extreme, example, as we saw in Chapter 8 Kantor's artistic vision led him to deal with the actor as object (Witts 2010: 21). In his production of *In a Small Country House* (1961) 'One could not clearly distinguish between the bags and the actors who also fell out from behind the closet doors' (in Klossowicz 2002: 142). Alongside this conscious aesthetic effect of alienated being Kantor's productions included the presentation of himself as 'conductor'. The staging of these versions of humanity exists within a viewpoint that sees the relations of spectator and actor as alienated (Witts 2010: 40). Now the stories of the processes that led to the productions also tell us about rehearsal-room tantrums (Witts 2010: 30, 46). So the staging of Kantor as 'conductor' in amongst body-objects, the making special of the director's role within alienated viewing relations, gives an aesthetic gloss to an actual relationship founded on a power differential that allows for occasional abuse of that power. Indeed one could say that the staging of Kantor in and by the artwork goes one step further than offering a gloss. The enactment of that which is dead and deadened, the testimony to the irrecoverable, becomes apparently more authentic if it emerges from a process of submission and cruelty. The abuses of power, the tantrums, are thereby made aesthetically necessary.

If Kantor's concern with himself as the artist is an example of limited application, we might consider Richard Maxwell's rather different approach to making shows that speak of an organisational attitude or indeed commitment. He has a recurrent interest in unpicking the technique, assumptions and value system of so-called 'Method acting'. The actors are to approach their work as a task rather than a creative activity drawing upon their own interiority. Spontaneity is not to be imitated but to be actual. To that end the processes are open-ended. Maxwell seems to take no one approach to the job of directing and the rehearsals seem not to arrive at a point of full closure. When he wrote *The End of Reality* Maxwell auditioned and cast the play before he had finished the script, then adapted the script to the actors. But if the playscript became fixed, the mise en scène did not: 'By repeatedly altering the *mise en scène*, Maxwell creates a working environment that forces his actors to achieve – rather than imagine – spontaneity.' What emerges from the repeated prohibition on acting as imitation is a performance in which the actors appear, to some reviewers, to be 'deadpan'. But it's more unsettling than simply being a display of non-acting. This is not a complete repudiation of Method so much as a staging of Method's assumptions and their limits: 'By asking actors to make judgements based on what they "feel" in the present moment, the approach engages with the terms and philosophies of Method acting while resisting the assumption that this necessarily produces a natural or realist effect' (Gorman 2010: 180, 188). The shows thus end up staging not only the open-endedness of the processes but a specific tussle with a system for organising the work of representation, the drama of being Methodical.

With Maxwell's company the distance from, or tension with, an organising system is part of the aesthetic effect, the process is made to show its open-endedness. But this can work for orderliness – and not just in the case of military processions – as well as disorder. Take Hytner's response to a fellow director: 'I admire productions by Howard Davies, for instance, because there seems to me to be an enormous sense of control, which is sometimes lacking in mine' (in Cook 1989: 58). And if organisation has aesthetic effect it can be regarded as part of the expressive machinery and manipulated as such. The appearance of ensemble playing from the Meiningen company through to the Compagnie des Quinze in the mid-1930s, and possibly well beyond into the next century, can be a result simply of directorial instruction. In this context Peter Sellars, for example, aims conspicuously to break the effect, which he notes is tough on critics 'who are used to a highly homogenised and beautifully cultivated sense of ensemble' (in Delgado and Heritage 1996: 225). In breaking the ensemble effect Sellars intends to make clear the actual diversity of the constitution of his company.

Sellars' adjectives suggest not simply a mode of playing but the thing that is played. As we noted above, what the ensemble effect has communicated in the past may be nothing to do with the actual working of a company and everything to do with a celebration of homogeneity and cultivation. Instead of actors upstaging each other competitively they show restraint and decorum, and as such may be taken to be homogenous with the preferred sense of self-identity of their cultivated audience. Ensemble may be said, in short, to be a performance of discipline, and in that lies much of its pleasure. So too, in a very different context, the political discipline and performed intelligence of Brecht's actors constituted a part of their authoritative theatrical effect. The 'sense of control' that Hytner found pleasurable may have a lot to do with how a whole range of shows work aesthetically. That control might be very obvious in the choreographed movement of masses of people, the filling and emptying of an arena, the commitment of participants or it might be a little less obvious in the precise distances, shapes and timings of a few performers on a stage. Sometimes the control – or lack of it – is what is being staged; most often it is there, less marked, simply as a texture to the show being done. And in those cases it is very difficult to name and define. When Hytner describes the concept of his production of *Don Carlos* he says: 'it would have been quite easy just to show the world of sixteenth-century Spain, but I think it should always be just one step beyond what you expect, not total dislocation or, worse still, decoration' (in Cook 1989: 59). When the feel of the show is 'one step beyond' there's a sense that it's being managed, framed, thought about. Sellars is after a similar sensation: 'Choreography is very important because I like structure. I want the audience to perceive structure' (in Delgado and Heritage 1996: 228).

Feeling that we are in the presence of something one step beyond, structured, controlled: to this list of words let's add one more. Here is Sarah Bryant-Bertail describing the Théâtre du Soleil's production of *Les Atrides*. She says that the mode of performance, with its gestic vocabulary of signs and 'écriture corporelle', was 'not just delineating a style or illustrating a text but haunting the ongoing action so that there can never be the sense of a pure present' (in Williams 1999: 181). She uses the word 'haunting' because she is interested in the recovery of a past. But for our purposes the word can take on a different meaning. Where audiences get the sensation of control, of structuring, the show might be said to be 'haunted by organisation.' The past that is always recovered is the history of the process. And as such there can never be a sense of the production having a pure present. For what is potentially always there at the same time is the feel of directedness. That thing always one step beyond is its direction.

References

Adams, Cindy (1980) *Lee Strasberg: The Imperfect Genius of the Artists Studio*. Garden City, New York: Doubleday & Company.

Alfreds, Mike (2007) *Different Every Night: Freeing the Actor*. London: Nick Hern Books.

Althusser, Louis (1971) *Lenin and Philosophy and Other Essays*. New York and London: Monthly Review Press.

Barba, Eugenio (2010) *On Directing and Dramaturgy: Burning the House*. London and New York: Routledge.

Barker, Clive (1978) *Theatre Games: A New Approach to Drama Training*. London: Eyre Methuen.

Belasco, David (1919) *The Theatre through its Stage Door*, ed. Louis V. Defoe. New York and London: Harper & Brothers.

Bering, Rüdiger (2003) 'Harold Prince and Stephen Sondheim: Adult Musicals', in Armin Geraths (ed.), *Creating the 'New Musical': Harold Prince in Berlin*. Frankfurt-am-Main: Peter Lang, pp. 41–57.

Bernheim, Alfred L. (1932) *The Business of the Theatre*. New York: Actors' Equity Association.

Bharucha, Rustom (1993) *Theatre and the World: Performance and the Politics of Culture*. London and New York: Routledge.

Bingham, Madeleine (1978) *Henry Irving and the Victorian Theatre*, fwd. John Gielgud. London: George Allen & Unwin.

Black, Malcolm (1975) *First Reading to First Night: A Candid Look at Stage Directing*. Seattle and London: University of Washington Press.

Bogart, Anne (2003) *A Director Prepares: Seven Essays on Art and Theatre*. London and New York: Routledge.

Boucicault, Dion (1926) *The Art of Acting*, intro. O. Skinner. New York: Columbia University Press.

Bradby, David and Sparks, Annie (1997) *Mise en Scène: French Theatre Now*. London: Methuen.

Braun, Edward (2000) *The Director and the Stage: From Naturalism to Grotowski*. London: Methuen Drama.

Brecht, Bertolt (1964) *Brecht on Theatre*, ed. J. Willett. New York: Hill and Wang.

Brockett, Oscar G. and Findlay, Robert R. (1973) *A History of European and American Theatre and Drama since 1970*. Englewood Cliffs, NJ: Prentice-Hall, Inc.

Brook, Peter (1988) *The Shifting Point: Forty Years of Theatrical Exploration, 1946–1987*. London: Methuen Drama.

Brown, John Russell (ed.) (2008) *The Routledge Companion to Directors' Shakespeare*. London and New York: Routledge.

Burnim, Kalman A. (1961) *David Garrick: Director*. Pittsburgh: University of Pittsburgh Press.

Caird, John (2010) *Theatre Craft: A Director's Practical Companion from A to Z*. London: Faber and Faber.

Callow, Simon (2004) *Being an Actor*. London: Vintage Books.

Calvert, Louis (1918) *Problems of the Actor*, intro. Clayton Hamilton. New York: Henry Holt and Company.

Carlson, Marvin (1978) *Goethe and the Weimar Theatre*. Ithaca and London: Cornell University Press.

Carter, Huntly (1964) *The Theatre of Max Reinhardt*. New York: Benjamin Blom.

Catron, Louis E. (1989) *The Director's Vision: Play Direction from Analysis to Production*. Mountain View, CA: Mayfield Publishing Company.

Caughie, John (ed.) (1981) *Theories of Authorship: A Reader*. London, Boston and Henley: Routledge & Kegan Paul.

Chaikin, Joseph (1972) *The Presence of the Actor*. New York: Atheneum.

Chothia, Jean (1991) *André Antoine*. Cambridge: Cambridge University Press.

Clurman, Harold (1972) *On Directing*. New York: Collier Books.

Cohen, Lola (2010) *The Lee Strasberg Notes*. London and New York: Routledge.

Cohen, Robert (2011) *Working Together in Theatre: Collaboration and Leadership*. Basingstoke: Palgrave Macmillan.

Coldewey, John C. (1977) 'That Enterprising Property Player: Semi-Professional Drama in Sixteenth-Century England', *Theatre Notebook* 31, pp. 5–12.

Cole, Toby and Chinoy, Helen Crich (eds) (1963) *Directors on Directing: A Source Book of the Modern Theatre*. Indianapolis and New York: The Bobbs-Merrill Company.

Common Ground (1985) *The Fence*, in *Peace Plays*, sel. and intro. by Stephen Lowe. London and New York: Methuen.

Condee, William F. and Irmer, Thomas (2008) 'Experiments with Architectural Space in the German Theatre', in Simon Williams and Maik Hamburger (eds), *A History of German Theatre*. Cambridge: Cambridge University Press, pp. 248–74.

Cook, Judith (1989) *Directors' Theatre: Sixteen Leading Directors on the State of Theatre in Britain Today*. London: Hodder & Stoughton.

Coward, Noël (1979) *Hay Fever*, in *Plays: One*, intro. Raymond Mander and Joe Mitchenson. London: Eyre Methuen.

Craig, Edward Gordon (1980) *On the Art of the Theatre*. London: Heinemann.

Daoust, Yvette (1981) *Roger Planchon: Director and Playwright*. Cambridge: Cambridge University Press.

Dean, Alexander and Carra, Lawrence (1974) *Fundamentals of Play Directing*. Holt, Rinehart and Winston: New York, 3rd edn.

Delgado, Maria M. and Heritage, Paul (eds) (1996) *In Contact with the Gods?: Directors Talk Theatre*. Manchester and New York: Manchester University Press.

Donnellan, Declan (2005) *The Actor and the Target*. London: Nick Hern Books.

Doyle, Brian (1982) 'The Hidden History of English Studies', in Peter Widdowson (ed.), *Re-Reading English*. London: Methuen & Co.

Elsom, John and Tomalin, Nicholas (1978) *The History of the National Theatre*. London: Cape.

Etchells, Tim (1999) *Certain Fragments: Contemporary Performance and Forced Entertainment*. London: Routledge.

Fernald, John (1968) *Sense of Direction: The Director and His Actors*. London: Secker and Warburg.

Foreman, Richard (1992) *Balancing Acts: Foundations for a Theater*, ed. Ken Jordan. New York: Theatre Communications Group.

Franko, Mark (2002) *The Work of Dance: Labor, Movement, and Identity in the 1930s*. Middletown, CT: Wesleyan University Press.

Freyer, Achim, http://www.goethe.de/kue/flm/prj/kub/lit/en(3951)016.htm (accessed 5 February 2012).

Gaskill, William (1988) *A Sense of Direction: Life at the Royal Court*. London and Boston: Faber and Faber.

Giannachi, Gabriella and Luckhurst, Mary (1999) *On Directing: Interviews with Directors*. London: Faber and Faber.

Goorney, Howard (1981) *The Theatre Workshop Story*. London: Eyre Methuen.

Gorman, Sarah (2010) 'Richard Maxwell and the New York City Players – *The End of Reality* (2006) – Exploring Acting', in Jen Harvie and Andy Lavender (eds), *Making Contemporary Theatre: International Rehearsal Processes*. Manchester and New York: Manchester University Press, pp. 180–201.

Granville Barker, Harley (1913) 'The Golden Thoughts of Granville Barker', *The Play Pictorial* 21: 126.

—— (1922) *The Exemplary Theatre*. London: Chatto & Windus.

—— (1923) Introduction to *The Players' Shakespeare: The Tragedie of Macbeth*. London: Ernest Benn.

—— (1927) *Prefaces to Shakespeare*. London: Sidgwick & Jackson Ltd.

—— (1964) *On Dramatic Method*. New York: Hill and Wang.

—— (1984) *Prefaces to Shakespeare: King Lear; Macbeth*, fwd. Sir John Gielgud. London: B.T. Batsford Ltd.

Guthrie, Tyrone (1961) *A Life in the Theatre*. London: Readers Union, Hamish Hamilton.

Hall, Peter (1999) *The Necessary Theatre*. London: Nick Hern Books.

—— (2000) *Making an Exhibition of Myself*. London: Oberon Books.

—— (2009) *Shakespeare's Advice to the Players*. London: Oberon Books.

Hauser, Frank and Reich, Russell (2003) *Notes on Directing: 130 Lessons in Leadership from the Director's Chair*. New York: Walker Publishing Company.

Hirsch, Foster (1989) *Harold Prince and the American Musical Theatre*. Cambridge: Cambridge University Press.

Hirst, David L. (2006) *Giorgio Strehler*. Cambridge: Cambridge University Press.

Hortmann, Wilhelm (2009) *Shakespeare on the German Stage: The Twentieth Century*. Cambridge: Cambridge University Press.

Houghton, Norris (1938) *Moscow Rehearsals: An Account of Methods of Production in the Soviet Theatre*. London: George Allen & Unwin Ltd.

Howe, P.P. (1910) *The Repertory Theatre: A Record and a Criticism*. London: Martin Secker.

Hunt, Albert and Reeves, Geoffrey (1995) *Peter Brook*. Cambridge: Cambridge University Press.

Ilson, Carol (1989) *Harold Prince: From Pajama Game to Phantom of the Opera*, fwd. Sheldon Harnick. Ann Arbor & London: UMI Research Press.

Innes, Christopher (2008) 'The Rise of the Director, 1850–1939', in Simon Williams and Maik Hamburger (eds), *A History of German Theatre*. Cambridge: Cambridge University Press, pp. 171–97.

Irving, Henry (1893) *The Drama: Addresses*. London: William Heinemann.

Itzin, Catherine (1980) *Stages in the Revolution: Political Theatre in Britain since 1968*. London: Eyre Methuen.

Kantor, Tadeusz (1993) *A Journey Through Other Spaces: Essays and Manifestos, 1944–1990*, ed. and trans. Michal Kobialka. Berkeley and London: University of California Press.

Kazan, Elia (2009) *Kazan on Directing*. New York: Alfred A. Knopf.

Kennedy, Dennis (2005) 'The Director, the Spectator and the Eiffel Tower', *Theatre Research International* 30:1, pp. 36–48.

—— (2008) *Granville Barker and the Dream of Theatre*. Cambridge: Cambridge University Press.

Klossowicz, Jan (2002) 'Tadeusz Kantor's Journey', in Rebecca Schneider and Gabrielle Cody (eds), *Re:Direction: A Theoretical and Practical Guide*. London and New York: Routledge, pp. 140–6.

Knowlson, James and Elizabeth (2006) *Beckett Remembering, Remembering Beckett: Uncollected Interviews with Samuel Beckett and Memories of Those Who Knew Him*. London: Bloomberg.

Kobialka, Michal (1993) 'The Quest for the Self/Other: A Critical Study of Tadeusz Kantor's Theatre', in Tadeusz Kantor. *A Journey Through Other Spaces: Essays and Manifestos, 1944–1990*, ed. and trans. Michal Kobialka. Berkeley and London: University of California Press, pp. 269–364.

Komisarjevsky, Theodore (1929) *Myself and the Theatre*. London: William Heinemann Limited.

—— (1935) *The Theatre and a Changing Civilisation*. London: John Lane The Bodley Head Limited.

Kracauer, Siegfried (1994) 'Girls and Crisis', in Anton Kaes, Martin Jay and Edward Dimendberg (eds), *The Weimar Republic Sourcebook*. Berkeley, CA: University of California Press.

Kuppers, Petra (2007) *Community Performance: An Introduction*. London and New York: Routledge.

Lash, Scott and Urry, John (1987) *The End of Organized Capitalism*. Cambridge: Polity Press.

Lavender, Andy (2001) *Hamlet in Pieces: Shakespeare Reworked by Peter Brook, Robert Lepage, Robert Wilson*. London: Nick Hern Books.

—— (2010) 'The Builders Association – *Super Vision* (2005) – Digital Dataflow and the Synthesis of Everything', in Jen Harvie and Andy Lavender (eds), *Making Contemporary Theatre: International Rehearsal Processes*. Manchester and New York: Manchester University Press, pp. 17–38.

Leach, Robert (2006) *Theatre Workshop: Joan Littlewood and the Making of Modern British Theatre*. Exeter: University of Exeter Press.

Leiter, Samuel G. (1991a) *From Stanislavsky to Barrault: Representative Directors of the European Stage*. New York: Greenwood Press.

—— (1991b) *From Belasco to Brook: Representative Directors of the English-Speaking Stage*. New York: Greenwood Press.

MacGowan, Kenneth and Jones, Robert Edmond (1964) *Continental Stagecraft*. New York: Benjamin Blom.

Macherey, Pierre (1978) *A Theory of Literary Production*, trans. Geoffrey Wall. London: Routledge & Kegan Paul.

Magarshack, David (1950) *Stanislavsky: A Life*. London: MacGibbon & Kee.

Mallarmé, Stéphane (1956) *Selected Prose Poems, Essays & Letters*, trans. and intro. Bradfield Cook. Baltimore: The Johns Hopkins Press.

Mamet, David (1998) *True and False: Heresy and Common Sense for the Actor*. London: Faber.

Mann, Charlie (1985) 'How to Produce Meerut (1933)', in Raphael Samuel, Ewan MacColl and Stuart Cosgrove, *Theatres of the Left 1880–1935: Workers' Theatre Movements in Britain and America*. London: Routledge & Kegan Paul.

Marker, Lise-Lone (1975) *David Belasco: Naturalism in the American Theatre*. Princeton, NJ: Princeton University Press.

Marowitz, Charles (1986) *Prospero's Staff: Acting and Directing in Contemporary Theatre*. Bloomington and Indianapolis: Indiana University Press.

Marshall, Norman (1947) *The Other Theatre*. London: John Lehmann.

—— (1962) *The Producer and the Play*. London: Macdonald.

Matthews, Brander (1914) *On Acting*. New York: Scribner.

Maugham, William Somerset (1961) *The Summing Up*. London: Heinemann.

McCaffrey, Michael (1998) *Directing a Play*. London: Phaidon.

McKinnon, Andrew (1995) *The Training of Theatre Directors: 1995 and Beyond*, A report to the National Council for Drama Training and The Gulbenkian Foundation November 1995: unpublished.

Meech, Anthony (2008) 'Classical Theatre and the Formation of a Civil Society, 1720–1832', in Simon Williams and Maik Hamburger (eds.), *A History of German Theatre*. Cambridge: Cambridge University Press, pp. 65–91.

Meyerhold, Vsevolod (1969) *Meyerhold on Theatre*, trans. and ed. with critical commentary by Edward Braun. London: Eyre Methuen.

Miles-Brown, John (1980) *Directing Drama*. London: Peter Owen.

Miller, Jonathan (1986) *Subsequent Performances*. London and Boston: Faber and Faber.

Mitchell, Katie (2009) *The Director's Craft: A Handbook for the Theatre*, fwd. N. Hytner. London and New York: Routledge.

Mitter, Shomit (1992) *Systems of Rehearsal*. London and New York: Routledge.

Monck, Nugent (2002) 'The Maddermarket Theatre and the Playing of Shakespeare', *Shakespeare Survey 12: The Elizabethan Theatre (1959)*. Cambridge: Cambridge University Press.

Osborne, John (1988) *The Meiningen Court Theatre 1866–1890*. Cambridge: Cambridge University Press.

Patterson, Michael (1990) *The First German Theatre: Schiller, Goethe, Kleist and Büchner in Performance*. London and New York: Routledge.

—— (2010) *Peter Stein: Germany's Leading Theatre Director*. Cambridge: Cambridge University Press.

Piscator, Erwin (1980) *The Political Theatre*, trans. and ed. Hugh Rorrison. London: Eyre Methuen.

Pitches, Jonathan (2012) 'A Tradition in Transition: Komisarjevsky's Seduction of the British Theatre', in Jonathan Pitches (ed.), *Russians in Britain: British Theatre and the Russian Tradition of Actor Training*. London and New York: Routledge.

Playfair, Nigel (1925) *The Story of the Lyric Theatre Hammersmith*. London: Chatto & Windus.

Rabkin, Gerald (ed.) (1999) *Richard Foreman*. Baltimore & London: The Johns Hopkins University Press.

—— (2002) 'Is There a Text on This Stage? Theatre, Authorship, Interpretation', in Rebecca Schneider and Gabrielle Cody (eds), *Re:Direction: A Theoretical and Practical Guide*. London and New York: Routledge, pp. 319–31.

Rae, Kenneth (1989) *A Better Direction*. London: Calouste Gulbenkian Foundation.

Ritchie, Rob (1987) *The Joint Stock Book: The Making of a Theatre Collective*. London: Methuen London.

Roose-Evans, James (1968) *Directing a Play*. London: Studio Vista.

Rossi, Alfred (1977) *Astonish Us in the Morning: Tyrone Guthrie Remembered*. London: Hutchinson.

Roudané, Matthew C. (1987) *Conversations with Arthur Miller.* Jackson and London: University Press of Mississippi.

Saint-Denis, Michel (1960) *Theatre: The Rediscovery of Style.* London: Heinemann.

Schechner, Richard (2002) 'Reality Is Not Enough: An Interview with Alan Schneider', in Rebecca Schneider and Gabrielle Cody (eds), *Re:Direction: A Theoretical and Practical Guide.* London and New York: Routledge, pp. 73–83.

Schechner, Richard, Hoffman, Theodore, Chwat, Jacques, Tierney, Mary (2002) 'An Interview with Grotowski', in Rebecca Schneider and Gabrielle Cody (eds), *Re:Direction: A Theoretical and Practical Guide.* London and New York: Routledge, pp. 236–46.

Schneider, Rebecca and Cody, Gabrielle (eds) (2002) *Re:Direction: A Theoretical and Practical Guide.* London and New York: Routledge.

Schwartz, Michael (2009) *Broadway and Corporate Capitalism: The Rise of the Professional-Managerial Class, 1900–1920.* New York: Palgrave Macmillan.

Selbourne, David (1982) *The Making of A Midsummer Night's Dream: An Eyewitness Account.* London: Methuen London.

Shaughnessy, Robert (2002) *The Shakespeare Effect: A History of Twentieth-Century Performance.* Basingstoke: Palgrave Macmillan.

Shepherd, Simon (2006) *Theatre, Body and Pleasure.* London: Routledge.

Maria Shevtsova and Christopher Innes (2009) *Directors/Directing: Conversations on Theatre.* Cambridge: Cambridge University Press.

Shyer, Lawrence (1989) *Robert Wilson and His Collaborators.* New York: Theatre Communications Group.

Sidiropoulou, Avra (2011) *Authoring Performance: The Director in Contemporary Theatre.* New York: Palgrave Macmillan.

Slowiak, James and Cuesta, Jairo (2007) *Jerzy Grotowski.* London and New York: Routledge.

Smith, A.C.H. (1972) *Orghast at Persepolis: An Account of the Experiment in Theatre Directed by Peter Brook and Written by Ted Hughes.* London: Eyre Methuen.

Stafford-Clark, Max (2004) *Letters to George: The Account of a Rehearsal.* London: Nick Hern Books.

Stanislavski, Konstantin (2008) *My Life in Art*, trans. and ed. Jean Benedetti. London and New York: Routledge.

Stoker, Bram (1906) *Personal Reminiscences of Henry Irving.* London: William Heinemann, 2 vols.

Stone, George Winchester, Jr. and Kahrl, George M. (1979) *David Garrick: A Critical Biography.* Carbondale and Edwardsville: Southern Illinois University Press.

Streitberger, W.R. (1994) *Court Revels, 1485–1559.* Toronto: University of Toronto Press.

Styan, J.L. (1977) *The Shakespeare Revolution: Criticism and Performance in the Twentieth Century.* Cambridge: Cambridge University Press.

—— (1982) *Max Reinhardt.* Cambridge: Cambridge University Press.

Suzuki, Tadashi (1986) *The Way of Acting*, trans. J. Thomas Rimer. New York: Theatre Communications Group.

Swain, Rob (2011) *Directing: A Handbook for Emerging Theatre Directors.* London: Methuen Drama.

Taylor, F.W. (1911) *The Principles of Scientific Management.* Harper & Brothers: New York and London

Tynan, Kenneth (2007) *Theatre Writings*, ed. Dominic Shellard. London: Nick Hern Books.

van Gyseghem, André (1943) *Theatre in Soviet Russia*. London: Faber and Faber.

Viagas, Robert (ed.) (2006) *The Alchemy of Theatre: The Divine Science: Essays on Theatre & the Art of Collaboration*. New York: Playbill Books.

Wallis, Mick and Shepherd, Simon (2010) *Studying Plays*. London: Bloomsbury, 3rd edn.

Weber, Carl (2002) 'Brecht as Director', in Rebecca Schneider and Gabrielle Cody (eds), *Re:Direction: A Theoretical and Practical Guide*. London and New York: Routledge, pp. 84–9.

Whitmore, Jon (1994) *Directing Postmodern Theatre: Shaping Signification in Performance*. Ann Arbor: The University of Michigan Press.

Whitton, David (1987) *Stage Directors in Modern France*. Manchester: Manchester University Press.

Williams, David (ed.) (1999) *Collaborative Theatre: The Théâtre du Soleil Sourcebook*, trans. Eric Prenowitz and David Williams. London and New York: Routledge.

Williams, Simon (2008) 'The Romantic Spirit in the German Theatre, 1790–1910', in Simon Williams and Maik Hamburger (eds), *A History of German Theatre*. Cambridge: Cambridge University Press, pp. 120–45.

Witts, Noel (2010) *Tadeusz Kantor*. London and New York: Routledge.

Worrall, Nick (2002) 'Meyerhold's Production of *The Magnanimous Cuckold*', in Rebecca Schneider and Gabrielle Cody (eds), *Re:Direction: A Theoretical and Practical Guide*. London and New York: Routledge, pp. 60–72.

REFERENCES: CHAPTER 6

Abirached, Robert (1995) *La décentralisation théâtrale vol. 3: 1968, Le tournant*. Paris: Actes Sud.

Anderson, Joel (2003) 'Directeur vs metteur en scène: Interviews with Stanislas Nordey and Brigitte Jaques', *Contemporary Theatre Review* 13: 3, pp. 47–58.

Attoun, Lucien (1999) *Profession Spectateur* (France Culture broadcast programme, 9 January 1999).

Banu, Georges and Tackels, Bruno (eds) (2005) *Le cas Avignon 2005: Regards critiques*. Vic-la-Gardiole: Entretemps.

Barthes, Roland (1958) 'Chroniques', *Théâtre Populaire* 30, pp. 80–3.

Benjamin, Walter (2008) *The Work of Art in the Age of Mechanical Reproduction*, trans. J. A. Underwood. London: Penguin Books.

Copeau, Jacques (1973) 'Lettre à Jean Schlumberger, 6 August 1919', in Denis Gontard (ed.), *La décentralisation théâtrale en France 1895–1952*. Paris: Société d'Édition d'Enseignement Supérieur (SEDES).

Darge, Fabienne and Salino, Brigitte (2005) '2005, l'année de toutes les polémiques, l'année de tous les paradoxes', *Le Monde*, 27 July 2005.

Dhomme, Sylvain (1959) *La mise en scène d'Antoine à Brecht*. Paris: Nathan.

Dort, Bernard (1988) *La représentation émancipée*. Paris: Acte-Sud.

Gontard, Denis (ed.) (1973) *La décentralisation théâtrale en France 1895–1952*. Paris: Société d'Édition d'Enseignement Supérieur (SEDES).

Grotowski, Jerzy (1968) *Towards a Poor Theatre*, ed. Eugenio Barba. London: Methuen.

de Jomaron, Jacqueline (ed.) (1992) *Le théâtre en France: Du moyen âge à nos jours*. Paris: Armand Colin.

Lang, Jack (1968) *L'État et le théâtre*. Paris: Librairie Générale de Droit et de Jurisprudence.

Osborne, John (1988) *The Meininger Court Theatre, 1866–1890*. Cambridge: Cambridge University Press.

Rolland, Romain (2003) *Le Théâtre du peuple*. Paris: Éditions Complexe.

Thibaudat, Jean-Pierre (1994) 'Tribulations de l'écriture dramatique en France', in *Le théâtre francaise*. Paris: Ministère des Affaires étrangères, pp. 5–33.

Van den Dries, Luk (2005) *Corpus Jan Fabre*. Paris: L'Arche.

Vilar, Jean (1955) *De la tradition théâtrale*. Paris: L'Arche.

Willett, John (1988) *The Theatre of the Weimar Republic*. New York: Holmes & Meier Publishers.

REFERENCES: CHAPTER 9

Ackerman, Marianne (1992) '*Alanienouidet*: Simultaneous Space and Action', *Canadian Theatre Review* 70, pp. 32–4.

Barthes, Roland (1992) *S/Z*, trans. Richard Miller. Oxford: Blackwell.

—— (1993) 'The Death of the Author', in *Image – Music – Text*, trans. Stephen Heath. London: Fontana Press.

Beauchamp, Hélène (1994) 'The Repère Cycles: From Basic to Continuous Education', *Canadian Theatre Review* 78, pp. 26–31.

Blankenship, Rebecca (2006) 'In Conversation', *Robert Lepage's Practice*, University of Manchester Conference, 30 May 2006.

Bureau, Stéphan (2008) *Stéphan Bureau rencontre Robert Lepage*. Québec: Amérik Média.

Burke, Seán (1995) 'The Ethics of Signature', in *Authorship: From Plato to the Post-Modern*, ed. Seán Burke. Edinburgh: Edinburgh University Press, pp. 285–91.

—— (1998) *The Death and Return of the Author: Criticism and Subjectivity in Barthes, Foucault and Derrida*. Edinburgh: Edinburgh University Press.

Carson, Christie (1993) 'Celebrity by Association: *Tectonic Plates* in Glasgow', *Canadian Theatre Review* 74, pp. 46–50.

Charest, Rémy and Lepage, Robert (1997) *Connecting Flights*, trans. Wanda Romer Taylor. London: Methuen.

Dundjerović, Aleksandar (2007) *The Theatricality of Robert Lepage*. Montréal and Kingston: McGill-Queen's University Press.

—— (2009) *Robert Lepage*. London and New York: Routledge.

—— (2010) 'Robert Lepage and Ex Machina – *Lipsynch* (2007) – Performance Transformations and Cycles', in Jen Harvie and Andy Lavender (eds), *Making Contemporary Theatre*. Manchester and New York: Manchester University Press, pp. 160–79.

Fricker, Karen (2007) 'Cultural Relativism and Grounded Politics in Robert Lepage's *The Andersen Project*', *Contemporary Theatre Review* 17:2, pp. 119–41.

—— (2008) 'Auteurship and Collaboration: Developments in Facilitated Creativity', round-table discussion, Central School of Speech & Drama, London, 19 November 2008.

Harvie, Jennifer (2002) 'Robert Lepage', in Hans Bertens and Joseph Natoli (eds), *Postmodernism: The Key Figures*. Massachusetts and Oxford: Blackwell, pp. 224–30.

Heddon, Deirdre and Milling, Jane (2006) *Devising Performance: A Critical History*. Basingstoke: Palgrave Macmillan.

Hiroshi, Takahagi (1995) 'Shakespeare at the Globe in Tokyo: A Crossroads of World Theatre', trans. Cody Poulton, *Canadian Theatre Review* 85, pp. 38–41.

Knowles, Richard Paul (1998) 'From Dream to Machine: Peter Brook, Robert Lepage, and the Contemporary Shakespearean Director as (Post) Modernist', *Theatre Journal* 50:2, pp. 189–206.

McAlpine, Alison (1996) 'Robert Lepage', in Maria Delgado and Paul Heritage (eds), *In Contact with the Gods?: Directors Talk Theatre.* Manchester and New York: Manchester University Press, pp. 130–57.

Pavis, Patrice (1998) 'Do We Have To Know Who We Do Theatre For?', *Performance Research* 3:1, pp. 82–6.

Pechey, Graham (1989) 'On the Borders of Bakhtin: Dialogisation, Decolonisation', in Ken Hirschkop and David Shepherd (eds), *Bakhtin and Cultural Theory.* Manchester and New York: Manchester University Press, pp. 39–67.

Shank, Theodore (1972) 'Collective Creation', *The Drama Review* 16:2, pp. 3–30.

W. K. Wimsatt Jr. and Monroe C. Beardsley (1995) 'From *The Intentional Fallacy*', in Burke, Seán (ed.), *Authorship: From Plato to the Post-Modern.* Edinburgh: Edinburgh University Press, pp. 90–100.

Index